Communications for Law Enforcement Professionals

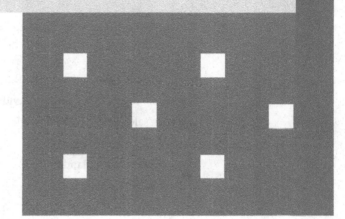

THIRD EDITION

John A. Roberts
Jeffrey S. Rosnick

emp

2010
Emond Montgomery Publications
Toronto, Canada

Emond Montgomery Publications Limited
60 Shaftesbury Avenue
Toronto ON M4T 1A3
http://www.emp.ca/highered

We acknowledge the financial support of the Government of Canada through the Canada Book Fund for our publishing activities.

Printed in Canada.
Reprinted September 2013.

The events and characters depicted in this book are fictitious. Any similarity to actual persons, living or dead, is purely coincidental.

Acquisitions editor: Bernard Sandler

Marketing manager: Christine Davidson

Director, sales and marketing, higher education: Kevin Smulan

Supervising editor: Jim Lyons

Copy editor: David Handelsman

Proofreader: Jamie Bush

Production editor and typesetter: Cindy Fujimoto

Indexer: Paula Pike

Cover image: © Moodboard / Maxx Images

ISBN 978-1-55239-388-8

The Library and Archives Canada CIP record for this book is available from the publisher.

Contents

Preface xi

INTRODUCTION

Importance of Communications in Law Enforcement 1
Learning Objectives 1
The Communication Process 1
Communicating in a Multicultural Society 2
Communicating with People with Disabilities 6
Working Together 6
Summary 9
    Diversity Component of Hamilton Police Service Officers' Evaluation 10

CHAPTER 1

Effective Listening 11
Learning Objectives 11
Introduction 11
Your Listening Profile 12
    Quiz 1 Analysis 12
    Quiz 2 Analysis 12
    Quiz 3 Analysis 14
Nine Rules for Effective Listening 14
    Rule 1: Decide to Listen 15
        Listening Keeps Us Informed 15
        Listening Keeps Us Out of Trouble 15
        Listening Makes Us Appreciated 15
    Rule 2: Avoid Selective Listening 16
    Rule 3: Give Acknowledgment and Feedback 16
        Reflective Listening 17
    Rule 4: Ask Appropriate Questions 17
        Broadening Questions 18
        Clarifying or Confirming Questions 18
        Questions That Change the Direction 18
    Rule 5: Look for Non-Verbal Cues 19
        Body Language 19
        Tone of Voice 19
    Rule 6: Listen with Your Whole Body 20
    Rule 7: Separate Fact from Opinion and Propaganda 20

Rule 8: Control Your Emotional Response 21

Rule 9: Make Notes 21

Some Additional Principles 22

Barriers to Effective Listening 23

Memory Techniques 23

Drawing It All Together 24

Spelling and Definitions 31

Mini-Puzzle 31

Word Search 32

CHAPTER 2

Spelling 33

Learning Objectives 33

Introduction 33

Improving Your Spelling 34

Word Search 39

Useful Spelling Rules 40

Rule 1 40

Rule 2 40

Rule 3 40

Rule 4 41

Plurals 41

Word Problems 44

Summary 56

Spelling and Definitions 57

Mini-Puzzle 58

Word Search 59

CHAPTER 3

Grammar Skills 61

Learning Objectives 61

Introduction 61

Grammar Pre-Test 62

Grammar Essentials: Sentences 66

Subject 66

Verb 68

Subject–Verb Agreement 70

Sentence Fragments 72

Run-on Sentences 75

Modifiers 77

Misplaced Modifiers 77

Dangling Modifiers 78

Pronoun References 78

Pronouns and Case 80

Ambiguous and Indefinite Pronoun References 80

Parallel Structure 81

Correlatives 82

Grammar Essentials: Punctuation and Capitalization 83

Commas 83

Apostrophes 84
    Possessives 84
    Contractions 86
Periods 87
Question Marks 87
Exclamation Points 87
Quotation Marks 88
Semicolons 88
Colons 88
Capital Letters 90
Voice 90
Summary 91
Spelling and Definitions 91
Mini-Puzzle 92
Word Search 93

CHAPTER 4

Summary and Paraphrase 95
Learning Objectives 95
Introduction 95
Writing a Summary 96
    Changing Direct Speech to Indirect Speech 98
    Counting Words 98
    Sample Summaries 98
Writing a Paraphrase 101
    Methods of Paraphrasing 101
    Bias in Reporting 104
Summary 107
Spelling and Definitions 108
Mini-Puzzle 109
Word Search 110

CHAPTER 5

From Words to Essay 111
Learning Objectives 111
Introduction 111
    Purpose 111
    Audience 112
    Figure 5.1   The Structure of an Essay 113
Paragraph 114
    Figure 5.2   Paragraphs and Topic Sentences 114
    Types of Paragraphs 117
Essay 117
    Getting Started 119
    Outline 119
    Thesis Statement 120
    Organizing the Essay 121
    Writing the Introduction 123
    Body of Essay or Support Paragraphs 124

Transitions 125
Writing Strategies 126
   Narration 126
   Description 126
   Exposition 127
   Persuasion 127
   Comparison/Contrast 127
Conclusion 128
Research Paper 130
Finding the Facts 130
Note Taking 130
Citing Sources 131
   MLA (Modern Language Association) Documentation Style 131
   APA (American Psychological Association) Documentation Style 136
Summary 139
Spelling and Definitions 142
Mini-Puzzle 143
Word Search 144

CHAPTER 6

Speaking Effectively

Speaking Effectively 145
Learning Objectives 145
Introduction 145
Effective Oral Presentations 146
Purpose 146
Selecting a Topic 146
Narrowing the Topic 147
Research 148
Preparation 150
Organization 152
Mechanics 152
Answering Questions 153
Nervousness 154
Visual Aids 155
Non-Verbal Communication 156
Visual Elements 156
   Eye Contact 156
   Facial Expression 156
   Gestures and Posture 157
   Body Orientation 157
Vocal Elements 157
   Loudness 157
   Rate 157
   Emphasis 157
Spatial Elements 158
Impromptu Speaking: Say What You Mean, SIR 159
A Last Word About Oral Presentations: Don't Read 160
One-on-One Communication 160
Dealing with a Difficult Person 160
Conferencing with Peers 162

Applications of Speaking Techniques 163
 Testifying in Court 163
Summary 173
Spelling and Definitions 173
Mini-Puzzle 174
Word Search 175

CHAPTER 7

The Memo Book 177
Learning Objectives 177
Introduction 177
Questioning to Obtain Information 178
 Effective Questioning 178
 How to Ask Questions 179
Note Taking 181
 Tips on Note Taking 182
 Use of Notes in Court 182
 Diagrams in Notes 183
 Figure 7.1 Common Symbols for Memo Book Diagrams 184
 Figure 7.2 Diagram of a Traffic Accident 185
Guidelines for Memo Book Entries 187
Summary 191

CHAPTER 8

Reports 195
Learning Objectives 195
Introduction 195
Parts of the Report 196
General Rules for Report Writing 197
Organization for Writing Reports 198
 Report Outline 199
 Composing the Report 200
 Figure 8.1 A Simple Report.. 200
Facts in Issue 202
 Figure 8.2 Facts in Issue 202
Common Errors in Report Writing 203
From Memo Book to Report 204
 Incident Report (Cover Page) 204
 Supplementary Report 204
Sample Incident Report and Supplementary 205
 Sample Incident Report 206
 Figure 8.3 Sample Incident Report 207
 Sample Supplementary 208
 Figure 8.4 Sample Supplementary Report................................. 209
Statement Forms 211
 Statement of a Witness 211
 Statement from Accused 212
 Motor Vehicle Accident Statement 212
 Figure 8.5 Incident Report 213

Figure 8.6   Supplementary Report 214
Figure 8.7   Statement of a Witness 215
Figure 8.8   Statement from Accused...................................... 217
Figure 8.9   Motor Vehicle Accident Statement............................ 219
The Crown Brief 224
Contents of the Crown Brief 224
Figure 8.10   A Crown Brief 226
Figure 8.11   Statement from Accused...................................... 236
Figure 8.12   Page from Officer's Memo Book 237
Additional Forms for the Crown Brief 238
Niagara Regional Police Service Reports 238
Summary 238

CHAPTER 9

The Written Communication Test

The Written Communication Test 243
Learning Objectives 243
Introduction 243
The Instructions 244
Figure 9.1   Sample Instructions 245
Figure 9.2   Sample Grading Sheet 246
The Fact Sheet 248
Figure 9.3   Sample WCT Fact Sheet Guide 248
Figure 9.4   Sample Scenario 249
Figure 9.5   Completed Fact Sheet 251
The Essay 252
Points to Remember 252
Figure 9.6   Scenario 1 and Sample Essay 253
Figure 9.7   Scenario 2 and Sample Essay 254
Summary 256

APPENDIX A

Memos

Memos 257
Introduction 257
General Purposes 257
Specific Uses 257
Is a Memo Necessary? 258
Format 258
Style 258
Headings 258
Subject Line 259
Closing 259
Content 259
Tone 259
Correctness 259
The "You" Approach 259
Writing Strategies 260
Direct Order 260
Figure A.1   Direct Order Memo 260
Indirect Order 261
Figure A.2   Indirect Order Memo 262

APPENDIX B

Letters 265
Introduction 265
Purpose 265
Formats 265
Style 266
    Headings 266
    Salutation 266
    Closing 266
    Content 266
    Tone 266
    Readability 266
    The "You" Approach 266
    Figure B.1   Modified Block Style with Modified Open Punctuation 267
    Figure B.2   Traditional Style with Closed Punctuation 268
    Figure B.3   Full Block Style with Open Punctuation 269
Letter-Writing Strategies 270
    Figure B.4   Direct Order Letter 271
    Figure B.5   Indirect Order Letter 272

APPENDIX C

Emails 273
Introduction 273
Purpose 273
Format 274
Style 274
    Headings 274
        To: 274
        Cc: 274
        Bcc: 275
        Subject: 275
        Attachments: 275
    Salutation 275
    Body 275
    Closing 275
Replying 275
    A Word of Warning 275
    Context and Clarity 276
Formatting and Attaching Documents 276
Spell Checks 276

References 277

Index 279

Acknowledgments 283

Preface

The third edition of *Communications for Law Enforcement Professionals* has been revised and expanded in response to feedback from students and instructors. Particular emphasis has been placed on new student activities throughout the text, as well as new material on report writing and a new chapter on the Written Communication Test. The new edition reinforces learning concepts and provides additional opportunities for a hands-on approach to topics, while developing students' skills in a wide range of communications venues.

This edition renews the emphasis on law enforcement agencies other than policing; examples are drawn from corrections, border security, and private security as well as policing. As in the previous edition, spelling and grammar skills are canvassed in separate chapters and then applied to summarizing, essay writing, listening, researching, and speaking, culminating in the use of these skills in law enforcement situations involving the memo book, reports, and the Crown brief. Notable changes to specific chapters are described below.

Introduction—Five new exercises have been added to the Introduction to help students understand the importance and challenges of communicating in a multicultural society and in teams.

Chapter 1: Effective Listening—A new section on memory techniques has been added to help students increase their retention and improve their effective listening skills.

Chapter 5: From Words to Essay—Modern Language Association (MLA) and American Psychological Association (APA) documentation guidelines have been updated to conform to professional standards.

Chapter 6: Speaking Effectively—The procedures for running a mock trial have been more fully explained and restructured and examples expanded. Additional information has been supplied to allow the participants in the mock trial to compose reports from the testimony provided in the exercise. A new exercise, "Communicating Effectively to Make a Good Impression," has been added.

Chapter 8: Reports—This chapter has been completely revised. New exercises have been included, extensive new information has been provided on methods of writing the incident report and the supplementary, and new sample reports have been included, along with instructions for completing the reports. Most importantly, the link between the information compiled in the memo book and the presentation of this information in a report has been strengthened. Overall, new case studies and new model reports have been included, along with a renewed consistency in the contents of exercises and an expanded explanation of reporting forms.

Chapter 9: The Written Communication Test—This chapter is new to the third edition. The Written Communication Test (WCT) is usually required for those wishing to enter a career in law enforcement. This chapter instructs the student on methods of writing the fact sheet and essay as part of the WCT, provides sample scenarios with answers, and includes a standard grading sheet. The chapter is structured to allow the student to study for the WCT outside of the classroom setting.

Appendix C: Emails—This new appendix has been included to explain protocol in electronic communications.

Thanks again to the crew at Emond Montgomery who have made previous editions of this book successful and to those who contributed to the third edition: Bernard Sandler, Christine Davidson, David Handelsman, Cindy Fujimoto, Jamie Bush, and Jim Lyons.

John A. Roberts
Jeffrey Rosnick
Hamilton, Ontario
Spring 2010

Importance of Communications in Law Enforcement

Learning Objectives

After reading this introduction, you should be able to:

- Understand the communication process and the barriers to it.
- Communicate with people from many cultures.
- Understand the importance of communicating as a member of a group.

The Communication Process

Everyone communicates. You speak, write, and make gestures, all of which can be considered methods of communicating. Even when you aren't speaking, writing, or gesturing to someone, communication takes place.

Communication involves more than one person. Even when your attempt to communicate feels quite unsuccessful, as if you're "talking to a brick wall," the person you're addressing does *receive* your communication. But perhaps he or she is not listening, or is not responding appropriately, or is not responding at all. In other words, your message isn't getting through, even though it's being received. No response, or an inappropriate response, is a form of feedback to your message. A traditional diagram used to illustrate this theory is set out in the following figure.

COMMUNICATION THEORY

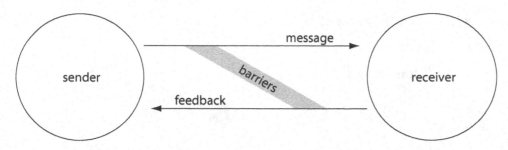

The person speaking, writing, or gesturing (the sender) sends a message to another person (the receiver). The receiver gives feedback to show that the message has been received and how the message has been received.

When someone doesn't respond to your communication or responds inappropriately, there are reasons for this breakdown; they are called *barriers to communication*. Possibly the receiver can't hear your message clearly; possibly the receiver doesn't agree with what you said and doesn't want to tell you so; or possibly the receiver is unable to respond for another reason. For example, your environment may be unsuitable for effective communication. Think of how difficult it might be to communicate with the victim of a hit-and-run accident in the following conditions: people around you are discussing the accident, it's raining, sirens are wailing, it's late at night, the victim is injured, and witnesses are trying to get your attention. These environmental factors are all barriers to communication, and make it difficult for you to obtain the information necessary to do your job.

Other situations involve different barriers to communication. Specific problems may occur, for example, when you are dealing with people who don't speak English or who have disabilities.

Communicating in a Multicultural Society

Immigration to Canada has increased significantly since 1991, and close to 25 percent of the total present-day Canadian population was born outside of the country. Therefore, law enforcement personnel in this country must frequently communicate with people whose first language is not English and it is essential that they be able to communicate in any cultural environment. Law enforcement officers, in particular, must be able to obtain information quickly, accurately, and in a non-threatening manner, regardless of their environment.

To communicate effectively within a multicultural environment, law enforcement personnel must be able to

- take responsibility for the communication
- withhold judgments
- show respect
- be empathetic
- tolerate ambiguity
- look beyond the superficial
- be patient
- recognize their own cultural biases
- be flexible
- send clear messages.

On a practical level, these communication skills can be applied in a number of ways:

1. Speak slowly and enunciate.

2. Face the person and speak directly to him or her, even when using a translator.

3. Avoid concentrated eye contact if the other speaker is not making direct eye contact.

4. Do not use jargon, slang, or idioms.

5. Avoid complex verb tenses.

6. Articulate key issues and questions in different ways.

7. Avoid asking questions that can be answered by "yes" or "no." Instead, ask questions that will produce answers that demonstrate understanding.

8. Use short, simple sentences; pause between sentences.

9. Supplement your spoken words with visual cues such as gestures, demonstrations, and brief written phrases.

10. Use active rather than passive verbs.

11. Pause frequently and give numerous breaks.

12. Use only one idea per sentence.

13. Respect the silence that non-native English speakers need to formulate their sentences and translate them in their minds. Be patient as they do so.

14. Check the other speaker's comprehension by having him or her repeat your words and instructions, and remember to summarize frequently yourself.

15. Provide positive feedback.

16. Listen attentively.

17. Don't speak louder; it won't help.

Non-verbal methods of communication are important in a multicultural environment. It is helpful to remember the following:

1. An officer's body language and non-verbal messages can override his or her words in high stress and crisis situations, especially for people whose first language is not English.

2. Different cultures have diverse ways of communicating stress, confusion, and uncertainty; a person who is silent and nervous and seems to be uncooperative may in fact simply be confused by the questions being asked.

3. Careful gestures and non-verbal cues from the officer can help the non-English-speaking person understand the verbal message.

EXERCISE 1

Analyze the following case study. Suggest ways in which the situation could have been handled better.

You are a loss prevention officer for a major department store chain. On a Saturday evening, you are on the job and notice that a couple of males are acting suspiciously in the electronics section. They take various CDs from the rack, examine them, and appear to replace them. As you continue watching them, one of the males appears to take one of the CDs and put it in his jacket pocket. The two then make a hurried exit from the store. You're not sure that the CD was not replaced, but from where you were standing, the CD could have been stolen. You follow the pair out of the store and confront them in the parking lot. You identify yourself as store security, and tell them that they are under arrest for stealing the item.

Both of the suspects are Asian, and claim not to speak English. By this time, a small crowd has gathered around, and you feel that the crowd is watching your next move. You want everyone to know that store security is on the ball, and that shoplifting won't be tolerated, especially shoplifting by immigrants. Even though you're not sure that they did steal the CD, and by this time you're not even sure which of the pair might have the CD, you begin to question them.

"You stole a CD from the store. Hand it over." Neither suspect says anything.

Standing less than an inch from the face of one of the suspects, you begin to raise your voice and stare into his eyes. "Come on! I know you have it! It'll go a lot easier on you if you admit it now!"

Again, neither suspect says anything, but both stand with downcast eyes, refusing to look you in the face, which you take as a sure sign of guilt. "You're going straight to the slammer. I know you can speak English; everyone can speak English. Now hand it over!"

You stand with your hands on your hips with your feet spread apart, hoping that you're presenting a no-nonsense attitude. You begin to speak louder, reasoning that, even if the pair doesn't speak English, you'll get your message through by raising your voice. "Okay, if that's the way you want it! We have laws in this country against people stealing things! I'm going to see that you get deported for this. We're going back to the security office and I'm going to call the police. I bet you won't like that very much. The police will get you to talk."

A woman who has been observing the confrontation steps forward, tells you that she speaks Cantonese and Mandarin, and offers to translate for you. You brush her off.

"No thanks, lady. I'll take care of this. Pretending not to speak English won't help them. Look how nervous they are. They look guilty to me. We'll teach them to play dumb!"

You roughly grab each suspect by the arm and lead them back to the store, keeping up a steady banter about people who come to this country and think that they can ignore our laws.

Officers should learn to avoid gestures or physical behaviour that another culture might find offensive or taboo. For example, the law enforcement officer should understand

- when touch is appropriate and when it is inappropriate;
- what different cultures consider to be a comfortable physical distance between two people;
- what are the protocols governing eye contact in different cultures, and what is meant by eye contact or lack of eye contact;
- how facial expressions are affected by culture;
- what are the inappropriate and appropriate gestures for a particular cultural group.

Below are examples of gestures and behaviour that people from other cultures could find offensive:

- In Canada, direct eye contact is thought to indicate honesty and reliability, whereas shifting one's gaze away is thought to indicate the opposite; however, in Latin America, direct eye contact is thought to indicate a challenge or aggression and shifting one's gaze away from a questioner is often used to indicate respect.

- In Canada, it is customary to smile for introductions and to indicate a friendly attitude even between strangers; however, in Japan, a smile is used as a polite expression of a range of emotions, from shame to anger. In Germany, smiles are reserved for family and friends.

- In Canada, we use the "OK" sign to indicate a positive response; however, this is a vulgar sign in some countries, including Turkey.

EXERCISE 2

EXPLORING PERSONAL SPACE

Divide the class into pairs. Have the pairs face each other at a distance of about 5 feet (1 1/2 metres). Ask one person in each pair to move gradually closer to the other. Have students monitor the effects of this exercise, particularly noting when they feel the other stepping into their "personal space."

EXERCISE 3

IDENTIFYING CULTURAL DIFFERENCES IN COMMUNICATION

The chances are good that your class consists of people from a variety of cultures. Have a class discussion on the variety of cultures in your class, and ask classmates from different cultures to volunteer information about their own cultures. What are some of the cultural differences in communication you found?

Also, be aware of problems that may arise from semantic differences across cultures and dialects. A single word within a language can have different meanings and nuances depending on its cultural context, and the way something is said is often more important than the words used. Remember, too, that law enforcement officials are viewed differently from culture to culture.

It is interesting to note that some police services have a diversity component as part of their officers' yearly evaluations. The section of the Hamilton Police Service evaluation form relating to diversity is shown on page 10.

EXERCISE 4

UNDERSTANDING THE POWER OF WORDS

Law enforcement officers must be effective communicators. Consider the phrase "Words have power." As a class, discuss the different meanings this phrase might have in a law enforcement context.

Communicating with People with Disabilities

Here are a few broad guidelines for communicating with people with disabilities:

1. *Recognize the existence of a disability.* People with disabilities may often use gestures to draw law enforcement officers' attention to their condition; they would prefer that their disabilities not be ignored.

2. *Understand the nature of the disability.* Some disabilities impair a person's ability to formulate and send a message; other disabilities impair a person's ability to receive and understand a message. Understanding the nature of the disability allows law enforcement officers to understand the barriers to communication and to shape their own efforts at communication accordingly.

3. *Be resourceful in attempting to establish communication.* For example, written notes are often the best way to communicate with a hearing- or speech-impaired person.

Working Together

Communicating is often a one-on-one situation. As was seen in the illustration of the communication process, a sender sends a message, a receiver receives the message, and the feedback indicates how much of the message was absorbed, understood, and accepted.

There are many situations, however, when you will be communicating with more than one person. After all, law enforcement is a group effort; for example, you don't usually solve crimes by yourself. You need the assistance of investigators, forensic specialists, civilian personnel, informants—an entire range of people to whom you must communicate vital information and from whom you must receive it. These people are members of your group. When mixed messages are sent between members of the group, or when various members interpret a message differently and fail to assist one another in the communication process, confusion usually ensues—another communication barrier.

EXERCISE 5

EVALUATING YOUR GROUP WORK STRENGTHS AND WEAKNESSES

Law enforcement officers must learn to work in teams. Group work is an essential way for you to learn teamwork skills. Use this brief quiz to identify your strengths and weaknesses. Rate yourself on a scale of 1 to 5 for each question (5 = I strongly agree; 1 = I strongly disagree). Compare answers with a partner, and discuss the reasons for them. Think about how you might improve in areas you are weak.

1. I am good at word processing.
2. I am a good presenter.
3. I am good at organizing people.
4. I am good at generating discussion.
5. I am good at keeping notes.
6. I know how to use presentation programs, such as PowerPoint.
7. I like to lead and inspire others.
8. I do my share.
9. I expect others to carry me along.
10. I expect to have my way.
11. I ask others what they think.
12. I am not afraid to disagree.
13. I am willing to take the time to solve problems.
14. I generally wait until the last minute to finish a project.
15. I need deadlines to focus my attention.
16. I practise presentations before I give them.
17. I do better working in groups.
18. I enjoy group work.
19. I have had bad experiences working in groups.
20. I want to learn to deal with group work.

EXERCISE 6

UNDERSTANDING THE CHALLENGES OF COMMUNICATING IN A DIFFERENT CULTURE

The Problem

What is it like to undergo questioning from an officer who doesn't understand your culture?

The Setting

You've been hired by a large multinational company, which is expanding its operations in Komanistan. You will be living there for one or two years, but you haven't had much to do with the local culture. You know you are experiencing culture shock.

Part A: Questioned in Komanistan

One night, you are walking in town with your guide, who suddenly darts into a shop and leaves you waiting on the street. While standing there, you witness a case of theft. A man grabs a woman's bag, throws her to the ground, and runs off. A security officer appears on the scene, and the woman points at you.

The remainder of the scenario is presented below and divided into numbered parts. For each part, determine how you would feel, and what you would be thinking.

1. The security officer is running toward you and shouting at you. He is using many Komani words you don't understand.

2. You look around for your guide, but you don't see him. You're on your own. Suddenly, you realize everyone is staring at you.

3. You call your guide's name, hoping for assistance. Immediately two older men come up to you and begin speaking in loud, agitated voices. They are waving their hands in the air. What are they talking about?

4. Now the security officer steps toward you so that he is almost nose to nose and says, "Passport!"

5. You glance around at the faces of the men who were staring at you. They are now looking toward the ground.

6. You hesitate, and look directly into the officer's eyes for understanding. Just then, your guide appears and begins arguing with the two agitated men in Komani.

7. You see the officer's expression change. He begins waving one hand at you and another toward his patrol car.

8. Your guide now addresses the officer: "Hi. Sorry about that. What's the problem, officer?" And then your guide looks down while he listens to the officer speak in Komani. Your guide looks surprised. Finally, he looks you up and down.

9. Your guide explains that the officer would like you to come to the station to make a statement as an independent witness to the theft.

Part B: Debriefing

Answer the following questions:

1. What did you learn from going through this experience?

2. How would you adjust your communication behaviour here at home when dealing with a recent immigrant from a different culture?

3. Form small groups and compare your answers with those of your group members.

   a. In what ways are your answers similar?

   b. In what ways are they different?

Summary

Everyone communicates, but the effectiveness of the communication process varies. Effectiveness is reflected in the types of feedback given and depends on how well the barriers to communication between sender and receiver are overcome. Law enforcement officers must be effective communicators. They must understand that certain barriers to communication, such as language difference or physical disability, present special communications challenges. People in law enforcement have a special need to communicate efficiently within a group.

DIVERSITY COMPONENT OF HAMILTON POLICE SERVICE OFFICERS' EVALUATION

10   Valuing Diversity:

Valuing Diversity is the ability to understand and respect the practices, customs, values and norms of individuals, groups and cultures other than one's own. It is not restricted to employment equity, but includes the ability to respect and value diverse points-of-view, and to be open to others of differing backgrounds or perspectives. It includes seeing diversity as beneficial to the Hamilton Police Service. It also implies the ability to work effectively with a wide cross-section of the community representing diverse backgrounds, cultures, and/or socio-economic circumstances.

Expectations:	☐ Requires Improvement ☐ Meets Exceeds: ☐ (d) ☐ (e)
(a) Accepts Diversity	Is willing to accept and respect the practices, customs, values and norms of other individuals or groups. Is open to others of different backgrounds or perspective. Responds openly when approached by others.
(b) Values Differences or Diversity	Values diversity and actively seeks out opportunities to gain new knowledge and understanding of individuals/groups through learning and active community participation and involvement. Recognizes prejudices and systemic barriers which may exist within the current environment.
(c) Monitors and Modifies Own Behaviours	Monitors and evaluates own beliefs and behaviours with regard to prejudices and personal bias. Practices new behaviours that reflect an understanding and appreciation of diversity.
(d) Challenges Others	Openly and directly addresses issues or situations that may not support diversity and tolerance of others. Holds people accountable for their actions to ensure that their behaviour reflects an appreciation and acceptance of diversity. Educates others of the value of diversity, and teaches tolerance and openness to diverse ideas and backgrounds.
(e) Actively Promotes Diversity	Actively promotes the value of diversity through planned and visible activities aimed at building sensitivity to, and support for, others. Actively promotes and supports programs that are designed to increase diversity within the Hamilton Police Service.

Supporting Evidence:

Comments:

CHAPTER 1

Effective Listening

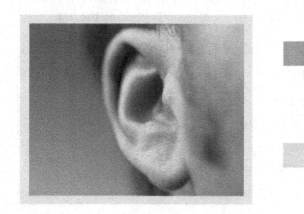

Learning Objectives

After completing this chapter, you should be able to:

- Recognize personal listening tendencies.
- Identify barriers to effective listening.
- Develop better listening habits.
- Understand the importance of listening skills for law enforcement professionals.

> *We have been given two ears and but a single mouth in order that we may hear more and talk less.*
>
> —Zeno of Citium

Introduction

"No one listens anymore!"

This is a complaint that many students have heard from their instructors, but is it correct? You sit in class and "listen" to what is being presented—except, of course, when you're looking out the window, or talking to someone, or daydreaming, or not concentrating because the room is too hot or too cold, or when you just don't feel like listening.

So, are you really listening? Are your instructors correct? Do the words go in one ear and out the other?

Listening skills are essential for law enforcement officers. You must continually listen to instructions from your superiors and to what is being said by victims, witnesses, accused persons, lawyers, colleagues, and many other people who will be part of your career. The best place to learn how to listen is in the classroom.

■ Your Listening Profile

This chapter includes three quizzes to help you rate yourself as a listener. There are no correct or incorrect answers. Your responses, however, will extend your understanding of yourself as a listener and show you where improvement is needed.

These are not particularly difficult quizzes, but your answers will reveal something about your listening skills in relation to others who have done the test.

> ## ▶ LISTENING PROFILE QUIZ 1
>
> ■ Circle the category that best describes you as a listener:
> excellent / above average / average / below average / weak
>
> ■ On a scale of 0 to 100 (100 being the best),
> how would you rate yourself as a listener? _____

QUIZ 1 ANALYSIS

■ Eighty-five percent of all people questioned rate themselves as "average" or worse. Fewer than 5 percent rated themselves as "excellent."

■ On the 0 to 100 scale, the extreme range of all respondents was 0 to 90, the general range was 35 to 85, and the average was 55.

> ## ▶ LISTENING PROFILE QUIZ 2
>
> On a scale of 0 to 100 (100 being the best), how do you think the following people would rate you as a listener?
>
> ■ Your best friend: _____
>
> ■ Your instructor: _____
>
> ■ An acquaintance: _____
>
> ■ Someone in your class: _____
>
> ■ Your girlfriend / boyfriend / spouse / partner: _____
>
> ■ Your employer, if you have a part-time job: _____

QUIZ 2 ANALYSIS

Most respondents rated themselves highest in the role of listeners to their best friends. In most categories, respondents rated themselves higher than they did in quiz 1.

What does this tell us? If people are in fact, as most of them suspect, strong listeners in relation to best friends, it is perhaps because such relationships, unlike others, necessitate good listening. It is interesting to note that most respondents felt that they were seen as poor listeners by spouses and partners. Does "familiarity breed contempt"? The results seem to indicate that respondents talk a lot to their partners but don't listen much.

The implications of all this for law enforcement personnel are startling. The quiz contains no categories for witnesses or victims, but if you assume that your overall listening performance would remain the same in connection with these people, you have to wonder how much information is being missed. What are you hearing? If you are an average listener, what happens to the information you missed, information that ought to appear on, say, a witness statement? Obviously, this information gets lost, and the implications can be serious. Being found guilty of a crime or at fault in a traffic accident can obviously affect a person's criminal record, insurance record, driving record, and employment status. The stakes are high.

▶ LISTENING PROFILE QUIZ 3

Choose one of the following answers for each of the questions below, and score yourself accordingly.

Answer	Score
Almost always	2
Usually	4
Sometimes	6
Seldom	8
Almost never	10

As a listener, how often do you ...	Answer	Score
■ consider a subject uninteresting?	_____	_____
■ criticize a speaker's delivery or mannerisms?	_____	_____
■ become passionate about something said by a speaker?	_____	_____
■ listen only for facts?	_____	_____
■ try to outline everything?	_____	_____
■ fake attention?	_____	_____
■ look for distractions?	_____	_____
■ ignore difficult material?	_____	_____
■ become antagonistic?	_____	_____
■ daydream?	_____	_____
	Total	_____

AT A LECTURE, ONLY 12 PERCENT LISTEN

Bright-eyed college students in lecture halls aren't necessarily listening to the professor, the American Psychological Association was told.

If you rang a bell at sporadic intervals during a lecture and asked students to record their thoughts and moods at that moment, you'd find the following:

- About 20 percent of the students, men and women, were pursuing erotic thoughts.
- Another 20 percent were reminiscing.
- Only 20 percent were paying attention to the lecture.
- Only 12 percent were understanding what was being said.
- The remainder were worrying, daydreaming, or thinking about something else.

— Paul Cameron, Wayne State University

QUIZ 3 ANALYSIS

The lower your score, the weaker are your listening skills. Think about it: if your listening skills are weak, what are you really hearing at your job?

Most of us engage in ineffective listening, an obvious barrier to good communication. People are generally poor listeners, usually out of habit, lack of attention or interest, or because the message is complex. Here are some suggestions about how to listen effectively.

Nine Rules for Effective Listening

Poor listening habits are the cause of more communication breakdowns than most of us realize; we tend not to think of listening as a communication skill. The first thing to realize about listening is what it's not. First of all, listening and hearing are not the same thing. Hearing is the physiological event of sound hitting the eardrum. Listening is complex; it involves receiving a message, interpreting the message, interpreting the speaker's feelings, eliminating personal biases, understanding what is being said, and practising other skills, which will be discussed in this section.

When someone else is speaking, usually you are not; there is silence from your side of the conversation. But if you are running over your reply in your mind and just waiting for the other person to finish so that you can jump in, that's not real listening.

Listening is a conscious act, and if you don't practise it actively, you simply cannot communicate effectively.

RULE 1: DECIDE TO LISTEN

Human beings deal with the noise in their environment by filtering out what doesn't interest them, so that they can concentrate on what does. For example, people who live on busy streets often claim that they don't hear the cars going by. The problem is that we often rely too heavily on this filtering mechanism and end up filtering out messages that we need to hear.

In law enforcement settings, we can't afford to let that happen, so we must actually *decide* to listen and then listen actively, with concentration and intent, using all of the skills that we'll be discussing in this section.

Why should we listen? Here are three good reasons: listening keeps us informed; listening keeps us out of trouble; listening makes us appreciated.

Listening Keeps Us Informed

"Nobody ever tells me anything around here!" This cry is usually heard just after someone has found out something that he or she should have known before. This exclamation reflects an attempt to blame others for one's own lack of knowledge. How often, on the other hand, have you heard someone say, "I never listen to anything that anyone says around here"? Make a point of paying attention to what's going on around you—of listening to messages and information from your colleagues—so that you will always be well informed. Knowledge is power; the best way to acquire knowledge is to listen.

Listening Keeps Us Out of Trouble

Perhaps you remember your mother saying, when you were quite young, something like, "I've told you over and over not to do that. Don't you listen?" The answer, of course, is that we didn't listen. We didn't realize it at the time, but we had more important things on our minds than instructions from Mom, so the information went, as my own mother used to say, in one ear and out the other.

Unfortunately, that situation isn't confined to childhood. Many of us carry poor listening habits into adulthood and the business world. If someone is giving you instructions and you don't listen well, there's a good chance that you won't be able to carry out those instructions properly. Over time, this can be detrimental to your career.

Listening Makes Us Appreciated

One of my best friends in university was very popular. More than once I heard people say that when they were with her, she made them feel as if they were the most important people in the world. They felt that way because she was a great listener. She listened with her ears, her eyes, her smile, her body, her mind—her whole self. When you put that much of yourself into the listening end of a conversation, the other person can't help but admire and appreciate you. Good listeners will often find themselves respected and trusted simply because other people enjoy working with them.

RULE 2: AVOID SELECTIVE LISTENING

Selective listening occurs when we listen only to what we want to hear: we select the message. In law enforcement, as in our personal lives, we can't afford to practise selective listening. The fact that we ignore bad news or uninteresting material doesn't make it go away or become irrelevant. In fact, things may well become worse if we act on just one part of a complex message.

One way we listen selectively is by not listening to all of what the other person is saying. We listen to half a sentence and then, assuming we know what the person is about to say, we respond without listening to the rest. Has anyone ever done this to you when you were speaking? Then you know how annoying it is. "That's not what I was going to say!" is like a dash of cold water in the listener's face, and it is well deserved.

A common cause of selective listening is personal bias or stereotyping against the speaker. As a customs officer, for example, you may attend a meeting of customs officials concerning procedures to eliminate the smuggling of illegal weapons across the border. While these procedures are being discussed, you overhear another customs officer whisper to another person, "This isn't going to work. We just don't have enough people to handle the inspections." Obviously, someone with this attitude is not going to listen to the presentation with an open mind, and in fact may not listen at all. That's selective listening.

It's also tempting to discount the opinions of people you simply don't like. If you feel yourself switch off when a certain person begins to speak, you are guilty of selective listening. Remember, the information may be valid and useful even if the person delivering it isn't someone you would have over for dinner—so listen up!

RULE 3: GIVE ACKNOWLEDGMENT AND FEEDBACK

You can encourage a speaker either through a verbal or a non-verbal response. A simple nod of the head, a smile, a raising of the eyebrows—these are all forms of non-verbal acknowledgment. They let the speaker know you are paying attention. Remaining silent at the appropriate times also indicates you're listening.

If you prefer to acknowledge the speaker verbally, you might interject encouraging words into the conversation, such as "Tell me more about it," "I didn't know that," or "I understand." Note that this indicates your understanding, not your agreement. Your chance to disagree will come later. You could also ask for clarification, with such expressions as "Are you saying that … ?" or "Do you mean that … ?" You may want to paraphrase the speaker's words, and begin your rephrasing with an expression such as "I hear you saying that … ." We'll look at the paraphrase in more detail in Chapter 4. These forms of acknowledgment let the speaker know that you understand what is being said. They demonstrate your interest and establish a rapport between the two of you. In a meaningful conversation, each party acknowledges the other's *feelings* as well as the actual words that are spoken.

For example, suppose that a co-worker is complaining about a seemingly trivial matter. She frowns and says angrily, "Why do they have so many rules and regulations? Why do they keep coming up with more? How does the security company expect me to pay attention to all of this paperwork? I almost feel like I need to be a lawyer as well as a loss prevention officer." If you simply agree with her, or say that you don't have a problem interpreting all of the new regulations, you might be missing the point. Respond instead with a statement such as, "This really seems to have you upset." This response opens up the possibility of further conversation. Indeed, you may find that the regulations aren't the problem so much as the fact that she feels overwhelmed with her workload, and is apt to view another piece of paper as the last straw. This is another example of how effective listening could contribute productively to the discussion.

Men and women tend to react differently to this type of acknowledgment. Of course, this is not always the case, but as a general rule, men are often reluctant to discuss their feelings, and are likely to deny them. When responding to a man in this situation, preface your remarks with phrases such as "It seems to me," or "Could it be," or "I wonder if." Women tend to be more direct about their feelings, although you still need to be careful.

It's important to watch the language you use in giving feedback. If you use preliminary phrases such as "My advice is" or "Your problem is," your feedback may not be welcome. You want to tune in fully to what is being said without offering your own judgment or ideas or feelings. If you give speakers the opportunity to talk a problem through, they will often come up with the answer themselves, which is much more effective than having you impose an answer.

Don't downplay a problem. Avoid responses such as "Don't worry" or "That's not so bad." These responses can be perceived as devaluing the speaker's concerns.

Reflective Listening

Reflective listening is a form of feedback that involves carefully rephrasing a speaker's message and returning it to him or her for confirmation, such as in the following exchange:

> *Richard*: "I'm fed up with issuing speeding tickets and seeing the speeder have the charge dropped in court."
>
> *Jerry*: "It sounds as if you're frustrated by not having more convictions. Is that right?"

That's reflective listening. It isn't suitable for all situations, and you have to avoid merely parroting what the speaker has said, but it can be a useful method of making sure, for example, that you have heard instructions correctly.

RULE 4: ASK APPROPRIATE QUESTIONS

Questioning is an important part of the listening process, because it helps the speaker convey his or her thoughts. By asking the right questions, you can greatly increase the scope of the conversation, which is the real art of listening. Compare the following modes of questioning:

1. *Inspector 1*: "Has Jenny been to work every day this week?"

2. *Inspector 2*: "How is Jenny doing now that she has a new partner?"

Here we see two different types of questions: **closed** and **open**. Employer 1 asks a closed question, which means that it can be answered with a simple "yes" or "no." Employer 2 asks an open question, which means that the other person must elaborate and give information in order to answer it.

If you want to develop and broaden a conversation, start by asking open questions. Then, as the need for confirmation arises, insert closed questions where appropriate. Let's continue with the sample dialogue from above:

Inspector: "How is Jenny doing now that she has a new partner?"

Sergeant: "Okay."

Inspector: "Do you think she's more satisfied with her job?"

Sergeant: "She seems a lot happier."

Inspector: "How so?"

Sergeant: "She used to take a lot of time off, complaining about headaches and stress. She didn't seem to be very happy. Now, she actually comes in early, is more outgoing than she used to be, and handles her reports quickly and efficiently."

Inspector: "And you attribute this to having someone new to work with?"

Sergeant: "Definitely."

Inspector: "I'm glad we were able to figure out the problem. What else do you think we need to do?"

Sergeant: "I think Jenny will be fine. We should look at the rest of our personnel and see if there are similar problems."

You can use both types of questions, closed and open, to broaden a conversation, to clarify or confirm meaning, or to move the conversation in another direction. Below are examples of questions that accomplish these three goals.

Additional information about the effectiveness of questions in law enforcement situation can be found in Chapter 6, "Speaking Effectively."

Broadening Questions

"Mary, you've told us about the new procedure they're using to inspect luggage at the Toronto airport, and it seems to be working well. How do you think we can adapt it to suit our conditions here?"

As you can see, this question calls for an analytical response that will bring in more information and broaden the discussion.

Clarifying or Confirming Questions

"What do you mean? Are you saying you agree with Doug's assessment?"

By asking questions like these, you give the speaker an opportunity to restate a position and clarify it for others.

Questions That Change the Direction

"We've discussed in depth your proposed procedure for handling young offenders and it seems to have merit. Can you tell us what impact it will have on the budget?"

The first sentence brings closure to one part of the discussion, and the ensuing question moves it on to another part.

Do you see how the open-ended questions elicit information, and the closed-ended questions serve to confirm information or opinion? Think about your own conversations. Do you use questions effectively? Questioning is a valid and helpful aspect of listening, so it's important to work on it.

RULE 5: LOOK FOR NON-VERBAL CUES

Suppose for a moment that you now live in a different place from the one where you grew up, and that you have gone home on vacation. For the first week you have spent every day and evening with your mother, and you have thoroughly enjoyed her company. Now, an old friend has invited you out for dinner. As you leave, you say, "Okay, Mom, I'm off. I'll probably be at Barbara's place for a couple of hours, so I won't be too late."

Instead of looking at you with her usual cheerful face, Mom looks down at the carpet, her head leans forward and down to one side, and her voice seems to slow down and age 20 years as she says in a world-weary tone, "Oh, don't worry. I'll be fine. Just you go ahead and enjoy yourself, and don't give a thought to me."

This is a classic case of the non-verbal cues—body language and tone of voice—being in direct conflict with the spoken words. Mom's non-verbal message is clear: "I don't want you to go, I'd prefer that you not enjoy yourself, and I have no intention of being fine!"

People send non-verbal messages in the workplace all the time, and effective listeners learn to "hear" them. How you decide to respond is not the issue here; the important thing is that you recognize the non-verbal message. Additional information on body language and non-verbal communication can be found in Chapter 6, "Speaking Effectively."

Body Language

Interpreting body language is not an exact science. There is danger in interpreting individual gestures and mannerisms according to a fixed set of rules; the meanings of gestures and mannerisms vary from one person to another. For example, we are told that folded arms indicate defensiveness or an unwillingness to be persuaded; however, many people fold their arms simply because it is a comfortable position.

It is important to look at "body language clusters" if you want to interpret body language accurately. If your sergeant stands in front of you with his arms folded and asks for information, it doesn't necessarily mean anything. But if he folds his arms while tapping his foot, frowning, and clenching his teeth, you can be sure that a problem exists.

What the good listener looks for is body language that *seems* to contradict the words of the speaker. When words and body language are in direct conflict, the body language is usually a truer indicator of meaning.

Tone of Voice

Have you ever heard a speaker stand up on a platform and begin a speech with the words, "I'm pleased to be here with you today," spoken in a flat monotone that indicated no pleasure at all? You probably noticed that the tone of voice didn't match the words, and you probably believed the tone. Most people would. What did that do for the speaker's credibility? Likely, not much.

Tone of voice plays a larger role in our conversations than we realize. On hearing their voices on a tape recorder for the first time, most people refuse to believe that they sound "like that." People don't realize that they speak in such a flat tone.

Alertness to tone of voice is another tool for evaluating the truth and sincerity of a person's actual words in relation to the real feelings behind them. Ideally, for a message to be clear and uncomplicated, the words, body language, and tone of voice should all be in agreement; in other words, they should all send the same message.

Effective listeners always pay attention to non-verbal cues because they are a vital component of communication.

RULE 6: LISTEN WITH YOUR WHOLE BODY

Picture this: something exciting happened on your shift today. When you and your partner sit down to dinner, you begin to relate the incident. Your partner doesn't look at you, doesn't say a word, shows no reaction—just keeps on eating. Do you feel listened to? Is your partner using the tools of lively listening? The fact is that that person might well be listening, might be taking in every word you say. But is it effective listening? No.

The effective listener not only takes in information, but also indicates in many ways that the speaker's message is getting through. If you want to make it clear that you are listening, use your entire body.

First, *look at* the person speaking. Give the speaker plenty of non-verbal feedback: nod your head, smile, frown, vary your expression to suit your response, lean toward the speaker; the speaker is encouraged to continue because you have made it clear that you're listening.

Using your body also helps you as the listener; if you're active, your attention is much less likely to wander. In other words, by physically indicating to the speaker that you *are* listening, you will actually improve the quality of your listening.

RULE 7: SEPARATE FACT FROM OPINION AND PROPAGANDA

The challenge of this rule is that you must learn to distinguish what is fact from what is merely opinion or what someone would like you to believe. People colour their words in many ways, which adds to the challenge of effective listening.

"These people are doing it. Why don't you join them?" This is the familiar message of what the advertising industry calls "lifestyle advertising": a group of happy, laughing adults enjoys a certain brand of beer. The implication, the suggestion, the unspoken message is that if you drink this brand of beer, you too can enjoy this lifestyle. You are encouraged to jump on the bandwagon.

We recognize this tactic in advertising, but we don't always notice it in normal conversation. Any time someone is trying to persuade you to do something or believe something, listen carefully for the facts and strip away the opinion.

Another way that facts can be distorted is with biased words and expressions. People sometimes have so much invested in their opinions being accepted that they sound like a circus pitchman in full swing. "This process will revolutionize the way our company operates!" This may well be true, but it may not be the kind of revolution you want. Or it may not be true at all. Learn to strip away the opinion and propaganda and listen for the facts before you respond.

RULE 8: CONTROL YOUR EMOTIONAL RESPONSE

We all have hot buttons. We all have attitudes and beliefs that make us respond with a quick flash of anger when people raise certain topics in particular ways.

What are your hot buttons? It's important to be aware of them so that you can decide how to react when someone pushes them in a conversation. As a lively listener, you need to take several steps to control your emotional response to what someone says to you.

First, you must recognize your response. When someone says something that makes you angry, what does it feel like? What happens in your body? Usually, one of the first things we notice is a change in our breathing pattern—breathing becomes shallower and faster. Perhaps you find that blood rushes to your face, and you feel heat there. Some people feel a headache suddenly begin; others automatically clench their hands into fists. How do you feel if one of your hot buttons is pushed? Take some time to really think about this, because it needs to be immediately recognizable to you if you want to be an effective listener.

How do you control an inappropriate emotional response? First, acknowledge it to yourself. Then, take a momentary pause and breathe deeply. This will change your physiological state while giving you time to consider what to say. In that brief interval, you can get control of yourself and choose your reaction.

Depending on various factors—the subject under discussion, the identity of the person who has upset you, the purpose of the conversation—you might take one of three paths:

1. *Ignore the comment and move on.* This will enable you to continue the conversation, but it might leave you simmering below the surface.

2. *Mention it and make an issue of the remark.* If the same person constantly pushes the same hot button, at some point you will need to do this just to clear the air. It is possible that the person is pushing your buttons unwittingly and only needs to have it mentioned in order to stop.

3. *Respond in passing and continue the conversation on the right track.* Say something like, "You may be right, but that's not what we're discussing."

An inappropriate overreaction can put an end to any conversation, so you would do well to learn how to control your emotional response.

RULE 9: MAKE NOTES

Notes can be on paper, on a computer screen, or just in your head, depending on the situation. If one of your colleagues is explaining a situation and asking for your help, begin by saying, "I'll just make a few notes as we talk," and make it obvious that you are doing so. The person now knows that you are really listening and paying attention, and the notes serve as focal points to help you formulate your response. Don't overdo the note taking. It's one thing to make occasional notes; it's quite another thing to write down every word and make the speaker feel as if he or she is being interrogated.

Of course, in order to decide which points need to be noted, you need to take steps we have already discussed: provide feedback, ask questions, and listen with your whole body. All these practices help elicit information that you can use to make effective notes. Note taking is a vital step in becoming an effective listener.

Guidelines for taking notes in memo books can be found in Chapter 7, "The Memo Book."

SOME ADDITIONAL PRINCIPLES

1. Remember that the listener's job is to assimilate information, understand the information, and act on it.

2. Don't ignore the speaker's silence. Silence is a behaviour that has meaning, and it's often important to discover that meaning. You might try the following question: "You seem reluctant to discuss this matter. What's on your mind?"

3. Organize your perceptions: decide whether the speaker is angry, unreasonable, or open to advice. Also, recognize stereotypes and prejudices in others. Keep your perceptions provisional.

4. Interpret the speaker in the speaker's own terms, not yours.

5. Get agreement: summarize what you've heard and have the speaker agree to your version.

EXERCISE 1

KNOWING YOURSELF AS A LISTENER

1. Identify some topics of discussion to which you listen attentively. Why do these topics interest you?

2. Identify some topics that don't usually cause you to listen attentively. Why not?

3. For those topics that don't compel your full attention, develop a list of strategies for listening more attentively to discussion of them.

Barriers to Effective Listening

There are a number of reasons why people don't listen effectively. These barriers to effective listening can affect both the message being sent and the message being received. They include the following:

1. **Lack of interest.** If you're not interested in what's being said, you don't listen; or you listen only to those things that interest you—in other words, selectively—and ignore the rest.

2. **Daydreaming.** Your mind is occupied by something other than what's being said.

3. **Emotional concerns.** You may be emotionally involved in the topic and therefore interested in only one point of view; or you may have recently suffered an emotional or traumatic experience in your personal life that is occupying your thoughts.

4. **Judgmental approach.** You hear what is being said through the distortion of your own ideas, judgments, or feelings. Your biases and prejudices take over.

5. **Environmental and physical distractions.** These include background noise, uncomfortable seating, heat, cold, cramped space, colleagues who talk while you're trying to listen, and many others.

6. **Lack of understanding.** You lack the background needed to fully understand the speaker's topic.

7. **Unclear presentation.** The speaker is discussing the topics in a vague manner and not providing elaboration.

8. **Incorrect interpretation of the message.** You misunderstand the motives behind the message, being unable to interpret others in their own terms.

9. **Lack of retention.** Statistically, we forget more than half of a message immediately, and remember only about 35 percent after eight hours.

Memory Techniques

Lack of retention is a serious barrier to effective listening. Learn to use the following memory techniques, or mnemonics (pronounced "ni-monniks"), to increase your retention.

- For a series of things to remember, try an acronym. For example, use the acronym RICE to remember the procedure for treating a minor injury: Rest, Ice, Compression, and Elevation.

- Another common technique is *chunking*—organizing ideas into groups. For example, a 10-digit phone number is better remembered in a series of three groups of numbers: 293 399 4834.

- Elaborative encoding makes connections between a list of things and our own experience. It is a personal approach to memorization, and works by association. For example, you associate a person with his or her name, address, car, etc.

- Telling a story (narrative) helps us remember in terms of characters, settings, actions, etc. The story you invent might be realistic or ridiculous; so long as it helps you remember, it doesn't matter. For example, tell a story that focuses on specific aspects of a character (describe a suspect's prominent nose), the setting (exaggerate the cold or heat on the night of the event), or the action (compare the amount of blood at the scene of an assault to a slaughterhouse).

- Making a mental picture is an ancient approach to memory. You can organize key images together in a sort of inner photograph. For example, reading the jumbled sentences of the Written Communication Test scenario (discussed in Chapter 9) and devising a picture in which you describe the scenario in chronological order is a good way to place the various facts of the scenario in context.

EXERCISE 2

EFFECTIVE LISTENING

Watch the film *12 Angry Men*. Which rules of effective listening are the characters following? Which are they not following? What barriers to effective listening can you identify? In particular, pay attention to their non-verbal cues, such as body language, and try to identify characters' hot button issues. Summarize your findings verbally or in a short report.

Drawing It All Together

Now that we have identified both the skills involved in effective listening, and some of the barriers to it, we can summarize the steps you need to take:

1. *Pay attention.* The speaker may be saying something you can use to your advantage. (Skill enhancer: *Efficiency*)

2. *Concentrate on the message.* The message conveyed is more important than what the speaker is saying. (Skill enhancer: *Clarity*)

3. *Hear the speaker out.* Let the speaker finish speaking before you make any judgments. (Skill enhancer: *Objectivity*)

4. *Listen for main ideas, principles, and concepts.* Be aware of the large picture. (Skill enhancer: *Perception*)

5. *Listen two or three minutes before taking notes.* Do not begin writing immediately. (Skill enhancer: *Ability to conceptualize and summarize*)

6. *Relax while listening.* Tension detracts from listening ability. (Skill enhancer: *Self-discipline*)

7. *Eliminate distractions.* Distractions are any barriers to listening, such as noise, which will detract from the message. (Skill enhancer: *Decisiveness*)

8. *Learn how to listen to difficult material.* Do not withdraw your attention when the factual or the emotional content is difficult. (Skill enhancer: *Perseverance*)

9. *Identify your own greatest word barriers.* Word barriers are words or concepts that trigger bias or negative attitudes. (Skill enhancer: *Objectivity*)

10. *Make your interpretation skills an asset.* Use the following techniques to assist you:

    a. Anticipate the next point to be made.

    b. Make comparisons and contrasts.

    c. Identify the speaker's evidence.

    d. Practise mental summarizing.

    (Skill enhancer: *Resourcefulness*)

EXERCISE 3

TRACKING YOUR LISTENING BEHAVIOUR

1. For the next five days, pay attention to your listening behaviour. Make note of the times you genuinely try to listen and understand what someone else is saying and of the times when you aren't listening.

2. Keep a record of this information. For each entry include

    a. the day and time

    b. the people involved

    c. the situation (the topic of conversation, the emotions involved)

    d. the outcome (how did your listening style affect the outcome?)

    e. your level of satisfaction with the situation.

3. At the end of the five-day period, ask yourself the following:

    a. Which of the listening styles described in this chapter did you use?

    b. In what situations did you use the various styles?

    c. Are you satisfied with your listening behaviour?

    d. What improvements do you need to make to your personal listening style?

EXERCISE 4

CASE STUDY

I didn't want to go to work today. It had been raining all weekend, but now the weather was great; it figures that Monday would be warm and sunny. But I had a meeting first thing in the morning, and my supervisor had been on my case to finish a couple of files, so I dragged myself out of bed, thought about calling in sick, realized that I was late, and rushed out of my apartment without stopping for breakfast. At least, I rushed as far as my car; it wouldn't start. I called a cab. The cab came right away, but when I got to the office, I discovered that I didn't have any money with me, so I had to find an ATM to get the cash to pay the cab driver. He was a bit peeved with me, because he had another call waiting. I guess I could have given him a bigger tip, but I didn't like his attitude. It's not as if it's my fault that my credit card was maxed out. I was a few minutes late, and my supervisor, Mary Kim, was already speaking. She always starts on time. She should consider people like me, who have good reasons for being late, and give us an extra few minutes. I had wanted to get to work early, because there had been a big party on Friday night and I wanted to catch up on the gossip. Now I had to sit there for an hour or so until I could find out what went on. So Mary droned on for another 15 minutes. She usually doesn't have anything to say in any case, so I ignored most of her presentation. I was thinking about how, now that I didn't have a car, I was going to get to the bank at lunch hour to pay some bills. I made up my mind to pay attention to the rest of the meeting, but Joel King was making a presentation, and as far as I'm concerned, there wasn't much he could tell me. What a sycophant! Always running up to the boss and asking if there's anything he can help with. It makes me sick! I think he's after my job. And the topic bored me to tears. Something about legal research or new government regulations or something like that. I can't imagine who'd be interested in that stuff. I don't remember much about the rest of the meeting. The room was stuffy; you'd think they could have opened a window. So I guess you could say that, as far as my attention level was concerned, the lights were on, but no one was home. I was catching up on some missed sleep, even though my eyes were open. I should paint some eyes on my glasses so everyone will think I'm awake. But my body was there even though my mind wasn't. That's all that counts in these big law firms.

ACTIVITY

Identify the barriers to listening in this case study. For each barrier listed, describe what could be done to overcome it.

EXERCISE 5

LISTENING IN SCHOOL

Take a look at the courses you're studying this semester. It is easy enough to determine those in which you are succeeding and those in which you are struggling. Analyze the "good" courses to determine why you are successful in them. Then, decide why you aren't successful or as successful in the others. How can you apply good listening skills to improve your grades? Before analyzing your own case, however, practise on the one that follows:

When I was in university, I had to take a biology course. I couldn't get out of it; everyone in an arts program had to take one science course. My problems were as follows:

1. I didn't like biology; I was an English major.

2. I didn't like cutting up animals.

3. The course was dull, dull, dull.

4. The members of my group all wanted to be biologists.

5. The classroom smelled like a funeral home.

6. The instructor was dull, dull, dull.

7. I had no skills in math or chemistry.

Believe it or not, I didn't do well in this course. Suggest ways in which I could have improved through active listening.

EXERCISE 6

LISTENING IN GROUPS: MOTIVATION

1. Select groups, with four to six participants in each group.

2. Appoint one referee per group.

3. Ask each participant to make a list of items—thoughts, feelings, complaints, wishes, plans—that he or she would be willing to share with other group members. It could be a to-do list, a wish list, a "things-that-bug-me" list, a "what-I'd-do-if-I-won-the-lottery" list, or something similar.

4. The referee will collect the lists from each member, shuffle them, and select one. The member whose list it is will be "it" and will speak first.

5. The referee will give each participant two minutes to tell the rest of the group what is on his or her list.

6. The rest of the group, while not being visibly rude, should do their best not to listen to the speaker. Group members can make occasional eye contact, but this should be minimal. The group members might, for instance, concentrate on their own lists as a way of ignoring the speaker. Group members should not speak to each other or to other members of the class.

7. The referee will also ignore the speaker, and will discourage nervous laughter from the group, attempts to distract the speaker, and the like.

8. When two minutes have elapsed, the referee will select another speaker, and repeat the process until all members of the group have been "it."

9. The referee will then lead a group discussion based on the following questions:

   a. How did you feel when you were "it"?

   b. How did being ignored affect or influence your motivation to continue speaking?

   c. How did being ignored affect your sense of self-esteem?

   d. How do you think others feel when you either don't listen to them or don't give them your full attention?

   e. How do you think your inattention would affect children, adults, co-workers?

   f. How did you feel when you weren't "it"?

LISTENING IN GROUPS: MEANING

Take several minutes to discuss strong feelings, moral convictions, and personal beliefs. Record the findings on the blackboard, on a flip chart, or by some electronic means. Topics may include, but should not be limited to, the following:

a. Whether to legalize "soft drugs" and invest the tax profits in education and health care;

b. Whether to legalize prostitution (both male and female) and invest the profits in health care and research;

c. Whether to ban all forms of corporal punishment for children (including parental "discipline");

d. Whether to ban smoking in automobiles;

e. Whether to make licences mandatory for the operation of motorized recreational vehicles such as snowmobiles and motorboats, and whether to restrict these licences to people 16 years of age and older;

f. Whether to stop funding any system of education that is not public (e.g., religious schools, other private schools);

g. Whether anyone caught with illegal possession of firearms while committing a crime should get an automatic ten-year prison term on top of what the judge imposes;

h. Whether religious institutions (e.g., churches, mosques, temples, synagogues) should be taxed and the profits invested in municipal infrastructures such as roads, sewers, and the like.

Having compiled a list of this sort, proceed with the following steps:

1. Select groups of three participants.

2. Appoint one referee from each group.

3. Ask the two others in the group to select a topic from the list (or come up with an alternative) that will produce a disagreement between them.

4. Ask one participant to explain to the other his or her point of view on the topic. Limit the speaker to two minutes and ask him or her to focus on a small number of points. The speaker will be allowed to continue later in the exercise if more points need to be made. The listener may not speak during this discussion or express disagreement by any gestures or expressions.

5. When the speaker's time is up, ask the listener to paraphrase what the speaker has said.

6. When the person who was listening is finished with the paraphrase, ask the person who first spoke, "Is this what you said?"

7. If the person who spoke first agrees that the paraphrase was accurate, the two participants will change roles. The person who listened first

becomes the speaker and gives his or her point of view on the topic. Repeat the process.

8. Go back to the person who spoke first, and ask whether he or she has any additional points to make or has a response to the second speaker. Repeat the process.

9. When both participants have finished, ask them to paraphrase what the other one has said.

10. The referee's role will be to keep the discussion on track, to limit the two-minute discussions to a few specific points, to make sure that the listener does not speak or gesture while the other participant is speaking, and generally to maintain order.

Participants can then discuss the feelings and attitudes they had while listening, how difficult it was to listen and not interfere, whether they changed their point of view on the topic after listening to the speaker, and how important it was to listen to the entirety of what the other had to say.

EXERCISE 8

LISTENING IN INTERVIEWS

Assume that you are the investigating officer in the Wainman case described in Chapter 8 on page 201. Have one person in your class assume the role of Muriel Wainman. Using the information supplied in Chapter 8, interview Wainman concerning the accident. Use some of the questioning techniques described in this chapter and, by practising good listening skills, attempt to find out exactly what happened. The person playing the role of Wainman is allowed to make up facts (e.g., "I was trying to tune into my favourite radio station when the blue car passed me ..."). She (or he) might also behave as if she were upset by the recent accident, straying off topic into unrelated family problems. Although the text does not say that there were witnesses to the accident, it does affirm that people were at the scene attempting to assist Wainman when the officer arrived. Interview them as well, and write down answers while the people you interview are speaking.

Summary

Listening skills are difficult to master because of the various distractions, external and internal, that exist in any listening situation. Understand your own listening habits, and learn how to improve any shortcomings in your personal listening skills. Proper questioning methods will likely result in more useful responses.

SPELLING AND DEFINITIONS

Be able to spell and define the following words:

abatement	corroborate	guardian	quash
attendance	decision	humiliate	remittance
behaviour	discrepancy	litigious	sophisticated
benefited	dissipate	perversion	testify
catastrophe	duress	poisonous	transitory
citizen	exaggerate	prejudice	trustee
correspond	grievance	promissory	urgent

MINI-PUZZLE

Complete the following crossword using the definitions given below it. The words are taken from the Spelling and Definitions list for this chapter.

Across

4. Highly developed, refined.
6. Calamity; disaster; final event.
7. To scatter, disperse, vanish.
8. To increase beyond expected limits; to represent beyond the truth.
9. Complaint or cause of resentment.

Down

1. The freeing of someone from a debt or punishment; the sending of money as payment.
2. A difference or inconsistency between two accounts.
3. Make a sworn statement in court.
5. Passing; moving from one place, state, or topic to another.

WORD SEARCH

The following contains words from the Spelling and Definitions list. Find these words and circle them. Words may be spelled backwards or forwards, and may run horizontally, vertically, or diagonally.

```
L  D  E  H  D  X  K  Y  M  R  P  E  O  E  T  L  M  J  H  H  G  Y  C  P  Z
H  N  T  A  I  K  M  Q  V  C  A  T  A  S  T  R  O  P  H  E  W  T  J  L  O
A  O  A  K  S  N  B  V  E  C  N  A  D  N  E  T  T  A  T  N  E  G  R  U  M
S  P  I  R  S  T  F  B  N  O  I  S  R  E  V  R  E  P  Y  E  H  T  P  E  G
U  S  L  T  I  J  E  C  N  A  T  T  I  M  E  R  G  I  T  R  D  O  T  H  P
O  E  I  O  P  W  A  Q  I  C  G  S  B  S  T  Z  M  A  R  E  U  Y  P  B  F
N  R  M  K  A  F  M  W  J  X  G  Y  J  A  Y  E  R  Q  T  R  C  R  G  I  F
O  R  U  Y  T  U  D  V  M  H  F  H  F  D  W  E  S  A  Y  N  O  A  X  H  P
S  O  H  U  E  H  I  P  X  J  O  I  D  K  G  Z  C  T  A  M  H  E  Q  R  V
I  C  D  I  G  Q  E  U  J  I  D  N  L  G  M  I  J  P  I  A  K  C  B  V  Y
O  Q  A  M  S  Y  R  O  T  I  S  N  A  R  T  K  E  S  Y  F  F  V  L  Z  N
P  B  E  N  E  F  I  T  E  D  W  X  H  S  L  R  S  X  T  J  Y  D  P  J  L
A  U  O  C  S  C  K  I  K  X  E  G  I  R  C  O  M  I  B  R  F  T  K  M  J
A  T  R  F  T  K  Q  S  X  Y  F  H  T  S  R  V  B  E  H  A  V  I  O  U  R
Y  U  H  F  Y  Y  C  V  C  L  P  X  I  Y  Q  D  F  T  Q  G  Q  X  B  Q  V
Y  G  O  V  G  T  C  N  Y  O  T  D  O  E  T  A  R  O  B  O  R  R  O  C  O
C  Z  N  F  Y  M  D  U  S  F  R  S  L  V  L  E  Q  T  O  X  M  Q  B  I  F
```

ATTENDANCE	BEHAVIOUR	BENEFITED
CATASTROPHE	CORRESPOND	CORROBORATE
DISCREPANCY	DISSIPATE	EXAGGERATE
HUMILIATE	PERVERSION	POISONOUS
PROMISSORY	REMITTANCE	SOPHISTICATED
TESTIFY	TRANSITORY	URGENT

CHAPTER 2
Spelling

Learning Objectives

After completing this chapter, you should be able to:

- Understand the importance of spelling to law enforcement professionals.
- Follow spelling rules.
- Spell troublesome words.
- Increase your personal vocabulary.
- Increase your professional vocabulary.
- Differentiate between words that are commonly confused.

Introduction

Spelling in English is difficult because the language contains so many words that defy the basic spelling rules. In addition, irregular verbs, double *l* words, *ou* words, irregular plurals, possessives, and contractions make spelling a chore.

However, the law enforcement officer must know how to spell. Poor spelling casts doubt on the quality of reports and evidence. Law enforcement personnel are expected to be professionals, and poor spelling brings their professionalism into question. Imagine the following scenario:

> *Defence lawyer*: "Constable, you wrote in your report that you raped the victim after you were called to assist her."
> *Officer*: "I didn't rape anyone!"
> *Defence lawyer*: "Can you verify that this is your signature and badge number at the bottom of this report?"

Officer: "Yes, I wrote the report and signed it."

Defence lawyer: "Well, you wrote, and I quote, 'I raped the victim in a blanket after I gave her medical attention and called for an ambulance.'"

Officer: "Oh, I meant 'wrapped.' I wrapped her in a blanket; I didn't rape her."

Defence lawyer: "But your report says you raped her."

Officer: "It was a spelling mistake."

Defence lawyer: "How many other errors, then, are in your report?"

In spite of the many spelling irregularities in the language, there are some basic rules. Some of these spelling rules are set out in this chapter. Also included are lists of difficult words to help you discover patterns in the spelling of single words and groups of words.

When you review the principles of good writing, you begin with the study of words and of grammar. This chapter of the book and the next one, therefore, deal with how words are spelled, how grammar applies to good writing, and how words are used in sentences.

You cannot write effectively if you are a poor speller. Poor spelling is the most noticeable of all writing faults. The complaints that schools and colleges hear about the writing of their graduates are mostly concerned with poor spelling.

Improving Your Spelling

Use a dictionary to find the correct spellings of uncommon or difficult words, but you should not need it for common words such as *recommend* or *receive*. You should know words like these, and you should be able to write them as correctly and as effortlessly as you write your own name.

The 400 words most commonly misspelled by college students are found on the following pages. These words are used so frequently that you should begin your review by learning how to spell them perfectly.

To study the spelling of a word, take the following steps:

1. **Look at the word carefully and examine its structure.** Does it have a common prefix (*un*necessary, *un*interesting, *dis*appointed, *dis*satisfied) or a common suffix (exist*ence*, differ*ence*, perform*ance*, attend*ance*)?

2. **Pronounce the word correctly.** Many students misspell words such as *government, candidate*, and *library* because they have always mispronounced these words.

3. **Pronounce the word by syllables.** Sounding out the word part by part can help you with its spelling (e.g., "ac-com-mo-date").

4. **Notice the hard spots.** Misspellings almost always occur in the same place within a given word, so watch out for these hard spots (e.g., per*severance*, sep*arate*).

5. **Use memory devices.** The following are helpful memory devices: "Lett*ers* are written on station*ery*," and "*i* before *e* except after *c*."

Write the words you are studying over and over, and practise them until the correct spelling becomes a habit. Learn them any way you can, but *learn* them.

◗ 100 TROUBLESOME WORDS

1. success	26. evidently	51. satisfied	76. suggestion
2. difference	27. convenient	52. completely	77. explanation
3. pleasant	28. transferred	53. advertising	78. authority
4. remember	29. minimum	54. apparently	79. affectionately
5. finally	30. instruction	55. absolutely	80. cordially
6. preferred	31. foreign	56. information	81. situation
7. usually	32. examination	57. further	82. purpose
8. consideration	33. envelope	58. material	83. committee
9. doubt	34. description	59. purchase	84. representative
10. appearance	35. statement	60. ridiculous	85. necessary
11. determined	36. guarantee	61. secretary	86. probably
12. decision	37. naturally	62. duly	87. cancellation
13. actually	38. regretting	63. interest	88. regarding
14. extremely	39. beautiful	64. mortgage	89. tentative
15. endeavour	40. practical	65. occurred	90. recently
16. advisable	41. unnecessary	66. capacity	91. organization
17. position	42. therefore	67. assume	92. recommendation
18. basis	43. additional	68. equipped	93. cancelled
19. clothes	44. inquiry	69. double	94. bureau
20. although	45. character	70. quantity	95. government
21. February	46. catalogue	71. acknowledge	96. unfortunately
22. annual	47. impossible	72. criticism	97. commission
23. partial	48. superintendent	73. occasion	98. bulletin
24. obliged	49. assistance	74. especially	99. attention
25. anxious	50. application	75. surprise	100. considerable

▶ ANOTHER 100 TROUBLESOME WORDS

101. exactly	127. financial	153. Wednesday	179. satisfactory
102. library	128. addressed	154. Saturday	180. practice (n.)
103. studying	129. possibility	155. women	practise (v.)
104. article	130. sufficient	156. American	181. exception
105. attached	131. correspondence	157. business	182. excellent
106. approval	132. schedule	158. undoubtedly	183. replying
107. equipment	133. response	159. beginning	184. immediately
108. hospital	134. exceedingly	160. realize	185. cooperation
109. insurance	135. special	161. imagine	(or co-operation)
110. estimate	136. available	162. opportunity	186. courtesy
111. memorandum	137. distribution	163. knowledge	187. appreciation
112. paid	138. sincerely	164. perhaps	188. requirements
113. freight	139. similar	165. experience	189. individual
114. remittance	140. arrangement	166. reference	190. accordance
115. forward	141. disappoint	167. necessity	191. merchandise
116. convenience	142. remit	168. grateful	192. various
117. earliest	143. judgment	169. general	193. effort
118. duplicate	144. extension	170. permanent	194. association
119. written	145. particular	171. certificate	195. circumstances
120. invoice	146. all right	172. temporary	196. prompt
121. thoroughly	147. mention	173. difficult	197. policy
122. campaign	148. proposition	174. definite	198. customer
123. benefit	149. planning	175. approximately	199. assure
124. community	150. balance	176. opinion	200. communication
125. acquaintance	151. shipment	177. specified	
126. familiar	152. either	178. length	

▶ 200 FREQUENTLY MISSPELLED WORDS

1. absence	34. cafeteria	67. disease	100. influential
2. accessible	35. calendar	68. division	101. insistence
3. accidentally	36. candidate	69. earnestly	102. intelligence
4. accommodate	37. captain	70. eighth	103. interfere
5. accumulate	38. carrying	71. electricity	104. interrupt
6. accurately	39. catalogue	72. embarrassed	105. invitation
7. achieve	40. certain	73. emphasize	106. laboratory
8. acquainted	41. characteristic	74. essential	107. lightning
9. acquisition	42. chocolate	75. exaggerate	108. literature
10. address	43. choice	76. excitement	109. loneliness
11. advantageous	44. column	77. exercise	110. maintenance
12. agreeable	45. compelling	78. exhausted	111. mathematics
13. allegiance	46. competent	79. extraordinary	112. mechanically
14. almost	47. competition	80. facilities	113. merely
15. already	48. compulsory	81. familiar	114. miniature
16. amateur	49. concentration	82. formula	115. mischievous
17. amount	50. concern	83. generally	116. mysterious
18. apparatus	51. confident	84. grammar	117. negligence
19. appetite	52. conquer	85. gymnasium	118. niece
20. approach	53. conscientious	86. harass	119. ninety
21. appropriate	54. continually	87. height	120. noticeable
22. argument	55. controlled	88. hindrance	121. obedience
23. associate	56. courteous	89. humorous	122. occasionally
24. athlete	57. dealt	90. hygiene	123. occurrence
25. athletic	58. deceive	91. illegible	124. o'clock
26. attendance	59. deficiency	92. illiterate	125. omelette
27. aviator	60. definition	93. imagination	126. omitted
28. awkward	61. dependent	94. immensely	127. original
29. bachelor	62. desperate	95. imitation	128. parallel
30. beneficial	63. development	96. inaccuracy	129. paralyze
31. biscuit	64. digestible	97. incidentally	130. pastime
32. bookkeeper	65. dining	98. inevitable	131. perform
33. boundary	66. disappeared	99. independence	132. permissible

▶ **200 FREQUENTLY MISSPELLED WORDS (concluded)**

133. perseverance	150. professional	167. rhyme	184. successfully
134. persistent	151. professor	168. rhythm	185. surround
135. perspiration	152. prominent	169. sacrifice	186. technical
136. persuade	153. pronunciation	170. sandwich	187. tenant
137. physically	154. pursuing	171. scarcely	188. tendency
138. physician	155. recipe	172. scissors	189. truly
139. picnicking	156. recognize	173. seize	190. twelfth
140. politics	157. recollect	174. sentence	191. unaccustomed
141. possession	158. recommend	175. separate	192. unanimous
142. practically	159. referred	176. sergeant	193. unusual
143. predicament	160. rehearsal	177. serviceable	194. vacuum
144. prejudice	161. relieve	178. severely	195. valuable
145. preparation	162. religious	179. shining	196. varied
146. presence	163. repetition	180. siege	197. vegetable
147. privilege	164. reservoir	181. specimen	198. villain
148. probability	165. respectability	182. strength	199. weird
149. procedure	166. restaurant	183. succeed	200. wholly

WORD SEARCH

Below the puzzle is a list of words taken from the above list of frequently misspelled words. Find these words in the puzzle and circle them.

```
Z  N  R  D  M  I  S  C  H  I  E  V  O  U  S  G  C  C  N  Q  W  P  H  N  A
M  L  L  I  G  H  T  N  I  N  G  Y  A  R  O  R  Q  L  T  B  G  N  M  S  C
W  Y  Y  C  H  R  L  I  A  L  A  D  E  Q  U  Z  S  C  F  F  U  U  E  G  V
Z  L  C  G  E  I  A  E  E  C  N  A  R  E  V  E  S  R  E  P  L  T  T  T  H
A  L  A  E  C  O  I  I  W  Z  W  G  P  U  Z  G  T  E  F  O  C  I  A  H  S
C  A  R  X  I  V  T  L  O  M  E  L  E  T  T  E  D  A  C  X  D  U  R  N  G
Q  T  U  H  O  R  N  N  Z  E  N  T  A  L  P  P  X  W  M  I  M  C  E  V  E
U  N  C  A  H  E  E  U  O  B  K  Y  A  J  R  N  R  Q  D  A  J  S  P  F  X
I  E  C  U  C  S  S  F  E  T  M  T  Z  R  L  E  M  O  R  E  N  I  S  A  R
S  D  A  S  K  E  S  N  W  O  I  Q  X  P  E  H  U  X  M  V  C  B  E  X  A
I  I  N  T  L  R  E  V  B  B  I  C  Y  O  R  T  J  Q  P  I  T  E  D  I  A
T  C  I  E  Y  F  M  G  P  R  J  X  E  Y  Q  M  I  A  N  J  N  K  I  X  P
I  C  A  D  I  Y  F  J  N  M  D  A  J  A  L  Q  A  L  R  O  W  E  K  V  R
O  A  L  C  X  L  U  X  U  R  I  O  U  S  B  A  Y  B  L  O  C  B  N  G  E
N  K  I  Q  B  U  R  D  I  S  U  H  T  N  Y  L  E  X  H  I  K  V  U  T  X
W  A  G  Y  H  R  J  E  Z  Y  L  A  R  A  P  E  G  R  A  M  M  A  R  H
L  A  I  B  B  P  O  L  I  T  I  C  S  Q  Y  H  L  C  T  O  X  R  B  B  M
```

ACCIDENTALLY	CHOICE	ESSENTIAL	LIGHTNING
PERSEVERANCE	ACQUISITION	COLUMN	EXHAUSTED
MISCHIEVOUS	POLITICS	AMATEUR	CONQUER
GRAMMAR	NOTICEABLE	PROMINENT	BENEFICIAL
DECEIVE	ILLITERATE	OMELETTE	LUXURIOUS
BISCUIT	DESPERATE	INACCURACY	PARALYZE
RESERVOIR			

Useful Spelling Rules

Because most of us learn to spell by studying and practising one word at a time, you may find that some spelling rules are more confusing than helpful. But these rules apply to thousands of words and therefore may help you avoid many common difficulties. Four useful rules are set out below.

RULE 1

If a word ends with a *y* preceded by a consonant (as in *copy* or *try*), change the *y* to an *i* before every suffix except *ing*.

copy	+	es	=	copies
copy	+	ing	=	copying
worry	+	ed	=	worried
worry	+	ing	=	worrying
try	+	ed	=	tried
try	+	ing	=	trying
lady	+	es	=	ladies

If the *y* is preceded by a vowel, do not change it (as in *valley* or *honey*).

valley	+	s	=	valleys
honey	+	s	=	honeys

RULE 2

Write *i* before *e* except after *c* or when sounded as *a*, as in *neighbour* or *weigh*.

> *i* before *e* : brief, piece, belief, chief
>
> *e* before *i* : receive, ceiling, deceive, freight, weight, sleigh

Exceptions to the rule:

> either, neither, seize, leisure, weird

RULE 3

If a word ends with a single consonant preceded by a single vowel (*stop*, *begin*) and you add a suffix beginning with a vowel (*-ed*, *-ing*, *-ance*), double the final consonant in the two situations described below:

1. The word has only one syllable:

stop	+	ed	=	stopped
trip	+	ed	=	tripped
rub	+	ing	=	rubbing
drop	+	ing	=	dropping

2. The word is accented on the last syllable:

confer	+	ed	=	conferred
begin	+	ing	=	beginning
omit	+	ing	=	omitting
remit	+	ance	=	remittance

Do not double the final consonant if the accent is not on the last syllable (*benefited, profited, exhibited*).

RULE 4

If the word ends with a silent *e* (*bite*, *use*) and you add a suffix, the following rules apply:

1. Drop the *e* if the suffix begins with a vowel.

bite	+	ing	=	biting
use	+	able	=	usable
desire	+	able	=	desirable
gaze	+	ed	=	gazed

2. Keep the *e* if the suffix begins with a consonant.

use	+	ful	=	useful
achieve	+	ment	=	achievement
love	+	ly	=	lovely
hope	+	less	=	hopeless

These rules have two exceptions:

1. Words such as *noticeable* and *courageous* retain the silent *e* to keep the preceding consonant (*c* or *g*) soft.

2. Words such as *truly* and *argument* drop the silent *e* that follows a vowel.

Plurals

With most words, you simply add *s* to form the plural.

bed	beds
book	books
pipe	pipes

Words ending in a sibilant *ch*, *sh*, *s*, *x*, or *z*, however, add *es* to form the plural.

boss	bosses
box	boxes
bush	bushes
buzz	buzzes
catch	catches
sash	sashes
dress	dresses
fox	foxes

There are two rules for words that end in *y*:

1. If a consonant precedes the *y*, change *y* to *i* and add *es*.

activity	activities
apology	apologies
duty	duties

2. If a vowel precedes the *y*, simply add *s*.

attorney	attorneys
monkey	monkeys
toy	toys

For words that end in *f*, either add *s* or change *f* to *v* and add *es*, depending on the particular case.

belief	beliefs
chief	chiefs
cliff	cliffs
half	halves
life	lives
leaf	leaves
self	selves
loaf	loaves
wife	wives

There are many irregular plurals, some of which are set out below.

ox	oxen
child	children
deer	deer
foot	feet
goose	geese
moose	moose
man	men
woman	women
mouse	mice

There are three types of nouns that end in *o*, and there is a different pluralizing rule for each type.

1. If a vowel precedes the *o*, simply add *s*.

boo	boos
stereo	stereos
radio	radios

2. If the word is a musical term, add *s*.

piano	pianos
solo	solos

3. For all other words ending in *o*, there is no rule. The plurals must be memorized.

echo	echoes
silo	silos
hero	heroes
poncho	ponchos
zero	zeroes
potato	potatoes
tomato	tomatoes

4. Certain plurals derive from their Greek or Latin roots.

crisis	crises
thesis	theses
datum	data
criterion	criteria

EXERCISE 1

FORMING PLURALS

Change the following singular nouns to their correct plural form:

1.	attorney	_____	26.	dress	_____
2.	kiss	_____	27.	paper	_____
3.	rodeo	_____	28.	loss	_____
4.	crisis	_____	29.	chimney	_____
5.	foot	_____	30.	miss	_____
6.	piccolo	_____	31.	mix	_____
7.	bed	_____	32.	knife	_____
8.	cargo	_____	33.	key	_____
9.	watch	_____	34.	laugh	_____
10.	buzz	_____	35.	wish	_____
11.	analysis	_____	36.	duty	_____
12.	canoe	_____	37.	tool	_____
13.	patio	_____	38.	roof	_____
14.	man	_____	39.	push	_____
15.	latch	_____	40.	mouse	_____
16.	basis	_____	41.	loaf	_____
17.	self	_____	42.	wall	_____
18.	apology	_____	43.	bus	_____
19.	zero	_____	44.	table	_____
20.	six	_____	45.	business	_____
21.	child	_____	46.	axe	_____
22.	baby	_____	47.	belief	_____
23.	goose	_____	48.	pass	_____
24.	try	_____	49.	donkey	_____
25.	box	_____	50.	penalty	_____

☐ Word Problems

Troublesome words fall into four broad categories:

1. **Homographs**: words that have the same spelling, but have different meanings or uses.

2. **Homonyms**: words that have the same pronunciation, but different spellings and often different meanings.

3. **Synonyms**: words with similar meanings.

4. **Antonyms**: words with opposite meanings.

The following list includes, in addition to words in these categories, a selection of words that are commonly misspelled or misused, and words that are overused.

▶ WORDS FREQUENTLY MISUSED

a, an   These words are *indefinite articles*, used with nouns. *A* is used with nouns that begin with a consonant sound. *An* is used with nouns that begin with a vowel sound.

accede, exceed   To *accede* to something is to go along with it. *To exceed* your limits is to go too far.

accept, except   To *accept* something is to receive it. *To except* something is to exclude it or leave it out. *Except* is also an adverb that means "excluding."

access, excess   *Access* is the way into something. *Excess* means "extra" or "too much."

ad, add   The word *ad* is an abbreviation of *advertisement*. It is best avoided in formal communications. *To add* is to combine or to take a total.

adapt, adept   To *adapt* is to change, either oneself or something else. *Adept* is an adjective meaning "skilled."

addition, edition   *Addition* is the process of adding, or the thing or person added. An *edition* is a version of something, usually a book.

advice, advise   *Advice* is a noun; it is the information that well-meaning people give you when they counsel or *advise* (verb) you.

affect, effect   To *affect* (verb) is to influence, or to put on an act. An *affect* (noun—a psychologists' jargon word) is an emotion. *To effect* (verb) is to make something happen, and an *effect* (noun) is the result of what happens.

all ready, already   *All ready* means "to be prepared." *Already* means "previously."

all right, alright   Fundamentally, *all right* means "all correct." The expression also has a variety of colloquial meanings. It should not be spelled *alright*.

all together, altogether   *All together* means "as a group." *Altogether* means "entirely." *All together* is also a colloquial expression meaning "rational."

all ways, always   *All ways* means "in every aspect" or "in every direction." *Always* means "forever."

allot, alot, a lot   To *allot* something is to distribute or assign it. *Alot* is a common misspelling of *a lot*, which is an informal way of saying "a great deal" or "a large amount." A *lot* is also a piece of property.

allude, elude   To *allude* to something is to refer to it. *Elude* means "to escape."

allusion, illusion   An *allusion* is a reference to something. An *illusion* is an unreal picture or idea.

aloud, allowed   *Aloud* means "audible, not silent or whispered." *Allowed* means "permitted" or, in some cases, "admitted" or "confessed."

altar, alter   An *altar* (noun) is a raised ceremonial area, usually in a church or other place of worship. *To alter* (verb) something is to change it.

◗ WORDS FREQUENTLY MISUSED (continued)

alternate, alternative   An *alternate* (noun) is a substitute, or a person or thing that replaces someone or something else. The verb *to alternate* means "to take turns"; as an adjective, *alternate* means "secondary." *Alternative* means "another option."

although   As a conjunction, *although* is synonymous and interchangeable with *though*. *Though* is also used as an adverb. *Tho* and *altho* are not acceptable spellings. *Although* means "in spite of the fact that." For example, "She is happy although she has no money."

among, between   *Among* means "surrounded by." It refers to a position in the midst of several or more. *Between* means "separating," and refers to the situation, or position, of being bounded by two people or things.

amount, number   The *amount* is the quantity, the sum total. It is not the same as *number*, which is the total of all the units.

annual, annul   *Annual* is an adverb meaning "yearly." *Annul* (verb) means "to cancel."

anyway, any way   *Anyway* is a colloquial form of "in any event" or "in any case." *Any way* means "any means" or "any path."

appraise, apprise   *To appraise* is to evaluate. *To apprise* is to let someone know something, to inform.

are, our, hour   *Are* is a present tense of the verb *to be*. *Our* means "belonging to us." An *hour* is a time unit of 60 minutes.

as yet   *As yet* often functions as a wordy synonym for *yet*.

assistance, assistants   *Assistance* means "help" or "aid." *Assistants* are those people or things who give help or aid.

attendance, attendants   Your *attendance* means "your presence." *Attendants* are those people who give assistance.

between   See *among*.

born, borne   *Born* means "given birth to" or "created." *To be borne* is to be carried.

brake, break   *To brake* (verb) means "to put a stop to something"; the *brake* (noun) is the device on a car or piece of equipment that makes it stop. *To break* something is to make it come apart or shatter.

canvas, canvass   A *canvas* is a heavy piece of cloth used to cover things, camp under, or paint on. *To canvass* (verb) means "to solicit," as in the case of opinions or money.

capital, capitol   As an adjective, *capital* means "important" or "chief." As a noun, it commonly means "the city in a province, territory, or country that is the centre of government." *Capitol* refers to the building where a legislature meets.

cease, seize   *To cease* is to stop. *To seize* is to take hold of or to capture. Note the spelling of *seize*, which violates the "*i* before *e*" rule.

cite, sight, site   *To cite* means "to refer to" or "to award." *To sight* is to see; a *sight* (noun) is what is seen. *To site* is to locate; a *site* (noun) is a location.

close, clothes   *Close* is a homograph; pronounced one way, and used as an adverb, it means "near" or "in the vicinity." Pronounced another way, and used as a verb, it means "to shut." *Clothes* are the garments you wear.

complement, compliment   *To complement* is to add something that completes or enhances, and a *complement* (noun) is a supply of something. *To compliment* means "to praise," and a *compliment* (noun) is a piece of praise.

comprise, consist of, constitute   *To comprise* means "to contain." It is used informally to mean *consist of*, which means "made up of." *To constitute* means "to compose" or "to form" or "to create." The phrase *is comprised of* is always grammatically incorrect; use *is composed of* instead.

conscience, conscious   Your *conscience* is your inner moral feeling. *Conscious of* means "aware of."

◆ WORDS FREQUENTLY MISUSED (continued)

continual, continuous   *Continual* means "occurring constantly, again and again." *Continuous* means "happening without interruption."

could of, should of, would of   These word combinations are ungrammatical. *Could, should,* and *would* combine with the verb *have: could have, should have, would have.*

council, counsel, consul   A *council* is a group of advisers, or *councillors. Counsel* means "advice," something a *counsellor* would give. A *consul* is a country's representative, whose office is a *consulate.* In a legal environment, *counsellor* is rarely used. The *counsel* is an outside adviser who is a lawyer.

credible, creditable, credulous   Something that is *credible* is something that can be believed. *Creditable* means "praiseworthy." *Credulous* means "easily deceived."

decent, descent, dissent   *Decent* means "morally proper" or "adequate." *Descent* (noun) is the act or process of descending, while *dissent* means "disagreement."

desert, dessert   A *desert* (noun) is a dry wasteland, while *desert* (verb), pronounced differently, means "to leave without permission." *Dessert* is what is served after the main course of a meal.

device, devise   A *device* is "an instrument" or "a means of achieving an end." *Devise* (verb) means "to plan" or "to put together."

discreet, discrete   *Discreet* means "tactful" or "inclined to keep things to yourself." *Discrete* means "separate and distinct."

dual, duel   *Dual* (adjective) means "consisting of two parts." A *duel* is a single-combat fight between two people.

elicit, illicit   *To elicit* something is to extract it or draw it out from some source, as when you ask for information. *Illicit* means "illegal."

elude   See *allude.*

emigrate, immigrate   To leave a country permanently and live in another country is to *emigrate*; to enter a country and live there permanently is to *immigrate.*

eminent, imminent   *Eminent* means "well known" or "famous." *Imminent* means "on the point of arriving."

employ, use   *To employ* is to use something or someone in a specified way, usually with the sense of paying someone a wage in return for services.

exceed   See *accede.*

except   See *accept.*

expand, expend   *To expand* is to increase in size. *To expend* is to use up or to spend.

farther, further   Both *farther* and *further* can indicate physical distance, but *further* is preferable when you mean "also," "to a greater extent," or "in addition to."

feel   Avoid the overworked expression *I feel* when you want to render an opinion. Instead use *I believe* or *I think.*

fewer, less   *Fewer* means "a smaller number," while *less* refers to quantity and means "a smaller amount."

firstly   An overused adverb, replaceable by *first.*

forth, fourth   To go *forth* is to go onward. To finish *fourth* is to arrive after three others.

four, for   *Four* is a number; *for* is a conjunction, a connecting word.

great, grate   *Great* means "large" or "renowned." A *grate* is a framework of bars, usually criss-crossed pieces of metal or wood.

if, whether   Both words are conjunctions. Use *if* in a conditional situation ("She will work if I pay her"); use *whether* when you are dealing with alternatives ("She will work whether or not I pay her," or "I don't know whether she will work").

illicit   See *elicit.*

illusion   See *allusion.*

◆ WORDS FREQUENTLY MISUSED (continued)

incidence, incidents   *Incidence* means "rate of occurrence" ("There was a high incidence of theft"). *Incidents* are events, occurrences.

imply, infer   To *imply* means "to insinuate," "to suggest something without saying it." To *infer* means "to draw a conclusion."

irony, sarcasm   *Irony* involves saying one thing but meaning something else, usually the opposite of what is said, and doing so in a subtle manner so that the real meaning may not be clear. *Sarcasm* is a form of heavy, often bitter irony that leaves no question that the real meaning is opposite to what is being said.

irregardless, regardless   There is no word *irregardless*. Use *regardless* to mean "despite everything," "in any event," or "heedless."

its, it's   *Its* is the possessive form of *it*. *It's* is a contraction for *it is* or *it has*.

knew, new   *Knew* is the past tense of *know*. *New* means "not old."

know, no   To *know* is to understand. *No* expresses negation or refusal.

last, latest, previous   The *last* comes after all the others; the *latest* is the most recent in a series; the *previous* one is the one that went before in time or order.

later, latter   *Later* means "afterwards." The *latter* is the second of two items.

lay, lie   To *lay* means "to put," and always takes an object. For example, "Lay the book down." *Lie* means "to recline," and never takes an object. For example, "Lie down if you are tired." To *lie* is also a verb meaning "to tell an untruth."

lead, led   To *lead* is to be first, to show the way, to be a distance ahead. The past tense is *led*, pronounced the same as *lead*, a metal.

liable, likely, libel, slander   *Liable* means "legally responsible" or "likely to do something" (usually something undesirable). It is used informally in the sense of *likely*, meaning "probable." A *libel* is a false written statement, damaging to someone's reputation. A *slander* is a false statement, spoken rather than written, that is damaging to someone's reputation. *Libel* and *slander* are not opposites.

like, as   *Like* and *as* are often used interchangeably as connectors ("He is the same as I am"; "He is like me"). *As* can be used as a conjunction or a preposition ("It is as dark as night") while *like* should only be used as a preposition ("She is like her mother"). *Like* is also a verb meaning "feel affection for."

loose, lose   *Loose* means "not tight." *Lose* is an antonym of win, and also means "to misplace."

maybe, may be   *Maybe* is an adverb, synonymous with "perhaps." *May be* is a conjugation of the verb *to be*, expressing possibility.

new   See *knew*.

no   See *know*.

number   See *amount*.

off of   *Off* alone does the job; it doesn't need the *of* ("He jumped off the bike").

pain, pane   A *pain* is something that hurts; a *pane* is a panel, usually of glass.

past, passed   *Past* can be a noun, an adverb, or an adjective ("She lives in the past"; "She ran past the tree"; "She thought of her past loves"). *Passed* is the past tense of the verb *to pass*, meaning "to go by" or "move beyond."

patience, patients   *Patience* means "forbearance" or "endurance." *Patients* are people under medical care.

peace, piece   *Peace* is an antonym of war. A *piece* of something is a part of it.

personal, personnel, personally   *Personal* indicates something owned by or affecting a person; something private. Employees are collectively known as *personnel*. The word *personally* is overused as a qualifying word, as in "Personally, I think he was wrong."

◆ WORDS FREQUENTLY MISUSED (concluded)

plane, plain   A *plane* is a flat surface or a flying machine or a tool for smoothing wooden surfaces. *Plain* means "unattractive" or "unadorned," as well as "a large expanse of usually flat land."

presence, presents   *Presence* means "being in a place" or "attendance." *Presents* are gifts.

principal, principle   *Principal* indicates "most important" or "first." *Principles* are implied rules or ethics.

quiet, quite   *Quiet* means "not noisy," "silent," "unassuming." *Quite* means "entirely" or "to a considerable degree."

raise, rise   *To raise* means "to make something move up" or "to grow," and always takes an object. For example, "I raise the flag." *To rise* means "to stand up" or "to move upward," and never takes an object. For example, "I rise in the morning."

regardless   See *irregardless.*

right, rite, write, wright   *Right* means "the opposite of left" or "a privilege." A *rite* is a ceremony, usually religious. *To write* is to form words on a page. A *wright* is a craftsperson who makes a specified thing ("wheelwright," "playwright").

role, roll   A *role* is a part played by an actor. A *roll* is, among various other things, a list or a bakery product. *Roll* as a verb means "to turn over."

sarcasm   See *irony.*

set, sit   *To set* means "to put something in position," and always takes an object. For example, "Set the book over there." *To sit* means "to take a sitting position," and never takes an object. For example, "Sit in the chair."

should of   See *could of.*

sight, site   See *cite.*

so   Don't use this word as a lone intensive: "She was *so* lucky." Use *very* instead.

stationary, stationery   *Stationary* means "not moving." *Stationery* refers to the materials used for writing, typing; office supplies.

than, then   *Than* is used in comparisons ("bigger than"). *Then* is used in time sequences ("now and then").

their, there, they're   *Their* means "belonging to them." *There* is a place. *They're* is a contraction of *they are.*

though   See *although.*

threw, throw, through, thorough   *Threw* is the past tense of the verb *to throw. Through* is an adverb expressing passage into and out of something, and an adjective meaning "finished." *Thorough* is an adjective that means "exacting," "done with care," "leaving no room for doubt."

to, too, two   *To* is, among other things, a preposition indicating a direction or destination. *Too* means "excessively" or "also." *Two* is a number.

weak, week   *Weak* means "not strong." A *week* is seven days.

weather, whether   The atmospheric condition is what we call the *weather.* We use *whether* to indicate a choice between, or a question involving, alternatives. ("He didn't know whether to buy the blue one or the grey one.") See also *if.*

who's, whose   *Who's* is a contraction of *who is. Whose* is the possessive form of "who" and can function either as an adjective ("Whose coat is that?") or as a pronoun ("Whose is that?").

would of   See *could of.*

write   See *right.*

your, you're   *Your* is an adjective, the possessive form of *you*, meaning "owned by you." *You're* is a contraction of *you are.*

EXERCISE 2

DISTINGUISHING HOMONYMS

Correct the following sentence:

Weather the weather be cold, or weather the weather be hot, we'll weather the

weather whatever the weather, weather we like it or not.

EXERCISE 3

CHOOSING THE CORRECT SPELLING

Correct the following passage:

When going for an interview, your wise too exercise patients. Be prepared. Find

out about the personal of the company, than any other peace of information

your likely to need if your asked about the company. Find out whose in charge. Be

through in your answers. Your more liable to be considered if you no the amount of

employees. Perhaps the boss is an imminent person in the community. Go further

in your analysis of questions than expected; the less number of things you know

about the company, the less likely youll feel grate about the interview. Irregardless,

its important that you do your best and ask for assistants if you can't answer a

question. Sight any awards you know the company has received, and complement

the company for its successes. Appear credulous to your interviewers, present

yourself as a descent person, use whatever devises you need to make your points,

and don't forget—wear proper close.

EXERCISE 4

SELECTING THE RIGHT WORD

Choose the correct word in each of the following sentences:

1. Counsel for the defendant has (acceded, exceeded) to the Crown attorney's request for additional information.

2. The judge prefers witness statements not to (accede, exceed) two pages.

3. The court documents will be delivered this afternoon. Please (accept, except) them on my behalf.

4. Everything is in the file (accept, except) the list of witnesses.

5. The divorce settlement awarded custody of the children to the wife, but the husband has (access, excess) to them on weekends.

6. If he drinks to (access, excess), however, he will lose this privilege.

7. Sometimes it seems that more television time is devoted to (ads, adds) than to programs.

8. The figures in this bill are wrong. Please (ad, add) them up again.

9. Correctional personnel must (adapt, adept) their communication styles to meet the needs of specific situations.

10. You need to be (adapt, adept) at comforting victims of crime.

11. Is this new task an (addition, edition) to my regular duties?

12. Please order the latest (edition, addition) of the *Globe and Mail Stylebook*.

13. The client is going to seek the (advice, advise) of counsel in this matter.

14. I strongly (advice, advise) you not to be late for your court hearing, as this judge is known to be impatient.

15. The new insurance regulations will (affect, effect) your premium for next year.

16. At the examination for discovery, the defendant displayed a confused (affect, effect).

17. The new manager is (affecting, effecting) many changes in procedure.

18. Poor communications skills will have a negative (affect, effect) on your career in law enforcement.

19. Mrs. Smith's will (allots, a lots, alots) various sums of money to all her beneficiaries.

20. We don't have (allot, alot, a lot) of time to prepare the case for court.

21. We expect (allot, a lot) of donations to the holiday fund.

22. We are (all ready, already) for the meeting (all ready, already).

23. I have (all ready, already) finished my report on the shoplifting suspect.

24. The documents are (all together, altogether) on my desk.

25. I'm not (all together, altogether) sure that this is true.

26. We agree in (all ways, always) that matter.

27. I will (all ways, always) remember my first job.

28. Rehearse your presentation (aloud, allowed) to determine how it sounds.

29. Driving without a licence is not (aloud, allowed) by law.

30. The judge (alluded, eluded) to the defendant's previous offences when she sentenced him.

31. They won't be able to (allude, elude) justice for long.

32. The speaker made constant (allusion, illusion) to the news of the day.

EXERCISE 4 (continued)

33. I was under the (allusion, illusion) that this would be an easy job, but I was wrong.

34. Too often, principles are sacrificed on the (altar, alter) of profit.

35. The witness wants to (altar, alter) her statement.

36. Each director appoints an (alternate, alternative) in case he or she cannot attend a meeting.

37. The classes (alternate, alternative) between Mondays and Wednesdays.

38. I took the (alternate, alternative) route because of construction on the highway.

39. The evidence left the jury no (alternate, alternative) but to convict.

40. (Though, Although) Joan writes excellent research reports, it's not her favourite part of the job.

41. The security firm had to choose (between, among) three excellent candidates for the investigator's position.

42. Just (between, among) the two of us, I'm looking for a new job.

43. A huge (amount, number) of accidents take place on this corner every year.

44. The large (amount, number) of snow that fell overnight made it difficult to drive to work this morning.

45. The association holds its (annual, annul) conference in June.

46. I'm afraid you don't have grounds to (annual, annul) the contract.

47. (Lie, lay) the petition on his desk.

48. (Rise, raise) the table a bit to put this book under the broken leg.

49. I don't have much chance of winning the race, but I'll enter it (anyway, any way).

50. I want you to be successful and I will help you in (anyway, any way) I can.

51. You need to have your property (appraised, apprised) early in the process of selling it.

52. As a police officer, you should keep your superiors (appraised, apprised) of any information you receive about criminal activity.

53. We (are, our, hour) expecting to arrive at (are, our, hour) destination in an (are, our, hour).

54. We requested (assistance, assistants) from the RCMP in the investigation.

55. Arthur is such a busy lawyer that he needs not one but two (assistance, assistants).

56. Your (attendance, attendants) at the meeting is essential.

57. The bride and her (attendance, attendants) looked radiant.

58. Please complete the application form by inserting the year you were (born, borne).

59. My belief in his innocence was (born, borne) out by the evidence presented.

60. This candy is hard enough to (break, brake) my teeth.

61. The accident happened when the car's (breaks, brakes) failed.

62. The team worked six hours without a (break, brake).

63. The new tents are much lighter than the old (canvas, canvass) ones.

64. I will (canvas, canvass) the staff to see what they think about taking up a collection for the victim.

65. The (Capitol, capital) is one of the main attractions in Washington, the (capitol, capital) of the United States.

66. The court ordered the company to (cease, seize) violating its competitor's copyright.

67. His assets were (ceased, seized) when he declared bankruptcy.

EXERCISE 4 (continued)

68. The lawyer (cited, sighted, sited) several precedents in her argument for the defence.

69. For the exhausted marathon runners, the finishing line was a welcome (cite, sight, site).

70. We have chosen an excellent (cite, sight, site) for our new cottage.

71. The course in English grammar (complements, compliments) the writing program I took last year.

72. The accused was represented in court by a formidable (complement, compliment) of seven lawyers.

73. The client (complemented, complimented) David on the fine job he did on the file.

74. The new firm (comprises, constitutes) 50 lawyers.

75. The thief showed no signs of a guilty (conscience, conscious).

76. Rebecca was very (conscience, conscious) of the importance of her job.

77. I can't rely on an assistant who (continually, continuously) arrives late for work.

78. Our softball team held the league championship (continually, continuously) for ten years.

79. The new town (council, counsel, consul) has vowed to clean up the streets.

80. This is a complex legal matter on which we must seek the advice of (council, counsel, consul).

81. If you should find yourself in trouble in a foreign country, seek help from the Canadian (council, counsel, consul) there.

82. He presented a great deal of evidence, very little of which was (credible, credulous).

83. He is so (credible, credulous) that he believes what he sees on television commercials.

84. Although he lost the race, he gave a (decent, descent, dissent) effort.

85. We are beginning our (decent, descent, dissent) into Toronto's Pearson International Airport.

86. Freedom of speech can result in loud expressions of (decent, descent, dissent).

87. Much of the land that is now (dessert, desert) was covered in water millions of years ago.

88. They say rats always (dessert, desert) a sinking ship.

89. Since I am on a diet, I won't have (dessert, desert).

90. A restraining order is a legal (device, devise) to keep offenders away from their victims.

91. Ms. Wilson (deviced, devised) a brilliant defence strategy.

92. The nature of their work demands that social workers be very (discrete, discreet).

93. A Crown brief can be a complex document with many (discrete, discreet) elements.

94. Since he has (dual, duel) citizenship, my father carries two passports.

95. Fortunately, arguments are no longer settled by a (dual, duel) at dawn.

96. Detectives need good interviewing skills in order to (illicit, elicit) needed information from clients.

97. The police discovered an (illicit, elicit) gambling operation in the basement of the old building.

98. Canada owes much of its development to the work of (emigrants, immigrants).

99. I left my home and (emigrated, immigrated) to Canada.

100. Everyone was pleased when an (eminent, imminent) judge agreed to take the case.

101. Final agreement was held up pending an (eminent, imminent) change in the regulations.

102. Our security firm continues to (expend, expand) with the addition of three new investigators.

103. Tom (expends, expands) a great deal of energy in his morning workout.

104. (Farther, Further) to our previous correspondence, I can now give you the closing date for the sale of the property.

105. Our destination is just a little bit (farther, further) along the highway.

106. We seized (less, fewer) drugs at the border last year than previously.

107. Although there were more accidents on this street last year, there was (less, fewer) loss of life.

108. Go (fourth, forth) proudly and accept your award.

109. The sprinter came in (fourth, forth), so he did not win a medal.

110. His (great, grate) powers of oratory made him formidable in court.

111. The sound of that squeaky door (greats, grates) on my nerves.

112. There was too great an (incidents, incidence) of this error for it to be accidental.

113. An unfortunate (incident, incidence) occurred when the two parties met outside the courtroom.

114. The client (implied, inferred) that he was going to change lawyers.

115. From speaking to witnesses, the prosecutor (implied, inferred) that the case would be complicated.

116. He displayed a fine sense of (sarcasm, irony) by wishing her happy birthday as he served her with divorce papers.

117. His use of (irony, sarcasm) is so continuous that it's hard to tell what he really means.

118. When you have everything in (it's, its) place, (it's, its) easy to find what you need.

119. The (new, knew) corrections officer has certainly been well trained.

120. I always like to get my favourite author's (last, latest) book as soon as it's published.

121. Her answer to the (last, latest) question in the text was wrong.

122. Jonathan and Christina are both excellent law clerks, but the (later, latter) deals particularly well with clients.

123. The meeting went longer than planned, so I had to catch a (later, latter) train.

124. Our service (lead, led) the way in promoting minorities to supervisory roles.

125. Seepage of (led, lead) into the drinking water has (lead, led) to lawsuits against the company.

126. If you lose the lawsuit, you will be (libel, slander, liable) for court costs.

127. The front page story resulted in a (libel, slander, liable) action against the newspaper.

128. The president gave incorrect information to a reporter, resulting in a (libel, slander, liable) action against the company.

129. If we (lose, loose) this case, it will do great damage to the cause of justice.

130. I don't like having papers (lose, loose) in a file; it's too easy to (lose, loose) them.

EXERCISE 4 (concluded)

131. (Maybe, May be) I'll try that new restaurant for lunch today.

132. It (maybe, may be) worth taking your complaint to a higher level.

133. The (pain, pane) of glass shattered, causing me great (pain, pane).

134. Elizabeth (past, passed) the position of company president on to her successor at the annual meeting. Elizabeth is now the (past, passed) president.

135. Proofreading a long document requires much (patience, patients).

136. Although he has been a doctor for only two years, Jack has already treated hundreds of (patience, patients).

137. In a democracy, the state does not interfere with (personnel, personal) religious beliefs.

138. The department that handles staff was once called (Personnel, Personal), but it's now known as Human Resources.

139. What he said may be hard to accept, but it's the (plane, plain) truth.

140. Use a (plane, plain) to level out the bumps in the wood.

141. He was such a charismatic leader that his (presents, presence) seemed to fill the room.

142. It is unethical for police officers to accept (presents, presence) from the public.

143. The presumption of innocence is a basic (principal, principle) of our legal system.

144. I was proud of my son when he took the (principal, principle) role in the school play.

145. Business tends to be (quite, quiet) in the summer, but it picks up (quite, quiet) a bit in September.

146. Even a criminal has certain (rights, writes, rites, wrights) under the law.

147. The high-school prom is a traditional (right, write, rite, wright) of passage out of adolescence.

148. A famous (playright, playwrite, playrite, playwright) asked us for a legal opinion about his (copyright, copywrite, copyrite, copywright).

149. The law clerk's (role, roll) often is to act as liaison between client and lawyer.

150. Each morning at camp began with a (role, roll) call.

151. He stood as (stationary, stationery) as a rock while the tornado passed.

152. The security company printed a new logo on its (stationary, stationery).

153. Where are (they're, their, there) books? (They're, Their, There) over (they're, their, there).

154. After a (threw, through, thorough) cross-examination, their witness was excused.

155. The professional basketball player (threw, through, thorough) the ball (threw, through, thorough) the hoop with amazing accuracy.

156. I wanted (too, to, two) go (too, to, two), but one taxi was (too, to, two) small to take us all, and we had to order (too, to, two).

157. It doesn't matter (weather, whether) you like the job or not; you're stuck with it.

158. The lawyer for the prosecution presented a (weak, week) case in court.

159. (Whose, Who's) turn is it to make the coffee?

160. You will (loose, lose) your footing on the ice if you're not careful.

EXERCISE 5

EXPANDING YOUR VOCABULARY

Be able to spell and define the following words:

1. abrasion	24. calibre	47. extenuating	70. perpetrator
2. accelerate	25. cartridge	48. fabricate	71. pertinent
3. accessory	26. circumstantial	49. felon	72. plaintiff
4. accomplice	27. civilian	50. fugitive	73. preliminary
5. accused	28. collision	51. grievous	74. provocation
6. acquit	29. complainant	52. habitual	75. recidivist
7. adjourn	30. concurrent	53. homicide	76. refute
8. adjudicate	31. condemn	54. incarcerate	77. reprieve
9. admissible	32. confession	55. incorrigible	78. resuscitate
10. affidavit	33. confiscate	56. inquest	79. supplementary
11. aggravate	34. corroborate	57. interrogate	80. surveillance
12. alcohol	35. credibility	58. judicial	81. tactical
13. alleged	36. culpable	59. jurisdiction	82. testimony
14. altercation	37. defendant	60. laceration	83. trajectory
15. analyze	38. delinquent	61. lenient	84. trauma
16. anonymous	39. deposition	62. litigant	85. truancy
17. apprehend	40. detention	63. malicious	86. velocity
18. arraign	41. deterrent	64. mandatory	87. verdict
19. assailant	42. disperse	65. mitigating	88. vicious
20. assault	43. embezzle	66. negligence	89. waiver
21. attorney	44. enforceable	67. nuisance	90. warrant
22. bailiff	45. evidence	68. occurrence	
23. boulevard	46. exhibit	69. pedestrian	

EXERCISE 6

LEARNING LEGAL VOCABULARY

The following terms are important for law enforcement professionals. Be able to spell and define these terms:

1. abeyance	15. citation	29. *prima facie*
2. abscond	16. civil	30. proceeding
3. acquittal	17. codicil	31. recognizance
4. action *in rem*	18. contributory negligence	32. *regina*
5. action *in personam*	19. defeasance	33. *res gestae*
6. ad hoc	20. disposition	34. retainer
7. admissible evidence	21. exhibit	35. solicitor
8. amendment	22. grievance	36. specimen
9. appeal	23. *habeas corpus*	37. statute
10. arbitration	24. indictable	38. subrogation
11. boycott	25. injunction	39. tort
12. brief	26. *mens rea*	40. waive
13. case law	27. preamble	
14. *caveat emptor*	28. precedent	

☐ Summary

The English language is complicated. While spelling rules apply to many words, there are certain words that, especially in their verb tenses and plural forms, do not follow these rules, and such words must be learned individually. Knowing how to spell is important, but you should also understand the meanings of words; it is of little value to be able to spell a word without knowing its meaning. Law enforcement professionals can make themselves more effective by learning the vocabulary that applies to the legal profession.

SPELLING AND DEFINITIONS

Be able to spell and define the following words:

accessible	ceiling	evidence	pamphlet
accuracy	conspicuous	government	stomach
acquaintance	description	identity	tangential
affirmative	disabled	liable	valuable
aggravated	disastrous	loitering	vigilance
analysis	eliminate	memorandum	youthful
belligerent	evasive	miscellaneous	zealous

MINI-PUZZLE

Complete the following crossword using the definitions given below it. The words are taken from the Spelling and Definitions list for this chapter.

Across

2. Having only an indirect connection or importance.
6. Several or different kinds.
8. Likely; responsible; likely to be legally punished.
9. A person who is known but not a close friend.
10. Easy to reach, enter, or obtain.

Down

1. How something or someone is known.
3. Easily seen.
4. Something that gives proof or reason to believe something.
5. Note from one person to another in an office.
7. Too eager or overbearing in beliefs.

WORD SEARCH

Below the puzzle is a list of words taken from the Spelling and Definitions list.
Find these words in the puzzle and circle them.

```
B  K  J  G  A  T  W  K  Q  D  U  S  U  O  U  C  I  P  S  N  O  C  T  X  D
A  P  H  S  P  Y  G  Y  I  T  Y  V  E  T  S  P  L  Z  E  X  T  G  C  B  Y
J  O  G  T  K  C  O  S  A  M  V  S  G  U  E  A  E  V  E  M  V  N  E  E  H
F  B  J  J  M  U  A  N  U  A  T  X  O  L  G  A  A  U  V  A  Z  I  I  L  T
M  H  D  Y  T  B  G  D  L  O  I  E  B  C  L  S  U  L  I  I  J  R  L  L  Y
K  C  H  H  L  E  N  U  M  U  N  I  E  O  I  I  D  P  T  E  R  E  I  I  P
M  U  F  E  N  A  A  A  A  A  S  C  U  V  C  W  K  K  A  M  W  T  N  G  E
T  U  D  T  R  B  C  N  L  S  N  S  E  C  R  Y  F  E  M  D  N  I  G  E  C
L  Q  I  O  L  H  A  L  E  J  X  D  F  T  N  E  M  N  R  E  V  O  G  R  N
E  A  M  E  X  L  E  C  N  A  T  N  I  A  U  Q  C  A  I  C  V  L  P  E  A
L  E  D  X  Y  C  C  A  G  G  R  A  V  A  T  E  D  J  F  N  R  X  A  N  L
M  B  K  S  S  A  O  D  E  S  C  R  I  P  T  I  O  N  F  E  G  Y  M  T  I
M  L  I  I  U  W  F  Q  C  A  C  C  U  R  A  C  Y  Q  A  D  X  K  P  C  G
W  S  M  N  U  X  B  Z  C  D  F  I  E  L  B  A  I  L  X  I  M  E  H  V  I
C  H  V  N  A  Y  T  I  T  N  E  D  I  C  T  D  K  Y  I  V  B  M  L  D  V
W  J  J  V  W  S  U  O  R  T  S  A  S  I  D  I  A  V  R  E  S  E  E  F  H
E  J  F  U  Y  E  J  F  U  P  E  L  I  M  I  N  A  T  E  R  A  K  T  W  F
```

ACCESSIBLE	ACCURACY	ACQUAINTANCE	AFFIRMATVE
AGGRAVATED	ANALYSIS	BELLIGERENT	CEILING
CONSPICUOUS	DESCRIPTION	DISABLED	DISASTROUS
ELIMINATE	EVASIVE	EVIDENCE	GOVERNMENT
IDENTITY	LIABLE	LOITERING	MEMORANDUM
MISCELLANEOUS	PAMPHLET	STOMACH	TANGENTIAL
VALUABLE	VIGILANCE	YOUTHFUL	ZEALOUS

CHAPTER 3

Grammar Skills

Learning Objectives

After completing this chapter, you should be able to:

- Identify parts of speech in a sentence.
- Identify the purpose of a sentence.
- Correct common grammar errors.
- Recognize different kinds of phrases and clauses.
- Identify common punctuation marks and their uses.

Introduction

Correct grammar is important because it helps people understand each other in the communication process. Conversely, poor grammar can be a significant barrier to communication, especially when it leads to misunderstanding and misinterpretation.

To begin this chapter, complete the following pre-test to check your knowledge of grammar usage. Doing so will help you locate your areas of weakness.

GRAMMAR PRE-TEST

EXERCISE 1

FINDING SUBJECTS AND VERBS

Underline the subject with one line and the verb(s) with two lines in the following sentences:

1. People are retiring from law enforcement agencies at an alarming rate.

2. In Canada, many law enforcement positions are unfilled.

3. Many reasons are given, but the main one is that baby boomers are retiring.

4. There has not been much attention given in the past to the impending personnel shortage.

5. Now law enforcement agencies must scramble to recruit new people without sacrificing standards.

EXERCISE 2

CORRECTING SENTENCE FRAGMENTS

Change the following sentence fragments into complete sentences. One of the examples is already a complete sentence.

1. While on routine patrol.

2. PC Dubois received a radio call about a break and enter in progress.

3. Two suspects running from a house.

4. At 198 Queen St.

5. Were apprehended near the scene.

EXERCISE 3

USING SUBORDINATION AND COORDINATION

Use subordination or coordination correctly to combine each of the following pairs of sentences. One of the sentences is already correct.

1. Upon arrival at King Street. The officer noticed a broken window.

2. A blue late model Chevrolet was stopped for customs inspection; the driver was acting suspiciously.

3. The inmate population of the Workplace Detention Centre increased dramatically, it was thought to be a major problem.

3. Store security observed a woman hide a candy bar in her purse; and they moved in to arrest her.

5. Perimeter security patrol of an abandoned building is boring. And dangerous as well.

EXERCISE 4

RECASTING RUN-ON SENTENCES

Correct the following run-on sentences. One of the sentences is correct as it is.

1. I was asked to take photographs of striking workers I decided to do so.

2. Strong competition exists among private security companies they are each trying to build up their business.

3. A female hailed the cruiser when she was approached she refused to identify herself.

4. At the start of the shift it's important to note details of stolen cars they might be encountered while you're on patrol.

5. Information that may prove useful during your shift may be discovered by means of searches in specific cell blocks.

EXERCISE 5

USING COMMAS

Correctly punctuate the following sentences with commas. One of the sentences is correct as it is.

1. White-collar criminals dishonest employees and Internet scam artists are surfacing in growing numbers.

2. Recent arrests especially among technology manufacturers have been making headlines.

3. Even owners of sports franchises have been charged.

4. Small fines short prison terms or absolute discharges have not been effective.

5. Corruption reduces public trust in business corporations affects the stock market and has an overall negative effect on the economy.

EXERCISE 6

USING OTHER PUNCTUATION MARKS

Place punctuation marks (colons, semicolons, quotation marks) where they belong in the following sentences. One of the sentences is correct as it is.

1. He was advised to plead guilty the evidence was stacked against him.

2. The key term, say lawyers, is plea bargain.

3. The *Highway Traffic Act* concerns the following motorists, passengers, and pedestrians.

4. Private security agencies have three areas of concern personal protection, technological protection, and intellectual protection.

5. The motto of the Associated Protection Agency is "We protect your assets."

EXERCISE 7

ENSURING SUBJECT–VERB AGREEMENT

Correct the errors in subject–verb agreement in the following sentences. One of the sentences is correct as it is.

1. The history of law enforcement go back thousands of years.

2. Some writers from ancient Rome has described a system of law enforcement in that city.

3. Laws were modified so that the people could understand them.

4. Each group of explorers who went to America were surprised at the codification of laws in certain cultures.

5. The Iroquois Confederacy were able to formalize rules of behaviour.

EXERCISE 8

ESTABLISHING PARALLEL STRUCTURE

All but one of the following sentences lack parallel structure. Revise to create parallel structure.

1. In the past, officers were expected to be male, have big muscles, and tall.

2. Having women in front-line law enforcement positions offers many advantages, and to have them achieve senior positions is better yet.

3. With good planning and lucky, retirement packages for law enforcement personnel can be quite lucrative.

4. Observing, waiting, and listening are in reality more common police activities than those depicted in the action-filled lives of police officers on television.

5. He was a good officer, a brave man, and he worked hard.

EXERCISE 9

EDITING SENTENCES FOR ERRORS

Each of the following sentences contains an error in grammar or punctuation. Revise each sentence so that it is complete and correct.

1. These sort of experiences are helpful when applying for promotion.

2. No one wants to spend all their time writing reports.

3. I haven't kept my memo book up to date however I know I'm going to need it for court.

4. The Breathalyzer technician plan to come during the next shift.

5. All of my partners is very friendly.

6. The *Criminal Code* is long complicated and important.

7. Guns are dangerous they can cause a lot of trouble.

8. The siren wailed and we covered our ears loudly.

9. The files were lost for three weeks before the assistant found it.

10. Is a great detective.

■ Grammar Essentials: Sentences

A sentence is a group of words that contains a complete thought. Every sentence must contain a **subject** and a **verb**.

SUBJECT

The subject of a sentence is the word or group of words that the sentence is about or that the sentence concerns.

Fred is a corrections officer.

The subject here is *Fred*. Fred is who the sentence is about. If you wrote *Is a corrections officer*, you wouldn't know that the sentence is about Fred. This type of subject is called a **simple subject**.

The simple subject may be a noun (Fred), a pronoun (he), or a word ending in -*ing*, also known as a *gerund* or *verbal noun*.

Reading is her favourite hobby.

In the previous sentence, *reading* is what the sentence is about, or the focus of the sentence.

The subjects in the following sentences are italicized.

> *I* am on the midnight shift.
>
> *Driving* is a chore.
>
> The *tree* fell in the storm.
>
> The *store* was robbed last night.
>
> *She* became a police officer.
>
> *Bill* is in jail.

A subject can consist of more than one word, in which case it is called the **complete subject**. The complete subject contains the simple subject.

> The man on the jury seems to be asleep.

Here, *man* is the simple subject, and *the man on the jury* is the complete subject. The complete subject describes the simple subject by distinguishing the particular man from all other men in the courtroom. In the following sentences, the simple subject is italicized, and the complete subject appears in parentheses:

> (*Pat* and *René*) are partners.
>
> (*Corrections officers* and *customs officials*) attended the seminar.
>
> (*Arresting criminals* and *testifying in a court*) are my favourite parts of my police work.

In every case, remember that for a sentence to be complete, it must have a subject or subjects. Without a subject, a sentence is called a sentence fragment, which will be discussed later in this chapter.

EXERCISE 10

ADDING COMPLETE SUBJECTS

Add complete subjects to turn the following fragments into sentences:

1. is responsible for border security.

2. were my favourite courses at college.

3. teaches law enforcement courses at the college.

4. takes emergency calls from the public.

5. manages the marine unit.

VERB

The verb is the action word in a sentence. Every sentence must have a verb; otherwise, as in the case of a sentence without a subject, a sentence fragment occurs, which is a grammar error.

The verb in the following sentence is italicized:

The attorney *impresses* the jury with her argument.

The subject of this sentence (*the attorney*) does something, or causes an action to take place (*impresses*). Therefore, *impresses* is the verb.

Ming *operated* the radio.

She *arrested* the offender.

Jane *questioned* witnesses on the stand.

The human resources officer *orients* the new recruits.

The **tense** of a verb indicates when the action took place (past), is taking place (present), or will take place (future).

Past: I *walked* to work every day.

Present: I *walk* to work every day.

Future: I *will walk* to work every day.

Many verbs in the English language are known as **regular verbs**; these can be changed from present to past tense by adding *-ed* to the present form of the verb. This is not true of **irregular verbs**, which are dealt with below.

Changing the present tense to the future tense usually involves adding a word such as *will* or *shall* to the verb:

I *will apply* to a small law firm.

She *shall obtain* her diploma.

There are some verbs that don't appear to be "action" words; the action isn't obvious. These verbs are called **linking verbs** because they link subjects to other parts of the sentence. They are as much verbs, however, as any action word. The most common linking verbs are various forms of the verb *to be*: *is, am, are, was,* and *were*.

The lawyer *is* efficient.

I *am* a private investigator.

They *are* guilty as charged.

The officers *were* on patrol.

These forms of the verb *to be* are irregular because they don't take the forms of most regular action verbs. For instance, instead of adding *-ed* to the present form of *to be* to form the past tense, use the following forms:

Present	Past
I *am*	I *was*
You *are*	You *were*
He, she, it *is*	He, she, it *was*
We, you, they *are*	We, you, they *were*

The various tenses of the irregular verb *to be* may combine with an *-ing* word, or present participle, to produce the progressive verb tense.

> I *am* running.
> He *was* training.
> They *will be* exercising.

These present participles, ending in *-ing*, form part of the complete verb; in the examples above, *am running*, *was training*, and *will be exercising* are complete verbs.

Another irregular verb is *to have*. Note that *to be* and *to have* are called **infinitives**. The infinitive is the "to" form of the word—the basic verb form, without inflections to show person, number, or tense.

Present	Past
I *have*	I *had*
You *have*	You *had*
He, she, it *has*	He, she, it *had*
We, you, they *have*	We, you, they *had*

Below is a list of some irregular verbs in their infinitive, present tense, and past tense forms.

Infinitive	Present	Past
to break	break	broke
to catch	catch	caught
to do	do	did
to drive	drive	drove
to eat	eat	ate
to give	give	gave
to go	go	went
to know	know	knew
to see	see	saw
to sit	sit	sat
to speak	speak	spoke
to take	take	took
to write	write	wrote

A final point to keep in mind is that there can be more than one verb in a sentence.

EXERCISE 11

CHANGING VERB TENSE

Underline the complete verbs in the following passage. Then rewrite the passage, changing the verbs from the present to the past tense.

At 2330, I arrive at the residence of Fred Goldman, 211 Quiet St., to check on a possible break and enter. I check each window, being as quiet as I can, and find that nothing is broken. Then when I am walking through the front yard, I find that the front door is open. I am thinking that I should call for backup, but since the lights are on in the house, I suspect that it might be a false alarm. I enter the house and find Mr. Goldman sound asleep in front of the television. I wake him up, and he tells me that he often leaves the front door open.

SUBJECT–VERB AGREEMENT

Subjects and verbs must agree in their person and their number. Follow the "rule of *s*." Put an *s* on the end of either the subject or the verb, but not both at once:

> Cars speed.
> A car speeds.

When trying to ensure that your subjects and verbs agree, take particular care in the following situations:

1. *Words intervening between simple subject and verb.*

   One of the pictures *shows* the wanted man.
   The *suspect* in the robberies *was* arrested yesterday.

2. *Subject following verb.*

   Have John and Solly started a new security firm?
   Around the corner *ride the cyclists.*

3. *Two or more singular subjects joined by* or *or* nor.

   John *and* Bill *work* in litigation. [Compound subject takes plural.]
   John *or* Bill *works* in litigation. [One of John or Bill, but not both, works there.]

4. *Collective noun (group word) subject.*

   The jury *is* ready with its verdict. [The entity is acting as a single unit.]
   The jury *were* not in agreement. [Individual actions within the whole entity are meant to be considered.]

5. *Nouns plural in form but singular in meaning.*

   The news *is* reporting that the bank was robbed.
   The West Indies *is* a group of islands.
   Politics *is* of no concern to the law.

6. *Periods of time, fractions, weights, amounts of money.*

    Three days *is* a long time to spend on a cross-examination.

    Three-quarters of the stash *was* seized.

    Fifty pounds of contraband *is* in that car.

    A hundred dollars *is* the fine for the bylaw infraction.

    If a fraction refers to a quantity ("three-quarters of the membership"), it is treated as singular; if it refers to a number, it is treated as plural ("three-quarters of the pencils").

7. *Relative pronouns.* These pronouns (*who, which, that*) agree with their antecedent (the word to which they refer or the word that they replace) in number.

    These are the *employees who are* always reliable. [The antecedent of *who* is *employees.*]

    Bill is one of the *employees who are* always reliable. [*Employees* is the antecedent of *who,* requiring the plural verb *are.*]

    George is the *only one* of the clerks *who is* on vacation. [*Only one* is the antecedent of *who,* requiring the singular verb *is.*]

    Lian is one of the *women who work* undercover. [*Women* is the antecedent of *who.*]

8. *Indefinite pronouns.* The following indefinite pronouns are always singular: *one, each, anybody, anyone, somebody, someone, everybody, everyone, nobody, no one, either,* and *neither.*

    One *is* not obliged to purchase a raffle ticket.

    Each of the students *has* an assignment.

    Anybody who works with him *knows* he couldn't have done it.

    Anyone who *wants* to join may do so.

    Somebody up there *likes* me.

    Someone *is* following them.

    Everybody *is* going for fingerprinting.

    Everyone in the room *is* a suspect.

    Nobody *cares* about that.

    No one *has* a salary increase.

    Either suspect *fits* the description.

    Neither Joe nor Dave *has* a girlfriend.

    The following indefinite pronouns are always plural: *both, many, few,* and *several.*

    Both of the cars *were* blue.

    Many of the students *speak* French.

    A few of the officers *are* at the scene.

    Several of the people *were* victims of the scam.

The following indefinite pronouns are singular for quantity and plural for number: *all, any, most, none,* and *some.*

Quantity (Singular)	Number (Plural)
All of the parking lot *was* full.	All of the parking spots *were* taken.
Any time *is* good for me.	Any days *are* good for me.
Most of the audience *likes* the show.	Most of the people *like* the show.
None of the laundry *feels* dry.	None of the clothes *feel* dry.
Some of the food *was* spoiled.	Some of the eggs *were* spoiled.

9. *Compound subjects that do not agree in number.* In a compound subject, where one subject is singular and one is plural, make the verb agree with the *nearest* subject.

> Either the manager or the *assistants are* at the workshop.

> Either the assistants or the *manager is* at the workshop.

SENTENCE FRAGMENTS

Since every complete sentence must have a subject, must have a verb, and must make a complete thought, any group of words without one of these three characteristics is a **sentence fragment**.

> She reads a training manual.

This is a complete sentence: It has a subject (*she*) and a verb (*reads*), and it is a complete thought; it makes sense, and it's understandable. However, if the subject were left out, the remaining words would be

> Reads a training manual.

This is a sentence fragment because the sentence now has no subject. Who reads a training manual? A subject is needed.

Examples of different kinds of sentence fragments are set out below.

> Parked in the centre of town. [What or who parked in the centre of town?]

> My report on my sergeant's desk. [What about the report on the desk?]

> With only my jacket. [What happened with the jacket?]

> Waiting for the shipment. [Who was waiting?]

Adding a subject and verb to these fragments makes them into complete thoughts.

> I parked in the centre of town.

> My report is on my sergeant's desk.

> With only my jacket, I fought off a swarm of bees.

> The mailroom clerk was waiting for the shipment.

Any group of words that contains a subject and a verb is called a **clause**. A sentence is a clause in most cases, but not always. There are two types of clauses: independent and dependent.

EXERCISE 12

REVISING: SUBJECT–VERB AGREEMENT AND PRONOUNS

1. Correct the errors in subject–verb agreement and any pronoun errors in the following passage:

   I think that a person who drinks and drives should be shot because they get in their car and do a lot of damage. You may be at a bar all evening and think you are okay, but when the person gets in their car, look out! Often when we have been drinking, you lose your ability to make rational decisions, the biggest decision being whether we should get in our car or take a taxi home. Often this is a difficult decision for the person because, like most people, they have stayed at the hotel until it is too late: all your money is gone, and a taxi is now out of the question. Maybe we should make this decision at the start of the evening when your head is still clear and one has money in their pocket. If a person does not have enough sense to do this, I would stop drinking altogether until you can learn to control yourself, for one's own safety and for the safety of those around us.

2. Complete the following sentences, using the correct present tense of the verb *to be*:

   a. Anyone _____.

   b. Each _____.

   c. Somebody _____.

   d. Neither _____.

   e. Either _____.

   f. No one _____.

   g. Something _____.

   h. Much _____.

   i. Anybody _____.

   j. Everyone _____.

An **independent clause** contains a subject, a verb, and a complete thought; therefore, independent clauses are also sentences.

He will answer for his crimes.

A **dependent clause** contains a subject and a verb, but it does not express a complete thought. It is a fragment that needs something else to complete it.

Because he was caught.

He is the subject, *was caught* is the verb, but the clause does not explain what happened because he was caught. Therefore, this group of words does not contain a complete thought and is a sentence fragment.

Because he was caught, he will answer for his crimes.

As shown here, a dependent clause at the beginning of a sentence must be followed by a comma. If the dependent clause falls at the end of a sentence, the comma is not needed.

He will have to answer for his crimes because he was caught.

Another type of sentence fragment to be considered is the "list" fragment.

Law enforcement professionals must be. Intelligent, resourceful, and cautious.

Both of these fragments are dependent. The first fragment has a subject and a verb, but it needs the list ("intelligent, resourceful, and cautious") to complete its meaning. The list doesn't have a subject or a verb. The straightforward solution is to combine the two:

Law enforcement professionals must be intelligent, resourceful, and cautious.

Two further examples of common sentence-fragment errors are set out below, along with their corrected forms.

Fragment: I like card games. Such as euchre, poker, and blackjack.

Complete: I like card games, such as euchre, poker, and blackjack.

Fragment: We went to court. Saw the judge, the bailiff, and the lawyer.

Complete: We went to court, where we saw the judge, the bailiff, and the lawyer.

Finally, be aware that commands, brief though they usually are, do not qualify as sentence fragments.

Stop!

The subject *you* is implied here, so the sentence is complete.

Remember, too, that an *-ing* word, also known as a present participle (e.g., *running, shooting*), can never be the complete verb in a sentence.

Fragment: I running to keep in shape.

Complete: I am running to keep in shape.

EXERCISE 13

CORRECTING FRAGMENTS

Form the following fragments into complete sentences:

1. I worked hard. So that I could get a promotion.

2. We went into law. Because we love helping people.

3. Tell me the truth. If you know it.

4. He was arrested; because he was drinking and driving.

5. I love facing danger. Wherever I find it.

6. You will find your shirt. In the drawer. Where you keep your socks.

7. Because the traffic was heavy.

8. If they get their act together.

9. While running for the bus.

10. .22 calibre, .32 calibre, .45 calibre.

RUN-ON SENTENCES

The **run-on sentence** is the opposite of the sentence fragment. While the fragment is part of a sentence, the run-on is two complete sentences or independent clauses that have been joined together in an inappropriate way.

> I always stop here for doughnuts it is my favourite place.

The sentence can be corrected in four ways. You could use two sentences.

> I always stop here for doughnuts. It is my favourite place.

You could use a conjunction.

> I always stop here for doughnuts because it is my favourite place.

You could use a semicolon.

> I always stop here for doughnuts; it is my favourite place.

You could use a dependent clause.

> Since it is my favourite place, I always stop here for doughnuts.

Keep in mind that an independent clause contains a complete thought, but only one complete thought. The run-on expresses more than one thought with no division between the thoughts.

EXERCISE 14

CORRECTING RUN-ONS

1. Correct the following run-on sentences:

    a. Just let me do the talking you'll get us a ticket if you don't keep quiet.

    b. The cabin was cold however it had a wood stove.

    c. A strong wind was blowing the boat from the yacht club nearly sank.

    d. Most people have 20/20 vision that is a requirement for a job here.

    e. Career opportunities are good for students in law enforcement some employers also demand volunteer experience.

2. Correct the run-on sentences in the following paragraph:

    Thank you for your attention to this matter if I can be of any assistance to you in collecting the necessary documents please contact me I will do what I can to expedite the process it is important that this be completed as soon as possible if any of the documents are missing your case could be dismissed you would still be liable for court costs.

Another type of run-on is the **comma splice**.

> **There is a leash law, no one obeys it.**

In this case, the comma is misplaced; two independent clauses can't be separated by a comma without a conjunction or linking word. A comma splice can be corrected in the same four ways as any other run-on.

You can use two sentences.

> **There is a leash law. No one obeys it.**

You can use a conjunction.

> **There is a leash law, but no one obeys it.**

You can use a semicolon.

> **There is a leash law; no one obeys it.**

You can use a dependent clause.

> **Although there is a leash law, no one obeys it.**

EXERCISE 15

CORRECTING MISPLACED MODIFIERS

Correct the misplaced modifiers in the following sentences:

1. The woman was stopped for speeding with the hat.

2. He made cookies for his friends with chocolate chips in them.

3. The lawyer being recruited vigorously believed it was time for a change.

4. The police chief led the parade in full dress uniform.

5. Customs officers intercepted the smugglers guarding the coast line.

6. The criminal laughed when she was almost convicted maliciously.

7. The man escaped before the fire spread barely.

8. We planned to start work early Christmas Eve a long time ago.

9. The defendant stood in the dock without any signs of cracking.

10. The suspect said he was at home with a bow tie.

MODIFIERS

A modifier is a word or phrase that refers to, describes, or explains another word in a sentence. Modifiers must be placed as close as possible to the word or words they modify. There are two types of sentence errors involving modifiers: **misplaced modifiers** and **dangling modifiers**.

Misplaced Modifiers

Misplaced modifiers are modifiers that are placed within a sentence in such a way that it is unclear what word they apply to.

> The audience cheered when we graduated from college excitedly.

The modifier *excitedly* is misplaced here because it is unclear whether it modifies *graduated* or *cheered*.

Consider these other examples, in which the misplaced modifiers are italicized:

> He protested at the noise of the siren wailing *angrily*.

> The police officer approached the hostile-looking dog *with a hockey glove on*.

> Our lawyer rated our chances of winning *without much enthusiasm*.

EXERCISE 16

CORRECTING DANGLING MODIFIERS

Correct the dangling modifiers in the following sentences:

1. Risking her life, the accident victims were rescued by the lifeguard.
2. Crossing the street, my hat blew away.
3. To pass the communications course, one essay every week is required.
4. Driving through the suburbs, several luxury vehicles were seen.
5. Jogging through the park, a dog bit me.
6. On receiving an offer of employment, tears filled his mother's eyes.
7. When learning the *Highway Traffic Act*, memorizing is often used.
8. Driving at night, his mind began to wander.
9. Being a qualified legal assistant, a framed certificate was proudly displayed.
10. While attending the theatre, the apartment was looted.

To correct the sentences, place the modifiers closer to the words they modify.

> He angrily protested at the noise of the siren wailing.

> With a hockey glove on, the police officer approached the hostile-looking dog.

> Without much enthusiasm, our lawyer rated our chances of winning.

Dangling Modifiers

The other form of modifier fault is the dangling modifier. A dangling modifier is one that doesn't logically modify anything in its sentence.

> Crossing the border, my bags were searched.

> Expecting a lot of work, extra help was requested.

In both of these cases, the modifier is dangling. In the first case, who was crossing the border? *My bags*? In the second sentence, *who* is expecting a lot of work? Correct the sentences as follows:

> When I was crossing the border, my bags were searched.

> Expecting a lot of work, we requested extra help.

To fix a dangling modifier, add a word to which the modifier refers, and put the modifier as close to that word as possible.

PRONOUN REFERENCES

A pronoun is a word that replaces a noun. It may be used as the subject of a sentence (the word that indicates who or what performs an action). A pronoun may also be the object of a sentence (the word that indicates upon whom or what an action is performed).

Noun:	Roy works in the traffic unit.
Pronoun:	*He* works in the traffic unit.
Noun:	Sylvie and Ruth conduct secondary vehicle inspections.
Pronoun:	Sylvie and Ruth conduct *them.*

Pronouns may also be used as both the subject and the object of a single sentence.

Nouns:	Joe writes his report.
Pronouns:	*He* writes *it.*

Joe is the subject of the sentence, which is replaced with the pronoun *he.* The thing being written, *his report,* is the object of the sentence, which is replaced with the pronoun *it.*

When replacing a subject, use the following personal pronouns:

Singular	Plural
I	we
you	you
he, she, it	they

When replacing an object, use the following personal pronouns:

Singular	Plural
me	us
you	you
him, her, it	them

Note the use of both subjective and objective personal pronouns in the following examples:

Nouns:	Rex ran away from the intruders.
Pronouns:	*He* ran away from *them.*
Nouns:	The police officer told Fred to move the van.
Pronouns:	*She* told *him* to move *it.*

EXERCISE 17

USING PRONOUNS

Underline the correct pronoun in parentheses in each of the following sentences:

1. We expect you and (they, them) at the meeting.

2. Wait for my partner and (I, me).

3. (He, Him) and Amad worked together.

4. The receptionist told you and (her, she) to stay here.

5. Everyone was at the party except (we, us).

6. You and (I, me) are both in line for promotion.

7. Professionals such as you and (he, him) should help younger employees.

8. Was it (she, her) that you saw?

9. I think that the shoplifter was (he, him).

10. It could have been (they, them) who won the race.

Pronouns and Case

The case (subjective, objective, or possessive) of a personal pronoun is determined by the function it serves in a sentence. Pronouns can be subjects or subject complements (subjective case); they can be direct objects, indirect objects, or objects of prepositions (objective case); or they can indicate ownership (possessive case).

Subjective pronouns	Objective pronouns	Possessive pronouns
I	me	my (mine)
you	you	your (yours)
he	him	his
she	her	her (hers)
it	it	its
who	whom	whose
we	us	our (ours)
they	them	their (theirs)

He (*subject*) made the donation for me (*object*).

With whom (*object*) did I (*subject*) see you last night?

Her (*possessive*) litigation caseload is much heavier than his (*possessive*).

A subject complement following a linking verb (*to be* [am, is, are, was, were, have been], *to act, to appear, to become, to feel, to grow, to seem, to look, to taste*) takes the subjective case; for example, "It was I who opened the file."

Ambiguous and Indefinite Pronoun References

It is important to eliminate ambiguity in pronoun references.

When Rebecca saw Jane, she was angry.

Which woman was angry? To indicate that it was Rebecca and not Jane who was angry, the sentence can be recast as follows:

Rebecca was angry when she saw Jane.

To indicate that Jane was the angry one, recast the sentence as follows:

When Rebecca saw her, Jane was angry.

Use a pronoun to refer to a single noun, not a group of words.

He admitted that he defrauded the client. This was welcome news.

Does *this* refer to the fact that he defrauded the client, or to his admission of the fact? Rewrite the sentence to remove this ambiguity:

He admitted that he defrauded the client. His admission was welcome news.

Avoid the indefinite use of *it* and *they*.

They say that private security is the career of the future.

Who is *they*? Rewrite the sentence to give *they* a face:

Economists say that private security is the career of the future.

EXERCISE 18

REMOVING AMBIGUOUS AND INDEFINITE PRONOUN REFERENCES

Correct the pronoun errors in the following sentences:

1. They did not see the Smiths arrive because they were having lunch.

2. I don't know what he said to him, but he was angry.

3. The girl's mother studied law, and she is going to be one when she grows up.

4. He began his career as a private investigator, which was terminated by his death.

5. In my first job, I learned to change a toner cartridge without getting it all over me.

6. I let my relatives help me with the new cars although they were rather dirty.

7. The assistant told her manager that whatever she did she could not please her.

8. They say that crime is decreasing in the city.

9. He fell while addressing the jury, which was embarrassing.

10. They have good traffic laws in Ontario.

PARALLEL STRUCTURE

Parallel structure involves joining similar structures together in a sentence.

> **writing, listening, speaking**

These *-ing* words all refer to forms of communication, and they are parallel in structure because they all end in *-ing*.

> **Svetlana is intelligent, witty, and charms people.**

This sentence does not use parallel structure. To obtain parallel structure, you must rewrite the sentence as follows:

> **Svetlana is intelligent, witty, and charming.**

Parallel structure should be used when phrases, clauses, or infinitives are connected by conjunctions:

Two phrases:	**up the hill and down the valley**
Two clauses:	**that he is a thief and that he is in jail**
Two infinitives:	**to go or to stay**

EXERCISE 19

USING PARALLEL STRUCTURE

Correct the parallel structure faults in the following sentences:

1. The day shift or the night is fine by me.

2. I don't enjoy foot patrol when it is raining or it snows.

3. He had trained himself in juggling and to type.

4. I knew all the risks of crime and avoiding them.

5. He didn't know the bylaw or the *Criminal Code*.

6. The sergeant taught us memo books, writing reports, and how to do summaries.

7. Every law enforcement officer is taught the value of following orders and how to think independently.

8. The inspector is influential and a popular person.

9. He is not happy nor satisfied with his job.

10. My dream is to have a job with Corrections Canada, a family, and buy a house.

CORRELATIVES

Correlative conjunctions are specific sets of words that require parallel structure when used together. Some common correlative conjunctions are the following:

> either … or
> neither … nor
> not … but
> not only … but also
> both … and

These groups of words don't have to be used if there is no parallel structure involved in the sentence:

> The job required *both* concentration *and* speed.
> I like both colours.

Grammar Essentials: Punctuation and Capitalization

COMMAS

As a rule of thumb, fewer commas are better than many. Don't use a comma if you're not sure you need one. However, there are certain rules for comma use that should be followed.

1. Use a comma to separate three or more items in a series.

   The warrant was signed, sealed, and delivered.

   Some people prefer not to use a comma before the word *and* in a series. The only firm rule is, Be consistent.

2. Use a comma between two independent clauses separated by the coordinate conjunctions *and, but, or, nor, yet,* and *so,* especially if the subject changes in the second clause.

   He was a kind man, and his life was an inspiration to many.

3. Use a comma after a long introductory element.

   After ten years with the company, Tom became president.

4. Do not use a comma if such an expression is put at the end of the sentence.

   Tom became president after ten years with the company.

EXERCISE 20

USING COMMAS

Insert commas where necessary in the following sentences:

1. Her alibi of course was completely ridiculous.

2. By the way you have been promoted.

3. The elderly man coughed staggered and fell to the ground.

4. She smuggled drugs was caught as she left the plane and now has to pay for the crime.

5. The court date is set for August 8 2004.

6. I live at apartment 5 216 Bold St. Toronto ON.

7. Tomorrow July 31 is the anniversary of the day I was hired.

8. That's the best way I think to take creases out of your uniform.

9. I said "Your last statement isn't the truth."

10. You have to comply with the court order or you'll be arrested.

5. Use commas to separate "interrupters" from the rest of the sentence. Interrupters are words or phrases that are not essential to the meaning of the sentence. Taking interrupters out of the sentence does not change the meaning of the sentence.

   I knew, *of course*, that I would be caught.

6. Use commas to surround material that is not essential to the sentence. The difference between this rule and the preceding one is that, in this case, the information surrounded by commas adds some substance to the meaning of the sentence.

   Police officers, although they have a reputation for eating a lot of doughnuts, are usually in good shape.

7. Use a comma to separate different parts of addresses and dates.

   198 Queen Street South, Hamilton, Ontario L8P 3S7
   November 10, 2002

8. Do not use commas unnecessarily in addresses and dates.

   198 Queen Street South, Hamilton, ON L8P 3S7 [A comma is not needed between the province and the postal code.]
   10 November 2002

9. Do not use commas with the 24-hour clock or when dates are written as numerals.

   1320 (1:20 p.m.)
   44.05.31 (31 May 1944)

10. Use commas before or after a direct quotation.

    She said, "I'm here for the Written Communication Test."
    "I'm here for the Written Communication Test," she said.
    He answered, "You must be joking!"

APOSTROPHES

The apostrophe shows possession. It is also used in contractions.

Possession:	John's [belonging to John]
Contraction:	Didn't [did not]

Possessives

The possessive indicates ownership or affiliation. Most possessives can be written by adding an apostrophe and an *s* to a singular noun.

Possession:	Theo's whistle [Theo owns the whistle.]
Affiliation:	Manny's club [Manny is a member of the club.]

It often helps in determining possessives to rephrase a sentence using the word *of* to show possession.

The whistle of Theo.

EXERCISE 21

USING APOSTROPHES

Use apostrophes correctly in the following sentences:

1. Junes mother works for the Ministry of the Attorney General.

2. Those are the employees [plural] records we seized.

3. The clerks salaries were up for review.

4. The rooftops slant made it difficult to repair the tiles.

5. Is that Carloss desk?

6. We will be there in about a minutes time.

7. The ropes mark on the corpse was a clue.

8. Jeff Saunders daughters will be married next week.

9. The lawyers offices had to be cleaned.

10. Tobaccos high cost is leading to more smuggling.

11. Its against the law.

12. Theyre coming with their lawyers this afternoon.

13. Youre going to be promoted.

14. Whos going to pay for the damage?

15. Its Russs car that was involved in the accident.

16. Weve been working late every night.

17. Thats the sergeants problem.

18. Theyve got a chance to carry drugs across the border.

19. Youll never get hired with that attitude.

20. Whats the problem?

When forming the possessive of plural nouns ending in *s*, add the apostrophe after the noun.

> The cars' noise [More than one car is making noise.]

Compare this to the singular possessive.

> The car's noise [One car is making noise.]

A review of various forms of the word *car* is provided below.

Word	Part of speech
car	singular noun
car's	possessive singular noun [belonging to one car]
cars	plural noun
cars'	possessive plural noun [belonging to more than one car]

The following rules will assist you in creating possessive nouns:

1. If a singular word ends in *s*, add *s* to the final letter.

   My boss's office [There is one boss with one office.]

2. Words that are already plural take an apostrophe followed by an *s.*

   My children's toys

3. Statements relating to time need apostrophes in certain situations.

   I am eligible for a week's vacation [a vacation of one week].
   I am eligible for three weeks' vacation [a vacation of three weeks].

4. Never use an apostrophe with the following pronouns:

my	your	yours	his
whose	their	theirs	her
its	our	ours	hers

Note that *it's* is a contraction meaning "it is" or "it has"; it does not show ownership or affiliation.

Contractions

Contractions are formed from a combination of two words. Both contractions and possessives use apostrophes, but contractions do not show ownership or affiliation. The contraction is formed by replacing a letter or group of letters with an apostrophe.

> *I am* becomes *I'm.*
>
> *You are* becomes *you're.*
>
> *It is* becomes *it's.*

Common contractions include the following:

I'm (I am)	they're (they are)
I'd (I had/I would)	they'd (they had/they would)
I'll (I will)	they'll (they will)
I've (I have)	we're (we are)
you're (you are)	we'd (we had/we would)
you'd (you had/you would)	we'll (we will)
you'll (you will)	who're (who are)
you've (you have)	who'd (who had/who would)
he's (he is/he has)	who'll (who will)
he'd (he had/he would)	it's (it is/it has)
he'll (he will)	it'd (it had/it would)
she's (she is/she has)	it'll (it will)
she'd (she had/she would)	let's (let us)
she'll (she will)	isn't (is not)

aren't (are not)	hadn't (had not)
wasn't (was not)	wouldn't (would not)
weren't (were not)	would've (would have)
don't (do not)	couldn't (could not)
doesn't (does not)	could've (could have)
didn't (did not)	shouldn't (should not)
hasn't (has not)	should've (should have)
haven't (have not)	

PERIODS

1. Use a period at the end of a sentence.

   We had a quiet evening at home.

2. Use a period after most abbreviations.

   Mr. (Mister)
   Oct. (October)

3. Note that certain organizations do not use periods in their abbreviated names.

   RCMP (Royal Canadian Mounted Police)
   CSIS (Canadian Security Intelligence Service)

4. Note that the names of most provinces have alternative abbreviations, some of which do not contain periods.

   Ont. or ON (Ontario)
   Alta. or AB (Alberta)

QUESTION MARKS

1. Use a question mark after a direct question.

   She asked, "Are you writing the promotion examination?"

2. Do not use a question mark in an indirect question.

   She asked whether I was writing the promotion examination.

EXCLAMATION POINTS

Use an exclamation point after an emphatic statement or command.

   Stop, or you'll go off the road!

QUOTATION MARKS

1. Use quotation marks to enclose the exact words of a speaker.

   I said, "I'm going on vacation next week."

2. Do not use quotation marks around an indirect quotation.

   I said that I'm going on vacation next week.

3. After quotation marks, use a capital letter unless the quotation is split.

   "I'm going on vacation," I said, "next week."

4. Use quotation marks to enclose the titles of short works. Short works include poems, essays, articles, short stories, songs, and radio or television programs. (Longer works, such as novels, are italicized.)

   I read the pamphlet "Better Reports" before my test.

SEMICOLONS

1. Use a semicolon to indicate connection between two independent clauses. In the following example, the two independent clauses can be either separated by a period or, if you want to stress the connection between the two statements, joined with a semicolon:

   I witnessed the accident. I will testify in court.
   I witnessed the accident; I will testify in court.

2. Certain conjunctions need to be preceded by a semicolon and followed by a comma. These conjunctions are the following:

however	otherwise	nevertheless
moreover	therefore	nonetheless

   I did not see the accident; however, I was asked to testify in court.

3. Do not use a semicolon with the coordinate conjunctions *and, but, or, nor, yet,* and *so.* When these coordinate conjunctions separate two independent clauses, a comma is used in preference to a semicolon.

   I witnessed the accident, but you will testify in court.

COLONS

1. Use a colon after an independent clause to introduce a list of particulars.

   I have three favourite career choices: police officer, customs inspector, and legal assistant.

2. The introductory clause may often conclude with the terms *the following* or *as follows.*

   The thieves stole the following: a camera, a television, and a computer.

EXERCISE 22

APPLYING THE RULES: GRAMMAR AND PUNCTUATION

Correct the errors in the following sentences:

1. Mrs Ames appeared to be ready to settle her lawsuit.

2. If I had to do it over.

3. Get away from me he yelled.

4. I warned my sister to "drive slowly on icy roads."

5. Stop you're going to hit that pole.

6. The first chapter of this book is entitled effective listening.

7. I have read: a book, a poem, and a short story.

8. I lost the following from my wallet; my money, my identification, and my credit cards.

9. There's 200 students enrolled in the legal program.

10. Prof Brown is the director of the law clerk program at the college.

11. He failed the grammar, and the spelling part of the communications course.

12. The instructor said both him and I should pass the course.

13. When I suddenly heard a car door slam and the sound of many voices.

14. The hearing was supposed to begin at noon yet however the witness had not arrived.

15. She was employed by a woman who owned a van named Mary.

16. They're are the children who were called to the principals office.

17. That's the forth traffic ticket I've received.

18. Each of the constables owns their own house.

19. Neither the defendant nor the witness impress the judge.

20. I don't mind postponing the trial. Because that's my time for vacation.

CAPITAL LETTERS

1. Capitalize the first word in a sentence.

   Capitalize the first word in a sentence.

2. Capitalize the first, last, and important words in a title.

   Communications for Law Enforcement Professionals

3. Capitalize the names of specific persons, places, languages, nations, and nationalities.

   Mayor Huang   Hamilton   French   Canada   Canadian

4. Capitalize the names of days, months, and holidays. Do not capitalize the seasons.

   Monday   November   Labour Day   summer

5. Capitalize the first word in a direct quotation.

   I told her, "The prison is located in Kingston."

6. Capitalize the word *I*.

   I mean what I say.

7. Capitalize the names of specific academic courses. Do not capitalize general words that refer to a type of course.

   I am taking Communications I.

   I am taking a communications course.

Voice

Voice is the form of a verb that indicates whether the subject of a sentence is the instigator of the action or the receiver of the action. There are two voices: active and passive. A sentence is in the active voice when the subject of the sentence initiates the action.

> He *sued* his former employer.
>
> Our client *cannot sell* his property because of liens against it.

A sentence is in the passive voice when the subject receives the action. When an active verb is made passive, a form of the verb *to be* is used.

> He *was sued* by his former employer.
>
> Property with liens against it *cannot be sold.*

The active voice is more forceful and direct than the passive voice, and should be used in most writing when possible. However, when it is the action itself that is important, and the person initiating the action is less important (or indefinite or even unknown), or when you wish to emphasize the receiver of the action rather than the person initiating the action, use the passive voice.

Summary

Studying grammar will help you understand that there are different ways of expressing yourself. While there may be more than one correct method of writing, grammar rules must be followed. Correct grammar helps you to write with clarity and to eliminate potential misunderstandings and ambiguities.

SPELLING AND DEFINITIONS

Be able to spell and define the following words:

awkward	enough	obstructed	signature
confidentiality	flexible	occurrence	statute
coroner	grievance	personnel	subpoena
courteous	humane	preamble	supersede
disappear	implement	punishable	toxicology
disposition	legible	qualification	vehicle
dissent	narcotic	questionnaire	
disturbance	nevertheless	receive	
domestic	objectively	regulations	

MINI-PUZZLE

Complete the following crossword using the definitions given below it. The words are taken from the Spelling and Definitions list for this chapter.

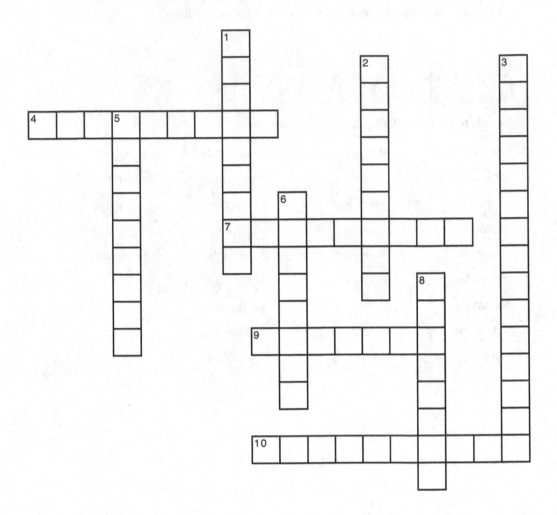

Across

4. All of the people employed by an organization.
7. Polite, considerate.
9. Clear; something that can be read.
10. Study of poisons.

Down

1. Complaint.
2. Put into practice.
3. Secrecy, privacy.
5. Take the place of; replace or supplant.
6. A written order to attend a court of law.
8. Bent easily; change to meet new conditions.

WORD SEARCH

Below the puzzle is a list of words taken from the Spelling and Definitions list. Find these words in the puzzle and circle them.

```
U  Z  H  H  U  M  A  N  E  T  T  V  E  H  I  C  L  E  W  N  Y  N  P  V  W
W  V  Y  T  X  E  N  O  U  G  H  I  A  W  K  W  A  R  D  L  O  K  E  C  O
P  C  C  O  M  I  A  I  D  I  S  A  P  P  E  A  R  A  E  E  X  Q  R  F  Z
O  R  E  X  S  V  L  N  E  L  E  G  I  B  L  E  N  V  C  T  O  U  S  E  Q
U  S  E  I  M  P  L  E  M  E  N  T  N  R  C  E  I  N  K  M  J  A  O  K  U
G  I  F  C  J  S  T  T  S  A  I  Q  G  F  O  T  A  D  Q  I  G  L  N  P  E
R  G  L  O  E  R  Z  O  U  N  D  T  X  P  C  B  U  O  I  O  B  I  N  U  S
I  N  E  L  D  I  H  R  P  N  M  S  B  E  R  C  O  O  Y  B  Q  F  E  N  T
E  A  X  O  C  T  V  W  E  A  L  U  J  U  U  D  E  C  F  S  H  I  L  I  I
V  T  I  G  O  Q  U  E  R  X  S  B  T  D  N  A  R  C  O  T  I  C  C  S  O
A  U  B  Y  R  J  Y  S  S  A  O  S  O  O  L  K  U  U  P  R  G  A  W  H  N
N  R  L  Y  O  I  T  J  E  F  I  I  N  M  M  L  I  R  A  U  Y  T  M  A  N
C  E  E  H  N  R  S  D  D  D  T  M  A  E  T  S  X  R  U  C  N  I  R  B  A
E  N  E  V  E  R  T  H  E  L  E  S  S  S  B  M  A  E  U  T  M  O  X  L  I
L  V  U  M  R  X  F  F  I  C  X  Z  T  T  C  H  A  N  P  E  V  N  I  E  R
E  C  O  N  F  I  D  E  N  T  I  A  L  I  T  Y  O  C  A  D  M  E  F  J  E
F  Y  O  Y  L  A  O  N  P  U  U  M  A  C  K  H  R  E  G  I  G  B  E  Y  Q
```

AWKWARD	CONFIDENTIALITY	CORONER	DISAPPEAR
DISTURBANCE	DOMESTIC	ENOUGH	FLEXIBLE
GRIEVANCE	HUMANE	IMPLEMENT	LEGIBLE
NARCOTIC	NEVERTHELESS	OBJECTIVELY	OBSTRUCTED
OCCURRENCE	PERSONNEL	PUNISHABLE	QUALIFICATION
QUESTIONNAIRE	RECEIVE	SIGNATURE	SUBPOENA
SUPERSEDE	TOXICOLOGY	VEHICLE	

CHAPTER 4

Summary and Paraphrase

Learning Objectives

After completing this chapter, you should be able to:

- Write summaries that contain the main ideas of the original works.
- Paraphrase for understanding.
- Detect bias in reporting.

Introduction

There are two different methods of shortening a piece of writing while keeping its main points: the **summary** and the **paraphrase**. Each is written differently, with a different emphasis.

In academic writing, summarizing and paraphrasing allow you to borrow from another source without plagiarizing. In law enforcement situations, both summary and paraphrase are used to condense witness statements, testimony, and other, sometimes lengthy sources of information.

Summarizing involves putting the main points of the written or spoken material into your own words. This produces a text that is significantly shorter than the original and that takes a broad overview of its contents.

The paraphrase, like the summary, involves putting the main ideas of the written or spoken material into your own words and is usually shorter than the original. But the paraphrase is a more detailed and subjective restatement than a summary; it includes your own interpretation of information and ideas expressed by another source.

▪ Writing a Summary

Law enforcement officers frequently need to summarize material. Witness statements need to be reduced to essentials; the most important information from memo books must be selected and included in reports—the need for summaries is constant. A summary allows the reader to know the contents of an original piece of writing without actually reading it. It is important to be able to summarize effectively.

The summary, which can also be called an abstract or a synopsis, teaches you three skills: to read carefully, to select wisely, and to write concisely. In the context of law enforcement, summarizing can help you not only with witness statements and reports but also when you need to take effective notes, to listen, or to describe an incident in the fewest possible words while conveying the maximum amount of information.

In order to summarize effectively, you must learn to

- pull out main ideas

- focus on key details

- use key words and phrases

- condense larger ideas

- write only enough to convey the essentials

- take brief, complete, and concise notes.

You must not try to

- write down everything in the original

- write down next to nothing from the original

- copy the original word for word

- copy complete sentences from the original.

The purpose of the summary, then, is to condense a piece of writing into your own words. The summary gives the reader the main ideas from the original, so that he or she doesn't need to consult the primary source. Remember, a summary is written in *your own words*.

There are a number of rules that apply to summary writing.

1. *Read the document carefully several times.* As you do so, note the thesis and any bias in the original.

2. *Underline the main ideas.* Eliminate anything that is not essential to the meaning of the original.

3. *Count the words in the original.* The summary should be about one-third or one-quarter the length of the original. It may consist of one sentence, one paragraph, or several paragraphs, depending on the length of the original. Do not use point form.

4. *Without looking at the original, write a draft summary.* Be sure that the essential points from the original appear in the summary. Although you should use your own words, the summary must reflect the intent of the

original passage. It should follow the order of the original and contain a number of supporting examples.

5. *Substitute single words for clauses and phrases.* Whenever possible, details should be summarized with generalizations. Following are some means of doing this:

   a. Change direct speech to indirect speech.

   b. Write in the third person if possible.

   c. Do not make critical comments; report the facts.

   d. Do not lift passages verbatim; you should not use more than three words at a time from the original.

   e. The amount of textual space given to the summarized ideas should be proportional to the amount they receive in the original (that is, one-quarter to one-third of the original space).

   f. Identify and eliminate minor supporting details.

   g. Eliminate wordy expressions. For example, change *as a result of* to *because* and *in the end* to *finally*.

   h. Identify and eliminate unimportant modifiers such as *extremely*, *huge*, and *friendly*.

6. *Look again at the original.* Check that you

   a. haven't quoted from the original

   b. have covered all the main points

   c. have excluded all non-essential material

   d. haven't included your personal point of view.

7. *Edit your summary for spelling and grammar.*

EXERCISE 1

REMOVING WORDY EXPRESSIONS

Find single words to replace the following phrases:

- conduct a discussion of
- perform an analysis of
- create a reduction in
- make a discovery of
- engage in the preparation of

- give consideration to
- make an assumption of
- is of the opinion that
- on account of the fact that
- carry out an investigation of

CHANGING DIRECT SPEECH TO INDIRECT SPEECH

The general procedures for changing direct speech to indirect speech are set out below.

1. *Direct words become an indirect statement, question, or command.* Quotation marks are eliminated.

   Direct: "I finished that file yesterday," she said.
   Indirect: She said she finished that file yesterday.

   Direct: "Where are you going?" he asked me.
   Indirect: He asked me where I was going.

   Direct: "Have all of the documents ready for the next hearing," the judge told me.
   Indirect: The judge told me to have all of the documents ready for the next hearing.

2. *Pronouns usually change from first to third person.* For example, *I* changes to *he, she,* or *it*.

3. *Verbs in the present tense usually change to some form of the past tense.*

COUNTING WORDS

Your summary should contain one-third or one-quarter the number of words contained in the original, depending on instructions given. Count the words in the original, then count the words in the completed summary. When counting words, observe the following rules:

1. Articles (*a, an, the*) count as one word.

2. Abbreviations count as one word.

3. Numbers count as one word.

4. Dates (23 October 2002) count as three words.

5. Compound words (e.g., *first-rate*) count as one word.

6. Words separated by a slash (e.g., *either/or*) count as one word.

7. Times (e.g., 7:10, 1430) count as one word.

SAMPLE SUMMARIES

Compare the following passage with the summarized version below it:

> We wish to acknowledge receipt of your letter of 22 September. We regret to inform you that we cannot fulfill your request at this point in time to bring a group of students to tour the city jail because the cell blocks are undergoing renovation. Within the next three months, we expect renovations to be complete and we will again allow civilians to visit the facility.
>
> We do not usually book appointments for tours this far in advance, but under the circumstances, if you are still interested in a tour when renovations

---

EXERCISE 2

PRACTISING SUMMARY

1. Summarize each of the following paragraphs into no more than two sentences.

    a. Gossip is a message that is not factual. It is not acceptable to consider gossip as fact. There may be several reasons for gossip: mischief, misunderstanding, boredom, or inattention by the person who is passing on the gossip. On the other hand, gossip may be offered as fact because people are in a rush, are busy, or simply don't get the message straight.

    b. It seems as if busy people attract business. There is always more to do for the busy person and more responsibility to accept. It is important that a law clerk keep active and busy when not on the job. The more a person becomes involved with things outside of work, the more that person learns. At the same time, one should not neglect other important things in life such as family and friends.

    c. Every law enforcement officer is faced with problems that need solving. He or she can take the easy way out by reporting each and every problem to the supervisor and then simply following instructions. A better idea, however, is to take some initiative and attempt to solve a problem before it has to be taken to a supervisor.

2. Look in your local newspaper for opinion-based articles on law enforcement issues. It will be especially informative to find articles that consider an issue from different points of view. Articles should be at least 300 words in length. Summarize the articles.

3. Summarize the article "How to Prevent Counterfeit Money from Falling Between the Cracks," which appears on the following page. The original article is 356 words long.

---

are complete, we would be happy to book an appointment with you immediately. I enclose a brochure concerning the city's law enforcement agencies with pertinent telephone numbers.

We hope that this arrangement will meet with your satisfaction.

———————————

Concerning your 22 September letter, we cannot meet your request since the cells are undergoing renovation and will not be ready for three months. We will, however, book an appointment for a student tour when renovations are complete. A brochure is enclosed for your information.

The following passage contains 183 words, the summary version below it 67 words. Main points in the original have been italicized.

> *The great defect in Jack's personality was a strong aversion to work as he defined it.* It wasn't because he lacked ambition or goals in life, for he would sit in a bingo hall, with 10 or 20 bingo cards on the table in front of him, and *play for*

▶ HOW TO PREVENT COUNTERFEIT MONEY FROM FALLING BETWEEN THE CRACKS

Counterfeiting investigators don't believe it's possible to produce foolproof counterfeit money.

With some training and a sharp eye, they believe, most merchants should be able to detect a phony bill when it crosses their counter.

The first line of defence is to recognize the subtle differences between phony bills and real paper—from the water marks to the fine print.

For example, the new $100 bill, with a picture of Sir Robert Borden, a former prime minister, has security features that would make it impossible for even the most sophisticated counterfeiter to replicate. It has water marks, a hologram, micro printing and other features that can't be reproduced on your ink-jet printers.

Retailers can obtain some helpful tips by phoning the Bank of Canada or visiting its website, www.bankofcanada.ca/en. On its website, the Bank of Canada suggests that anyone who comes across a counterfeit bill should keep the note and record its details. The person should contact the police and give them any details about who gave them the note. The Bank of Canada does not reimburse counterfeit notes.

But it has free booklets, videos and DVDs that teach merchants how to detect counterfeit notes and what to do with the bills.

Customized training seminars are also offered free of charge. The best way to detect a phony bill is to examine it under a magnifying glass beside a genuine bill.

That will reveal details like micro printing or the concentric circles in the Queen's eyes. It would also show differences in colour which are hard to reproduce with an ink-jet printer.

You should also pay attention to the feel and texture of the paper. Real Canadian money is now printed on 100 percent cotton paper, much different than even the best copy paper.

Genuine bills also have raised printing at specific spots and Braille characters that can be felt by running your fingers over the paper. Phony bills usually have a flat surface.

Merchants have been buying devices which detect phony bills by exposing them to an ultra-violet or black light. It's believed that a phony bill will light up when exposed to the black light while a real bill won't react to it. But police caution the machines aren't foolproof.

Source: From "How to Prevent Counterfeit Money from Falling Between the Cracks," 29 July 2004, *Hamilton Spectator*, p. A6.

hours without a murmur, even though he would *not be encouraged by a single win. He would stop by at the betting shop* during his rounds *every day*, even in the worst weather, *to place a few bets on horses that never seemed to win.* He would *never refuse to assist a drunk* who held his hand out for a few coins and was a *leader in community events*, such as organizing garage sales and fundraisers for the local school. *The local petty criminals*, too, *used to employ him to run their errands and to do odd jobs that their less obliging partners would not do* for them. In a word, Jack was *ready to take care of anybody's business but his own*; but as for *holding a job*, he found it *impossible*. (183 words)

Jack disliked ordinary work. He would play bingo for hours without a win and bet on horses every day without much luck. However, he would never refuse to help a drunk and was always a leader in community events. He would do odd jobs for criminals that no one else wanted to do and helped everyone but himself, finding it impossible to do an honest day's work. (67 words)

Writing a Paraphrase

The paraphrase and the summary are often thought to be the same. Both are summaries, but with a difference: the main point of the summary is to condense the basic concepts of a longer passage into a specific number of words. The summary is true to the meaning and tone of the original, but significantly reduced. A paraphrase translates a written passage or discussion into simpler terms; it entails a more radical "rephrasing" or rewording of the original. It does not have to be true to the tone or mood of the original, and *it need not be reduced in length*, but it should offer the reader or listener a clearer understanding of the original. Paraphrasing is one of the methods of effective questioning mentioned in Chapter 1 of this book.

A paraphrase, then, is:

- The rewriting of original material in your own words, not necessarily reduced in length.

- Not merely a restatement of the original's main points; it is an attempt to establish understanding of them.

- An attempt to interpret the original message so as to determine its intended meaning.

When someone is speaking to you, you may use a paraphrase to show the speaker how you are interpreting what has been said. For example, if you ask a person for a telephone number, that person might say, "The number is 905-555-1111." Your response might be, "Did you say 905-555-1111?" The reply might be, "Yes, that's right."

If you state in your own way what another person has said, that person can determine whether or not the message has been getting through. If the speaker thinks that you have misunderstood the message, the parts that seem to be causing difficulty can be reworded or repeated.

Paraphrasing has two additional benefits: it lets the other person know that you are interested in what has been said; and, since you appear to be interested in the other person's views, your own views may also be more readily accepted.

METHODS OF PARAPHRASING

There are a number of steps to follow when paraphrasing a written passage:

1. Reread the original passage until you understand its full meaning.

2. Set the original aside, and write your paraphrase on a note card.

3. Write a key word or phrase at the top of your note card to indicate the subject of your paraphrase.

4. Check your paraphrase against the original passage to make sure that your version expresses all of the essential information of the original.

5. Indicate, with quotation marks, any material you have borrowed directly from the original.

6. Record the source of your material.

Consider and compare the following examples of summary and paraphrase:

ORIGINAL: Students frequently overuse direct quotation in taking notes, and as a result they overuse quotations in their final paper. Probably only about 10 percent of your final manuscript should appear as directly quoted matter. Therefore, you should attempt to limit the amount of exact copying of source materials while taking notes. (51 words)

PARAPHRASE: In research papers, students often quote excessively, failing to keep quoted material down to a desirable level. Since the problem usually originates during note taking, it is essential to minimize the material quoted directly. (34 words)

SUMMARY: Students should take only a few direct quotations from sources to help minimize the amount of quoted material in a research paper. (22 words)

Source: From *Writing Research Papers: A Complete Guide* (pp. 46-47), James D. Lester, 1976, Glenview, IL: Scott, Foresman.

There are several ways of successfully paraphrasing a speaker's words:

1. Use the speaker's own words in your restatement.

ORIGINAL: "I hate paperwork!"
PARAPHRASE: "You say you hate paperwork?"

2. Restate the speaker's words in your own words.

ORIGINAL: "I hate paperwork!"
PARAPHRASE: "You have some really negative feelings about paperwork."

3. Talk about an experience of your own that is similar to the speaker's. This self-reference is designed to show the speaker that you understand, not to switch the focus to your own concerns.

ORIGINAL: "I hate paperwork!"
RESPONSE: "I know what you mean. When I used to do a lot of paper-work, I had trouble keeping everything straight, and I always seemed to be confused."

4. Identify the underlying implications of the message. This might lead to a deeper understanding of the speaker's message.

ORIGINAL: "I hate paperwork!"
RESPONSE: "Are you concerned that you won't be able to do your job properly?"

Since the function of paraphrase is to explain what someone has said and to demonstrate that you understand the speaker's or writer's message, it is important to check that your interpretation is correct.

EXERCISE 3

PARAPHRASING

1. Working in groups of three, select a legal topic, and ask the members of your group their opinion on that topic. Paraphrase what the other people have said in an attempt to reach understanding.

2. Paraphrase the newspaper article "Police Fume at Security Firms."

▶ POLICE FUME AT SECURITY FIRMS

Business improvement associations want to see more police walking the beat, but the police say they don't have the time. So private security guards are hired to do it.

Homeowners want more attention paid to speeders and people who run stop signs in their neighbourhoods, but police say traffic violations aren't a priority. So city council asks the province for permission to use red-light cameras at intersections in residential areas.

It's becoming more common for individuals and groups, unable to get the police to do what they'd like, to find other ways to get those services.

While the debate among Canadians rages over the benefits and dangers of two-tiered health care, a kind of two-tiered policing has become a reality.

"There's no turning back on this, it's a question of ensuring it works well," said Nathalie Des Rosiers, president of the Law Commission of Canada, about what she calls the "blending" of security and police ... .

Police and their supporters say citizens are in danger from the dramatic expansion of the largely unregulated "rent-a-cop" industry, which is taking over many traditional police roles. This is happening, the police union says, because politicians underfund the police.

Security guards, often paid little more than minimum wage and with no special powers, now do a wide range of jobs from prisoner transport to fraud investigations to patrolling streets and arresting drug dealers ... .

Security firms argue they are providing services citizens want and police don't or can't do—and for a better price ... .

Whether public money spent to keep citizens safe could be more effectively spent by divvying up jobs between the police (doing the dangerous difficult jobs) and private security (taking care of low-level tasks) is something that should be examined, the law commission's Des Rosiers says.

"There's no doubt the citizen would prefer to see a full-fledged police officer come to his or her door, but they want them to come within a reasonable time," Des Rosiers said. "And the dilemma is do they want to spend all the dollars needed to have that or do they want to have health care (as well)."

Source: From "Police Fume at Security Firms," by Kerry Gillespie, 19 October 2003, *Sunday Star* [Toronto], p. A1.

BIAS IN REPORTING

You're likely aware by now that not everyone agrees with everyone else all the time. In fact, you can have as many different points of view as there are topics to discuss. Most people have a particular point of view because they are biased about certain things or have strong opinions that can't be easily changed.

A bias does not necessarily involve a prejudice. The statement "I don't like people with brown hair" expresses a prejudice, defined as an unfavourable opinion or feeling, formed beforehand without knowledge, thought, or reason. A bias, on the other hand, can be favourable or unfavourable, but it indicates a strong opinion one way or the other, often based on experience.

The following example, taken from a local newspaper, shows two opposite biases on a single subject: dogs running free in local parks.

> Dear Editor:
>
> There are too many dogs running free in local parks while their owners just stand there and watch. This is against the law. Parks are for people. The bylaw states quite clearly that dogs are supposed to be on leashes, and people are supposed to "stoop and scoop" when dogs leave their droppings. Just the other day, I stepped in a pile of droppings that some ignorant owner didn't bother to pick up. Enforce the law! Leash your dogs, or lose them.
>
> —An unhappy taxpayer
>
> _____
>
> Dear Editor:
>
> Why can't parks be leash-free? Most dog owners, like parents of children, are very responsible and take care of their pets, picking up after them and keeping them under control. The animal shelter sells us stray and unwanted pets, but doesn't give us a place to exercise them. Then, Animal Control comes around to the parks and issues tickets to owners of dogs not on leashes. How hypocritical! We're taxpayers too. Give us a place to exercise our pets. Parks are for everyone, including dog owners.
>
> —An unhappy taxpayer

Both letter writers are unhappy taxpayers, but each looks at the issue of dogs in parks from a different point of view. Both are biased: the first writer wants dogs leashed, while the second writer doesn't. Who is right? I guess it depends on whether you own a dog, and whether you decide to obey local bylaws.

EXERCISE 4

UNDERSTANDING BIAS

Other than the leash law mentioned above, there are numerous bylaws that cause controversy. Research some of your local bylaws and try to imagine the biases that might result from their enforcement or their neglect. What might be the reasons for the different points of view?

Bias in the media goes beyond letters to the editor; it is seen in many newspaper articles and reports. The two articles by Rondi Adamson and Linda McQuaig are written from opposite points of view on the topic of the Canadian justice system. The bias in the first article is that the Canadian justice system is too soft on violent crime, while the second article takes the stand that cutting social programs increases criminal activity.

▶ IS CANADIAN JUSTICE SYSTEM TOO SOFT ON VIOLENT CRIME?

Pro

Thugs know they won't be severely punished

There isn't any question that looking at the "root causes" of crime, and funding programs designed to prevent people from turning to violence, are worthy endeavours. But there also isn't any question that once someone belongs to a gang, or is willing to murder, carjack, rape or steal, root causes are pretty much points rendered moot.

Once the crime has been committed, the fact that the perpetrator may come from a bad neighbourhood or have been the victim of racism or be young, no longer matters. ...

"I think," said Prime Minister Paul Martin, commenting on the Boxing Day killing [in Toronto] of 15-year-old Jane Creba, "more than anything else, the shootings demonstrate what are, in fact, the consequences of exclusion."

I beg to differ. I think, more than anything else, the shootings demonstrate that Canada's justice system is too soft on violent crime, and brutes out there know it.

In downtown Toronto, drug dealing, petty crimes and gang activity go on publicly with the perpetrators oblivious to reprisals. I doubt any of this was "exported from the United States," to quote another great thinker this week.

Passing the buck won't help, but more cops walking the proverbial beat, would. Allowing them to do their job would be useful, as well. Why not subject someone using drugs on a street corner to more scrutiny and police officers to less? The Youth Criminal Justice Act needs changing, too—tougher sentencing for lesser offences, and eliminating "alternative" sentencing (such as attendance in community programs) for offenders. ...

Rather than banning handguns, assuming that were possible, or wasting money on a gun registry (how many of the Boxing Day offenders do you suppose would co-operate with that?), how about a mandatory prison term for gun crimes?

Creba's death was the 78th homicide in Toronto this year [2005]. In November, when Amon Beckles was attending the funeral of murder victim Jamal Hemmings, he was shot to death outside the church. [Toronto] Mayor David Miller referred to Beckles' assailants as "despicable thugs." He talked tough, and truthfully. I'd like to hear more of that from every level of government—and reforms to our overly generous justice system.

Source: From "Is Canadian Justice System Too Soft on Violent Crime? Pro," by Rondi Adamson, 1 January 2006, *Sunday Star* [Toronto], p. A16.

Con

There is a deadly cost to cutting social programs

Ten years ago, [Ontario Premier] Mike Harris slashed Ontario's welfare rates by 22 percent, thereby cutting by almost one-quarter the incomes of Ontario's most vulnerable families.

The young kids in those vulnerable families are now teenagers. Recently, there's been an upsurge in violent crime by gangs of teenagers. Is it far-fetched to think there might be a connection?

There's ample research to show that conditions of poverty, economic disparity and social marginalization are among the factors that lead to crime, notes Wendy Cukier, who teaches justice studies at Ryerson University.

But in recent years, our ruling elites have steadfastly ignored such well-documented and intuitively obvious connections, as they've redirected an even bigger share of the national income to themselves, via tax cuts.

That was why Harris cut welfare rates—to deliver tax cuts, with the biggest tax savings going to the richest members of society. The Harris policies took money from the poor and handed it to the rich.

Did we really think this wouldn't affect poorer children, who already faced more difficulties than their schoolmates? ...

The Harris government also cut spending on an array of programs aimed at ensuring disadvantaged kids integrate into the mainstream. It cut funds for teaching English to immigrants, for social workers in the schools, for community recreation.

And when some kids behaved badly, it banned them from school with a "zero tolerance" policy. Where did we think they would go?

For an angry teen who feels excluded from the mainstream, a gang offers a sense of belonging, prestige, dignity and status among his peers. The mainstream offers less and less.

Of course, the mainstream offers jail. The Boxing Day slaying [of Jane Creba] has renewed calls for toughening up our criminal justice system.

That's understandable. But it's also what we've been doing for the past decade. We've toughened up our laws considerably, including mandatory minimum sentences for gun-related crimes.

The courts generally deal harshly with violent criminals—as they should.

But if we really want to make this a liveable society, not just enjoy the satisfaction of locking up bad people, we should intervene much earlier.

We still don't seem to grasp the connection between slashing social supports and social breakdown, including violent crime.

In the midst of the current [federal] election campaign [December 2005/January 2006], the Liberals and the Conservatives are promising massive tax cuts, rather than massive social reinvestment.

Tax cuts may put more cash in our pockets. But are we really better off if we have more cash for shopping—yet no longer feel safe to go shopping?

Economics teaches us that there's no such thing as a free lunch. Recent experience in Toronto should remind us there's no such thing as a free tax cut.

Source: From "Is Canadian Justice System Too Soft on Violent Crime? Con," by Linda McQuaig, 1 January 2006, *Sunday Star* [Toronto], p. A16.

EXERCISE 5

SUMMARIZING AND COMPARING

1. Look in your library for newspaper or magazine articles that contain opposing points of view on the same topic. For instance, there have been many articles supporting the *Youth Criminal Justice Act* and just as many stating that the new Act lets young offenders off too easily. There are many such articles in the media about a wide range of legal topics.

   Write an essay comparing and contrasting two articles that take opposite points of view on the same issue. In your opening paragraph, state the theses put forward by the opposing authors. Next, either in block form or point-by-point form, summarize the contents of these two articles, pointing out the bias in each and citing the examples each provides. Finally, write a concluding paragraph telling which article was more effective and why.

   The length of your essay will be determined by the length of the articles you use. You must follow the rules of summary writing: each summary should be about one-third of the article's original length. Your articles must be opinion-based, not report-based (there's not much bias in a brief newspaper article reporting the latest fender bender), and should be at least three hundred words.

2. Write an essay on a law enforcement topic about which you feel strongly. Research the topic to gather whatever facts you need. Point out your bias and the reasons for your bias. Remember, it's your opinion that counts, but you must back up your opinion with facts.

Summary

The ability to summarize and paraphrase is an effective communication tool for the law enforcement professional. In summaries, you put other people's words, substantially reduced, into your own words while retaining the meaning of the original. When paraphrasing, you demonstrate your understanding of a speaker's or writer's meaning. In most newspaper or popular magazine articles, authors reveal a particular point of view, or bias, on a topic. Facts supporting this bias are used to persuade the reader of the author's point of view.

SPELLING AND DEFINITIONS

Be able to spell and define the following words:

citation	distorted	preamble	subordinate
colleagues	emotional	process	traumatic
complainant	immediately	prosecutor	trespassing
compromise	impediment	proximity	vandalism
controversial	lenient	regulation	vehicle
corporation	minority	reputed	vindicate
desperate	nuisance	secretary	
distended	overrule	statutory	

MINI-PUZZLE

Complete the following crossword using the definitions given below it. The words are taken from the Spelling and Definitions list for this chapter.

Across

2. Not severe in judgment or punishment.
5. Disputable; generally supported but with some doubt.
6. Mutual concession.
8. Enter privately owned land or property without permission.
9. A person, thing, or situation that causes annoyance or inconvenience.
10. False or dishonest; misrepresented.

Down

1. Nearness.
3. Deeply and unforgettably shocking.
4. A legal action in all its stages.
7. Swollen because of pressure from inside.

WORD SEARCH

Below the puzzle is a list of words taken from the Spelling and Definitions list. Find these words in the puzzle and circle them.

```
M  D  R  P  G  N  I  S  S  A  P  S  E  R  T  T  P  Z  N  F  E  E  Y  Y  K
Y  X  R  P  J  Z  Y  U  T  I  V  O  E  H  M  I  L  A  N  O  I  T  O  M  E
F  M  P  R  J  A  X  Z  G  R  C  H  C  C  M  Y  P  P  F  C  M  H  R  O  O
I  W  F  C  C  T  T  Z  R  J  A  E  W  O  N  K  R  R  P  N  W  W  J  P  S
E  G  V  I  N  D  I  C  A  T  E  U  M  F  N  A  Z  A  O  W  O  M  P  K  O
I  M  M  E  D  I  A  T  E  L  Y  S  M  D  P  T  S  V  T  C  E  K  L  R  S
E  Y  T  I  M  I  X  O  R  P  I  W  E  A  C  Y  R  I  H  E  E  I  T  P  Q
T  Y  T  I  R  O  N  I  M  L  J  D  T  D  T  O  L  O  U  E  R  S  Y  A  O
A  H  T  G  D  B  V  D  A  O  N  N  G  B  E  I  M  K  V  N  V  C  S  V  B
N  M  C  N  B  E  W  D  S  E  E  M  G  V  E  T  C  P  F  E  J  B  E  D  G
I  N  I  P  A  R  N  T  T  I  C  C  G  N  E  X  R  R  R  V  R  R  K  S  X
D  P  Q  D  O  A  T  S  N  Y  L  A  Q  T  H  H  S  O  S  O  R  S  M  G  V
R  M  W  I  V  T  I  E  A  F  K  W  M  W  C  V  I  L  T  U  M  U  I  W  W
O  E  Y  A  Z  D  L  P  L  T  C  G  C  U  E  L  W  C  L  S  J  I  S  A  U
B  E  T  A  R  E  P  S  E  D  J  Y  R  U  S  J  T  E  L  F  I  Q  S  U  L
U  I  M  R  O  T  U  C  E  S  O  R  P  P  I  R  U  W  X  E  I  D  M  E  A
S  Z  A  R  Y  C  U  F  J  F  T  Y  T  N  A  N  I  A  L  P  M  O  C  J  E
```

COMPLAINANT	COMPROMISE	CONTROVERSIAL	DESPERATE
DISTENDED	DISTORTED	EMOTIONAL	IMMEDIATELY
LENIENT	MINORITY	NUISANCE	OVERRULE
PROCESS	PROSECUTOR	PROXIMITY	SECRETARY
SUBORDINATE	TRAUMATIC	TRESPASSING	VANDALISM
VEHICLE	VINDICATE		

CHAPTER 5

From Words to Essay

Learning Objectives

After completing this chapter, you should be able to:

- Consider your audience and your reason for writing.

- Construct a paragraph containing a topic and a thesis.

- Understand how different types of paragraphs are written.

- Write an essay using an effective introduction, support paragraphs, and conclusion.

- Use transitional words and phrases between parts of your essay.

- Document your research.

Introduction

Why do you write? People have many purposes in writing, but whatever their particular purpose may be, writers who hope to communicate their ideas must transmit them in a form that their readers will recognize and accept.

PURPOSE

In college, you most likely write because your instructor has given you an assignment. The purpose of these assignments is to teach you how to process information, how to be accurate, and how to convey a message in understandable prose and in the proper written form.

These components are essential to any type of law enforcement writing you may do. You likely won't have to write an "academic" essay while on the job as a law enforcement officer; however, you'll most certainly have to write an essay as part of applying for a law enforcement career. If you plan to pursue your education beyond the college level, perhaps in a university criminology program, knowledge of essay-writing skills will be essential:

> While the essay is required in any number of courses—law enforcement, business studies, office administration, technology, social sciences, journalism, broadcasting, and the like—its value transcends the requirements of a post-secondary level course. Writing essays can equip you with the skills you'll need to write corporate reports, evaluations, summaries, research papers, letters, memos, and job applications. Forms of writing vary, but the essay is still the basic form. Good spelling, grammar, and logic, essential features of an effective essay, remain paramount in all forms of writing, as does the ability to express yourself clearly. (Adapted from Lipschutz, Roberts, Scarry, & Scarry, 2004, p. 175)

In general, a writer seeks to *inform*, to *explain*, to *persuade*, or to *put something on record*, and to do so as efficiently as possible. To determine which of these aims applies to your writing, ask yourself, "What do I want to happen as the result of my writing?"

AUDIENCE

It is important to analyze your audience before beginning any writing assignment. Ask the following questions:

1. Who will be reading this?

2. What does the reader want to hear?

3. What do I want to tell the reader?

4. How can I best arrange and present the message?

In the case of a college assignment, the answers to some of these questions are obvious. Good grades depend on identifying and fulfilling the instructor's expectations. Many of these expectations are identified in this book. You are asked to write a report, for example, based on the guidelines established in Chapter 8. This is what the instructor expects, and your grade for that assignment will depend on your ability to follow those guidelines.

Of course, the world of law enforcement brings a different audience. Different people will approach your written work differently, with diverse agendas. Consider the following, for example:

- Your sergeant will want to see that your writing is clear, concise, factual, and complete.

- The defence lawyer will examine your written work carefully, with an eye to any mistakes in spelling, grammar, or facts, which may bring your report into question and aid the defence.

- The Crown attorney will want to use your written work as a basis for prosecution, and will be looking to see that facts are not omitted, that opinion and hearsay aren't treated as facts, that spelling and grammar errors don't occur, and that you haven't been sloppy.

- The insurance company will examine your material with a view to determining fault and deciding on a possible settlement.

Your written words must be so effective that every person reading them can visualize the situation as you saw it. The only way to learn how to write is to write. Writing begins with a letter, then a word, then a sentence, then a paragraph. From there, it evolves to the essay, the report, or another longer format. Figure 5.1 shows the structure of an essay.

FIGURE 5.1 THE STRUCTURE OF AN ESSAY

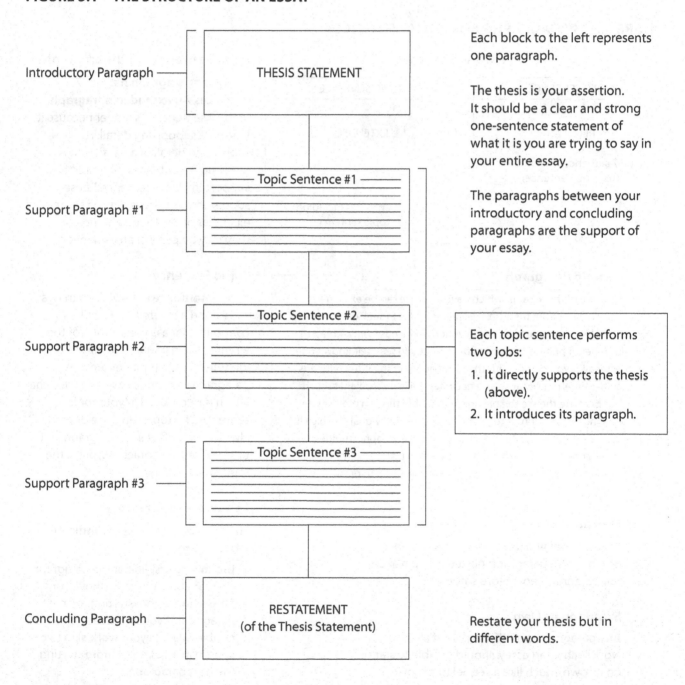

Source: Adapted from Lipschutz, Roberts, Scarry, & Scarry (2004), p. 176.

■ Paragraph

A paragraph is composed of a number of sentences. Each paragraph contains one main idea, either as part of a longer piece of writing, such as an essay or a report, or as an independent unit. There is no prescribed length for a paragraph. But the paragraph must be long enough to fully express your main idea or your purpose for writing. Generally, paragraphs are from 5 to 12 sentences in length.

You express the paragraph's main idea in a *topic sentence* (see Figure 5.2). Every other sentence in the paragraph supports, describes, or explains the main point you are expressing in the topic sentence.

FIGURE 5.2 PARAGRAPHS AND TOPIC SENTENCES

Two Paragraph Types

TOPIC SENTENCE
REGULAR (5–7 sentences including the topic sentence)

TOPIC SENTENCE
EXTENDED (8–12 sentences including the topic sentence)

Regular or Extended Paragraphs

A **regular paragraph** has 5 to 7 sentences. An **extended paragraph** (8 to 12 sentences) is longer because it has more supporting detail. The supporting detail of a paragraph is made up of sentences that directly support the topic sentence. These supporting sentences may be specific examples of the topic sentence, or they may be parts of an explanation.

Sample Paragraph

One of the areas in which having choice can be extremely valuable is that of friends. Like leaving home to seek greater knowledge of yourself, picking your own friends from a greater number of people can aid in your journey to seek self-knowledge. After all, if you go out with the same group of small-town friends all the time, not because you necessarily like them all that much but because they're the only ones available, this can prove quite limiting when it comes to your growth as an individual. The big city, on the other hand, offers an endless number of opportunities to meet people of like interests. You're much more likely to cultivate relationships with people who help you to grow.

Topic Sentence

A **topic sentence** includes two things: a *topic* and a *controlling idea*. The controlling idea is the attitude of the writer of the paragraph toward the topic identified in the topic sentence. A paragraph contains *one single idea*—that which is introduced in your topic sentence. The topic sentence does not always appear first in a paragraph, but until you are well practised, place the topic sentence first.

Transitions

Transitional words or phrases are used to organize the paragraph better and to make the paragraph flow more smoothly.

Stands on Its Own

Any paragraph, even if it is part of a longer work such as an essay, should be able to stand on its own, much like a sequel to a movie.

Paragraph Indication

There are only two ways **to indicate a new paragraph**:

1. **Indent** the first line of the paragraph (see sample paragraph above), or
2. **Skip a line** before starting the next paragraph. If you are already double-spacing your work, skip two lines, instead of one, before starting the next paragraph.

Source: Adapted from Lipschutz, Roberts, Scarry, & Scarry (2004), p. 158.

Most paragraphs begin with the topic sentence, although it does not have to appear at the beginning. Examine the following paragraph:

> Growing up near a police station had a profound influence on my life. Every day I'd watch the police cruisers leave the station. I'd wonder where they were going and what adventures awaited them. I'd hear the sirens in the middle of the night and jump out of bed to watch the flashing lights disappear down the street. I'd watch people entering the police station and wonder what problems they had. I grew up considering myself part of the daily routine.

The topic sentence in this paragraph is the first sentence. The main idea is that the writer grew up near a police station and was greatly influenced by what he or she saw. Every other sentence supports this main idea: the references to the cruisers, the sirens, the people, all contribute to the notion that proximity to the station had a profound influence on the writer's life.

You will see later on in this chapter that every essay has a topic (what is being written about) and a thesis statement (the writer's point of view on the topic). Like the essay itself, each paragraph has a topic and a thesis, in this case called a *controlling idea*. The controlling idea expresses the writer's point of view on the paragraph's topic. Consider the following topic sentence:

> Working as a customs officer for the summer was both rewarding and frustrating.

Here the author is writing about his or her summer job as a customs officer (the topic). It was at once rewarding and frustrating (the controlling idea, describing how the author experienced the job). The remainder of the paragraph should provide details about how the job was both rewarding and frustrating.

A topic sentence can have a wide variety of controlling ideas, depending on the writer. A summer job as a customs officer could have been rewarding yet frustrating for one writer and exciting, or boring, or challenging for other writers.

Once you have chosen your topic and have written a topic sentence reflecting your controlling idea, it is necessary to substantiate your topic sentence with *supporting details*. These are the sentences that support the main idea through detail and example. The previous example, "Growing up near a police station," illustrated how supporting details work within a paragraph. The writer of that paragraph used examples to demonstrate the main idea of influence.

Examples are specific illustrations or evidence that support the controlling idea. They must be clear and specific. The following paragraph lacks specific examples; it uses no specific information, and, in the end, it is clear that the paragraph as a whole does not support the topic sentence and controlling idea. The topic sentence is set out in italics:

> *Police officers are lazy.* All they do is sit around and eat doughnuts all day, or they drive around ignoring everyone. Sometimes I see them writing in a little book, but they're likely making up their grocery list. And you can never find a cop when you want one. Just the other day, I called the police station to report my bike missing. It took forever for the officer to arrive to take the report. Boy, was I angry. It's a good thing I remembered I left it at my friend's house.

EXERCISE 1

WRITING TOPIC SENTENCES

For each of the topics below, write a possible topic sentence with a controlling idea. Look at the examples before proceeding.

Sample topic: Canada's justice system
   Possible topic sentence:
   Canada's justice system is among the fairest in the world.

Sample topic: Hand-held electronic devices
   Possible topic sentence:
   Banning cellphone use while driving will reduce road accidents.

Sample topic: Restorative justice
   Possible topic sentence:
   Restorative justice is a new method of dealing with offenders.

1. *Topic*: Choosing a career in law enforcement
Topic sentence:

_____

_____

_____

2. *Topic*: The *Criminal Code*
Topic sentence:

_____

_____

_____

3. *Topic*: Two years as an auxiliary police officer
Topic sentence:

_____

_____

_____

4. *Topic*: The Law and Security/Police Foundations Program
Topic sentence:

_____

_____

_____

5. *Topic*: Young offenders
Topic sentence:

_____

_____

_____

_____

EXERCISE 2

USING SPECIFIC EXAMPLES

Rewrite the paragraph about the laziness of police officers. Compose a topic sentence and give specific examples to support your controlling idea. You can adopt the existing point of view, take an opposing point of view, or develop an entirely new controlling idea. Whatever point of view you take, be sure to use specific examples.

TYPES OF PARAGRAPHS

There are five main strategies for writing paragraphs: *narration* (tells a story), *description* (describes something using the senses), *exposition* (explains how something is done), *comparison/contrast* (points out similarities and differences between two or more subjects), and *cause and effect* (describes the result of something taking place). Following are topic sentences in each category and suggestions of ways in which to develop them.

Narration
When I transferred into the Police Sciences course, I knew that I had found my career. [*Then tell the story of how you came to choose the Police Sciences course.*]

Description
The line of cars waiting to clear customs inspection was long. [*Then describe the length, the line, and the attitudes of drivers.*]

Exposition
Loading and unloading a handgun is a simple process if you know what you're doing. [*Then give a step-by-step account of the process, being careful not to leave out anything important.*]

Comparison/contrast
American prison guards are trained differently from Canadian prison guards. [*Then point out similarities and differences.*]

Cause and effect
An ineffective parole system leads to increased crime on the streets. [*Then give specific examples of increased crime on the streets and how it is caused by an ineffective parole system.*]

Essay

The essay is the basic form of writing in many academic programs, and an essay is often required for the successful completion of law enforcement testing.

The essay helps prepare you for other forms of writing: the report, the summary, the job application, the letter, and the memo. Spelling, grammar, clarity, and proper structure are all essential parts of the essay.

An essay is a form of writing that contains a number of paragraphs. Writing one may also involve research, citations, and documentation to show the origin of

---

EXERCISE 3

WRITING DIFFERENT KINDS OF TOPIC SENTENCES

Write a topic sentence and controlling idea for the following topics, using the strategy in parentheses following the topic. An example is provided.

Example: Locker room (description):
   The locker room was a picture of chaos.

1. My first week at college (narration):

_____

_____

2. Prison guards (description):

_____

_____

3. How to write a resumé (exposition):

_____

_____

4. Police chiefs of Toronto and Vancouver (comparison/contrast):

_____

_____

5. Illegal handguns (cause and effect):

_____

_____

Write a whole paragraph based on one of the topic sentences you have written above.

---

facts used in the essay. An essay can be written on any topic, but whatever the topic, the essay always consists of a number of paragraphs in which you consider a topic much more thoroughly than you could in a single paragraph.

The essay may be *narrative* (it tells a story), *descriptive* (it describes something), *expository* (it explains something), or *persuasive* (it tries to convince the reader of the writer's point of view).

All essays must have an introduction, a body, and a conclusion. The introduction and conclusion are usually one paragraph each, although they may be longer.

The purpose of the *introduction* is to explain your essay to the reader and to capture his or her attention. This paragraph contains a topic sentence (what the essay is about) and a thesis statement (your point of view), which can be combined into one sentence. The opening paragraph "introduces" your essay.

The *body* of the essay is made up of the paragraphs between the introduction and the conclusion, and it provides the evidence to support your thesis. The body of the essay usually consists of at least three paragraphs that are connected by transitions.

The *conclusion*, usually one paragraph in length, summarizes the proofs that you have supplied in support of your thesis.

GETTING STARTED

What to write about? Usually this isn't a problem: Your instructor will ask for a 2,000-word essay on the topic of the death penalty, or a job application will ask for a brief essay about "why you want to work for Corrections Canada." In some situations, the choice of topic is left up to you. The remainder of this chapter will tell you how to write the essay, but before beginning to write, you must choose a topic or develop some ideas about an assigned topic, and decide how to express these ideas.

One of the best ways to collect ideas is through *brainstorming*. Brainstorming is simple. It can best be accomplished in groups of four or more people, but the number of people involved isn't as important as the number of ideas you generate. The steps in brainstorming are as follows:

1. Come up with as many ideas as you can and write them down.

2. Don't initially criticize any idea. You can weed out poor ideas later.

3. Develop alternatives. If any ideas generate objections, work on varying the ideas rather than simply discard them.

4. As you come up with ideas, discuss them. Your discussion will generate other ideas.

5. Make sure that everyone in the group completely understands the ideas generated.

6. Put your list of ideas aside for a while. Think about them occasionally, at your convenience. This "backburner" approach will often generate further ideas.

Select your best ideas, use them as possible topics or thesis statements, and begin to prepare an outline.

OUTLINE

An outline is the logical starting point in the writing process. An outline can be considered as a sketch, a plan, a focus, a framework, or a method of organization. It gives you an opportunity to organize your ideas into a plan or a pattern. It provides a framework for your facts, your main ideas, and your supporting points. Begin by developing a thesis statement that expresses your essay's overall message to the reader. You can organize your research, ideas, and facts around this thesis statement.

EXERCISE 4

BRAINSTORMING

Assume that you must submit a report on one of the following topics:

- maintaining discipline in a Law and Security class
- causes of car accidents
- problems with drugs
- ethical behaviour for law enforcement officers
- changes to the *Highway Traffic Act*.

In groups of no fewer than four people, take ten minutes to brainstorm the topics. Have someone record the ideas you come up with, and be prepared to present them to the class.

THESIS STATEMENT

The thesis statement expresses the essay's main idea. It usually conveys the writer's position on the topic and is especially important in the persuasive or expository essay. The thesis statement is a single, complete sentence that can be found anywhere in the introductory paragraph, but it is usually found at the beginning or end. It tells the reader what will be explained, described, proven, or answered in the essay, and it clearly states what position the writer is taking.

It is not enough to write "The crisis in our correctional system" as a thesis statement. This is a topic, or possibly a title, but the words do not meet the requirements of a thesis statement, which must

- be a complete sentence and
- express the writer's point of view.

A thesis statement might take the following form:

> The correctional system is facing a shortage of trained personnel, a situation that can be remedied only if more funding is allocated for training.

Other sentences in the introductory paragraph should supplement this thesis statement with details, as in the following example:

> Corrections Canada is facing a crisis. While the number of inmates in Canada's prisons is rising, the number of guards and administrators in the system is declining. [*The writer may wish to quote the source of this fact here or give actual figures later in the essay.*] The correctional system is facing a shortage of trained personnel, a situation that can be remedied only if more funding is allocated for training.

In order to write an effective thesis statement, the writer should consider the following advice:

1. *Make sure the scope of the topic is not too broad.* For example, Canada's customs service is too large a topic for an essay. You may either limit or qualify the topic:

   Limited topic: **Customs officers should not be allowed to carry firearms. [Topic limited to firearms only, not other issues relating to customs officers.]**
   Qualified topic: **Surveillance has increased at border crossings since 11 September 2001. [Topic suggests a function of customs officers, and the discussion will be limited to that one function.]**

2. *Use a controlling idea.* State a personal point of view that you feel you can support with research.

   There has been a dramatic, but necessary, increase in surveillance at border crossings since 11 September 2001.

3. *Indicate the strategy to be used in the essay.* While you may have facts to support the idea that border surveillance has increased and is necessary, you need a method of presenting this point of view and research. Your strategy may be implied, though not stated, in your thesis statement or elsewhere in your introductory paragraph. Strategies include:

   Comparison/contrast: **A description of surveillance before and after 11 September 2001.**
   Cause and effect: **An analysis of what caused increased surveillance and what effect it has had.**
   Advantages/disadvantages: **An analysis of how increased surveillance has both helped and harmed cross-border traffic.**
   Reasons: **A statement of reasons why surveillance at borders must increase.**
   Persuasion: **An argument that even those drivers caught in long lineups at inspection stations must agree that surveillance was too lax in the past.**

ORGANIZING THE ESSAY

Now that you have your thesis statement, you can go ahead and organize your research, your facts, and your arguments, keeping in mind that the thesis statement forms the focus of your organization. There are many ways of organizing the essay into a coherent unit. Some possibilities are as follows:

1. *Logical pattern.* Organize whatever notes, index cards, ideas, or research you have into what you consider to be a logical pattern. You might pick out major ideas and put them in sequence, then arrange information supporting these ideas.

2. *Generalities to specifics.* Organize your material so that it moves from general to specific facts.

3. *Order of importance.* Organize your material according to the importance of the various facts or ideas you may be using.

EXERCISE 5

WRITING A THESIS STATEMENT

Develop a thesis statement for each of the following topics:

■ Prevalence of crime in Canada

_____

_____

_____

■ Drinking and driving

_____

_____

_____

■ Capital punishment

_____

_____

_____

■ Conjugal visits for prisoners

_____

_____

_____

■ Fraud against senior citizens

_____

_____

_____

4. *Chronology.* Organize your material chronologically.

5. *Strategy.* Organize your material in relation to comparison/contrast, cause and effect, or any of the other strategies discussed thus far.

The nature and content of your essay will determine the best organization. For example, a narrative essay lends itself well to a chronological format. An outline based on your strategy selection will give the essay the beginnings of an organized look. You may notice areas that need more research or supporting facts, and you will see how the various parts fit together.

You may wish to organize your outline according to one of the two patterns set out below.

Introductory paragraph		Introductory paragraph
	or	
1. First major point		1. Major heading
2. Supporting material		a. Minor heading
3. Second major point		2. Major heading
4. Supporting material		a. Minor heading
5. Third major point		3. Major heading
6. Supporting material		a. Minor heading
Conclusion		Conclusion

WRITING THE INTRODUCTION

Once the outline has been organized, you can begin writing the introductory paragraph. You have now decided on a topic and thesis statement along with a writing strategy. In the introductory paragraph, the topic and thesis are stated. A pattern for the essay must be developed, something that will attract the reader's interest while allowing you to implement your strategy.

There are various ways to write an introductory paragraph:

1. Select a general subject that can be narrowed down to a specific topic.

   The need for prison reform seems to be generally recognized these days, and the one problem that needs immediate attention is that of overcrowding in prisons. With hundreds of inmates crowded into prisons built for half that number and with prison cells filled beyond their intended capacity, small problems become large problems very quickly.

2. Begin with an anecdote. A short, possibly amusing, personal story can lead into your topic.

   I was arrested once. When I was in my final year of university, a couple of friends insisted that we go out for a few drinks. A few led to a few more, and we ended up in the drunk tank overnight. After what I saw that night, I resolved never to do anything that would get me sent to jail again. I also resolved to do what I could to help people who can't afford legal assistance. I met a few of those people that night.

3. Give a definition.

   Restorative justice is an approach to justice that has healing as its focus.

4. Make a statement that is sure to attract attention.

   A Justice Canada white paper being shopped around provincial governments and police forces suggests cops should be empowered to commit crimes ranging from drug trafficking to violent assaults, if they believe they need to in order to nurture an investigation. This is getting nervous looks from the legal community (Beazley, 2000).

5. Be contrarian: start by echoing a widely held point of view, then take the opposite view.

> Imprisoning people who break the law has many goals. Imprisonment shows society's abhorrence for certain anti-social behaviours and incarceration removes people from the community for a certain period of time. Imprisonment is supposed to alter criminal behaviour. Yet time served in prison being time to deter criminal behaviour is without empirical support (Gendreau, Coggin, & Cullen, 1999).

6. Start with a quotation.

> "Prison is not the place to grow old." Prison used to be for young people, but in the past two decades, the number of offenders over 50 years of age in Canada's prisons shot up dramatically, and continues to grow (Sheppard, 2001).

7. Start your essay with a description.

> Imagine you are in your car at a border crossing, inching ahead with what seem to be hundreds of other cars waiting to be inspected. It's hot, your motor is overheating, and cars in the other lanes always seem to be moving faster than yours. You don't care about possible terrorists entering the country. You've had a long drive, you're irritable, and all you want to do is answer the question, "Anything to declare?" and be on your way.

8. Ask a question.

> Are private security companies more effective than official law enforcement agencies? While the teaching and tools of private security have become more technical, the overall mission has remained the same for the past 300 years—the protection of assets, be they human, material, or technological. To complete this mission, private security personnel can do things that would be considered illegal if carried out by law enforcement agencies (Ingerman, 2001).

BODY OF ESSAY OR SUPPORT PARAGRAPHS

The number of paragraphs in an essay depends on the number of points you need to make. It's not a question of how long an essay is supposed to be, but of how many words, sentences, paragraphs, or pages are needed to make the point defined by your thesis.

There is going to be an introduction and a conclusion: that's two paragraphs. The body of the essay will contain the number of paragraphs required to support the thesis of the essay. While there is no formula for length or quantity of paragraphs or words, the development of your essay will involve at least three other paragraphs (and likely more) to support your thesis.

EXERCISE 6

ORGANIZING TOPICS WITHIN THE ESSAY

You've been assigned an essay project entitled "Causes of motor vehicle accidents." Listed below are some of the topics you can use for this essay. Using as many topics as you consider relevant, organize them logically under headings that you create.

- acts of God
- aggression
- alcohol and drugs
- anger
- back-seat drivers
- bare feet
- bumblebees in car
- confusing traffic signs
- daydreaming
- distractions
- drivers' medical emergencies
- short drivers
- tall drivers
- drivers under emotional strain
- drivers unfamiliar with car
- cellphones
- fog
- glare
- immature drivers
- impaired drivers

- lateness
- long hair
- mechanically unfit vehicles
- suicide
- pedestrians
- poor driver skills
- poor eyesight and hearing
- poor mirrors
- poor seat adjustment
- poor tires and steering
- poorly lit roadways
- poorly marked highways
- potholes
- racing
- reckless driving
- road construction
- road hazards
- snow and ice
- student drivers
- other

TRANSITIONS

Transitions are words or phrases that connect thoughts within a sentence, between sentences, and between paragraphs. In other words, they form links between ideas. For example, in the sentence below, the words "instead of" are used to contrast two things within a sentence:

He spent his time investigating accidents instead of writing reports.

Transitions are used to show the logical connection between ideas. The transitions are italicized in the following sentences:

Before drawing your weapon, be sure you have cause.

Finally, with all my reports typed and filed, my shift was finished.

I tried again to reach her by phone, *but* I had no luck.

The anonymous phone tip mentioned only a one-armed man; *nevertheless*, it was still a good lead to follow up.

To the left of the prison stood a coffee shop.

WRITING STRATEGIES

Narration

Narration tells a story. The best way to tell a story is to start at the beginning and continue to the end; in other words, use chronological order. Tell what happened first, then what happened next, until you reach the end of the story.

Useful transitions for narrative essays include words that indicate the passage of time and the sequence of events, such as the following:

- after
- at once
- before
- first
- immediately

- next
- now
- suddenly
- then
- usually

Description

Description portrays something. The best way to describe something is to be concrete and appeal to the five senses. There are many adjectives and adverbs that can be used descriptively. While you can't appeal to every sense in describing a person, place, or thing, you can appeal to a number of them. A description of a handgun, for example, might engage all your senses. Before embarking on such a description, you might ask yourself the following questions:

Sight: What kind of handgun (revolver, automatic), and with what features?

Sound: What sound does it make when fired, or when a cartridge is being loaded?

Touch: Is it cold, plastic, smooth?

Taste: Can you taste burnt powder on your tongue when the gun is fired?

Smell: What about the smell of the oil used to preserve the weapon, or the smell of spent gunpowder?

When describing something, start with a specific part of the item you wish to describe, and go in a specific direction: top to bottom, left to right, outside to inside. For example, in describing a person, your order might be as follows:

1. shape of head
2. hair colour
3. hair style

4. shape of ears
5. eye colour
6. shape of mouth

Exposition

Exposition tells how something is done. This type of essay is sometimes called the *process* essay. You use this mode for telling your reader how to complete a task (for example, how to apply to the Ontario Provincial Police [OPP] for a job) or how an institution such as the Canada Border Services Agency (CBSA) was formed.

This type of essay requires that you include all the steps in the correct order. There is no use telling the reader the requisite steps for applying to the OPP if you omit some steps, such as obtaining a St. John Ambulance certificate or a driver's licence. Without these items, the applicant will certainly be rejected for employment.

There are a number of transitions helpful in writing the expository essay, including the following:

- after
- begin with
- finally
- finish with
- first
- next
- start with
- the first step
- the second step
- then

Persuasion

Persuasion involves an attempt to change a reader's viewpoint, or to convince a reader of your point of view. There are procedures to use when writing the persuasion essay:

1. Define a clear thesis statement.

   Canada must reform its prison system.

2. Use examples.

3. Use authorities. Quote others who support your point of view.

4. Be aware of the opposition. Because some readers will disagree with you, attempt to address potential disagreement in your essay. Don't ignore arguments. Deal with them.

5. Point out the options. Let your reader know the consequences of not accepting your point of view.

   If Canada fails to reform its prison system, overcrowding in our prisons will only get worse.

Comparison/Contrast

Comparison emphasizes similarities between things, while contrast emphasizes differences. Comparison and contrast essays can be organized according to either the *block method* or the *point-by-point method*. For example, consider the following:

Thesis: Applying for a job with Corrections Canada is similar to applying for other law enforcement positions, but there are also many differences in the process.

Block method: Describe the entire process of applying for employment with Corrections Canada, then the entire process of applying to another law enforcement agency, so that the body of the essay is divided into two parts.

Point-by-point method: Each paragraph in the body of the essay discusses Corrections Canada and another law enforcement agency in connection with a particular aspect of the application process. For example, begin with the requirements for both agencies in one paragraph, then the application process for both agencies in the next paragraph, then the interview process in another paragraph, and so on.

Some useful transitions are set out below.

Comparison	*Contrast*
■ like	■ unlike
■ similarly	■ conversely
■ likewise	■ otherwise
■ also	■ but
■ on the one hand	■ on the other hand
■ generally	■ however
■ usually	■ instead
■ in keeping with	■ as opposed to

CONCLUSION

Writing a good concluding paragraph is difficult. It is not enough to say, "In conclusion" and then repeat the thesis statement.

Thesis: Crime is on the increase in Canada because not enough criminals are stopped from entering the country.

Inadequate conclusion: In conclusion, crime is on the increase in Canada because not enough criminals are stopped from entering the country.

There are a number of methods you can use to write a successful conclusion:

1. Rework and elaborate on the contents of your introductory paragraph. Reword your thesis statement and the introduction's main idea.

   Customs officers need more tools to do the job. They are restrained by a lack of technology, and their lack of public recognition compared with other law enforcement officers tends to minimize their effectiveness in the fight against crime. Much has been done, yet much remains to be done, to make our borders safe.

2. Summarize. Repeat the main points of your essay.

   Law and Security programs are now found in every provincial community college, as well as in private training institutions. Coordinating these programs is essential if students are to graduate with acceptable minimum requirements acknowledged by all law enforcement agencies. Possibly the provincial government should step in.

EXERCISE 7

DEVELOPING AN OUTLINE

Using the contents of the following paragraph, develop an essay outline for each of the strategies discussed above (narration, description, exposition, persuasion, and comparison/contrast):

Customs officers are commonly seen as the opposition, threatening to confiscate that bottle of overproof rum you brought back from your Caribbean vacation. As they see it themselves, they are just enforcing rules made up by the government. Their chief targets are people who want to make exorbitant profits at the expense of their fellow citizens. But even the innocent feel intimidated. Confronted by a uniformed customs officer, most returning travellers feel guilty even if they don't have an undeclared jar of Uncle Sid's pickles hidden in their luggage.

1. Tell a story about an incident at customs that involved you. (Use narration.)

2. Describe a search of your luggage and car at a border. (Use description.)

3. Describe the procedure for a secondary customs inspection. (Use exposition.)

4. Convince a customs officer that you have nothing to declare. (Use persuasion.)

5. Describe how the duties of a customs officer differ from those of another law enforcement officer. (Use comparison/contrast.)

3. Offer solutions. After making a number of points in the body of your essay, offer a solution to the problem you've presented, or make a prediction about what might happen if your advice isn't followed.

The need for private security has increased dramatically as law enforcement agencies become overwhelmed owing to rising crime rates and underfunding. However, formal training for private security officers has not improved with the demand for their services. The training should meet a minimum standard sanctioned by the government in cooperation with police, customs, and corrections agencies. In this way, private security could play a more important and more respected role in law enforcement.

4. Tell a story that illustrates your thesis.

Frederich Dumont, a convicted murderer, was on the streets of Saskatoon after having served less than two-thirds of his sentence. Two days later, he seriously injured a variety store owner in a failed robbery attempt and was arrested in the store. This is but one more brutal incident showing the need to reform the parole system.

EXERCISE 8

WRITING CONCLUSIONS

Return to the previous exercise in which you developed outlines for each of the five writing strategies discussed in the chapter. Write a conclusion for each strategy based on the outline you developed.

Research Paper

The research paper and the essay are written in much the same way, except that with the research paper, you rely more heavily on facts from outside sources and use them in your paper. These facts must be documented—that is, you must list your sources in a bibliography, Works Cited, or References section at the end of your paper, and cite them in the paper itself. In this way you identify the sources of direct quotations, indirect quotations, and any ideas or other specific facts you have obtained from elsewhere.

FINDING THE FACTS

The nature and sources of information you'll need for your writing project will vary with the situation. In most cases, the facts and information you need are readily available in your college library. All you have to do is find them.

But the research paper does not just involve finding great chunks of information from outside sources and inserting them into your research paper. Rather, you will try to match what you already know or suspect with facts established elsewhere. For example, if you have the opinion that the number of homicides has decreased in your city, you can search for sources that deal with the topic of homicides and look for information that confirms your belief. Sometimes, in the course of your research, you will discover an abundance of evidence that changes your belief—you may discover that the number of homicides has in fact risen in your city. In such cases, you may decide to change your thesis and take an opposite position. Local newspapers, magazine articles, visits to the police station, and other sources such as the Internet will provide you with the information you need. In another situation, you might want to investigate the job prospects with, say, the Calgary police force. You'll need to research different sources to find this information.

NOTE TAKING

Identify as many relevant sources as you can. As you come across what looks like useful information, jot down, on an index card or in a notebook specifically designated for this task, things such as call numbers of books, titles, chapters, page references, the names of journals, tables of contents, Internet addresses—in short, the names and locations of potentially useful material. This is the first step.

Next, go over your sources to collect facts. If you have accurately listed your sources the first time around, it won't be a problem retrieving them. Extract specific information, jotting down ideas, direct quotations, links to other sources, and any information that is relevant to your topic. You might want to summarize or write a précis of a newspaper article, journal article, or Internet article. Never lose track of your sources, because you must acknowledge them in your research paper. Failure to attribute the source of your material constitutes plagiarism.

For example, if you are writing a paper on police use of force, your note might look like this:

> Edward J. Hedican. "The Ipperwash Inquiry and the Tragic Death of Dudley George." *The Canadian Journal of Native Studies*, vol. XXVIII, no. 1, 2008, pages 159-174.
> - "at approximately 9 p.m. the Ontario Provincial Police closed the roads leading to the park"
> - see p. 164
> - in campus library

Put quotation marks around any material you've taken directly from the source. Later, when you're writing your paper, you'll know whether you've used the source directly or paraphrased or summarized it.

Once you have your research together, you're ready to begin writing an outline for your paper. The outline will help you determine which sources go where, and whether or not you have enough information for each area.

CITING SOURCES

MLA (Modern Language Association) Documentation Style

MLA style is mainly used by students in English, history, and other programs in the humanities. As you write your research paper and use your sources, you must remember that anything taken from another source must be cited—that is, you must acknowledge in the text of your research paper that the material you are using is not your own. This applies to facts, direct quotations, indirect quotations, and even ideas. If you're following MLA style, you must acknowledge the source in two places:

1. In the body of the assignment, at the point where you quote or use someone else's idea. You acknowledge the source by providing a brief reference to the source of the material, called a *parenthetical reference*, which means that the reference is enclosed in parentheses.

2. At the end of the assignment, in a *Works Cited list*. Here, you provide complete publication information on the source.

The references within the text of your assignment and the Works Cited list function together. The initial, parenthetical reference indicates the author of the source and the page number of the material you've used. This enables the reader to identify the source of an idea quickly and easily. Knowing the author's last name, a reader can locate the complete publication information for that work in the alphabetically arranged Works Cited list at the end of your assignment. The reference in your text must point clearly to a specific source in the Works Cited list.

Following are some guidelines for recording parenthetical references in MLA style:

- Choose the appropriate format: page number (if the author's name is mentioned in your own introductory words); author and page number (if no mention of the author is made in your own text); or author, abbreviated title, and page number (if your paper cites elsewhere another work by the same author).

- Omit punctuation between author and page number.

- Omit the page number if a source lacks page numbers, as many Internet sources do.

- Don't use the word "page" or the abbreviations "p." or "pp."

Let's say, for example, your topic is "criminal responsibility" and you have paraphrased a paragraph from page 4 of the book *Murder: Whodunnit* by J.H.H. Gante and Robin Odel.

Your parenthetical reference would look like this:

> **Criminal responsibility must include both action and intent. In common law, there must be both a guilty act and a guilty intent. Every crime, therefore, has two parts (Gante and Odel 4).**

And your entry in your Works Cited list would look like this:

> **Gante, J.H.H., and Robin Odel. *Murder: Whodunnit.* London: Harrap, 1982.**

Following are some examples of the different parenthetical references required for different modes of citation.

- Facts or ideas are rephrased in your own words and the author's name is not mentioned.

> **When investigating a murder, detectives must look for both the criminal act and the intent (Gante and Odel 4).**

- Facts are quoted directly from the source and the author's name is not mentioned:

> **Under the common law, "simply committing an act does not of itself constitute guilt unless there is guilty intent" (Gante and Odel 4).**

- Facts or ideas are expressed in your own words and you mention the author's name or the title of the work in your own text. Since you have already identified the source, you include only the page number in the parenthetical reference:

> **Gante and Odel state that *actus reus* and *mens rea* have to be present in order for criminal responsibility to exist (4).**

The references in the three examples given above point the reader to the publishing information on the Gante and Odel book that is listed in the Works Cited list at the end of your assignment.

FORMATTING QUOTATIONS

Quotations of four lines or less are enclosed in quotation marks and incorporated in your own text:

> Gante and Odel define criminal responsibility as "*actus reus*, which in murder is the physical act of killing a person, and *mens rea*, which is the guilty mind or intent" (4).

Quotations of more than four lines are indented in a freestanding block. Do not use quotation marks around the block. Begin the block on a new line indented 10 spaces from the left margin. The parenthetical reference follows the last line of the quotation as part of the block and is placed outside the final period:

> Criminal responsibility is defined by the terms *actus reus*, which in murder is the physical act of killing a person, and *mens rea*, which is the guilty mind or intent. It is held in common law that simply committing an act does not of itself constitute guilt unless there is guilty intent. Thus every crime has two parts— *actus reus* and *mens rea*. (Gante and Odel 4)

GUIDELINES FOR PREPARING A WORKS CITED LIST

A Works Cited list

- contains complete publication information for all the sources you cited in the body of your assignment

- is placed at the end of your assignment on a separate page entitled "Works Cited."

The basic rules for preparing a Works Cited list are as follows:

- Double-space within and between entries.

- Begin each entry at the left margin. If the entry runs more than one line, indent subsequent lines half an inch or 5 spaces.

- Invert author names (last name first). If a work has more than one author, invert the name of the first author only.

- Arrange the list alphabetically by the first word in each entry (usually the last name of the author).

- If no author is given for a work, begin the entry with the title of the work. If the title has "a," "an," or "the" as the first word, alphabetize the title on the basis of the second word.

- Capitalize each significant word in all titles (that is, do not capitalize articles, prepositions, or conjunctions).

- Italicize the titles of books, magazines, journals, newspapers, film or video recordings, and websites.

- Use quotations marks around the titles of articles in magazines, journals, and newspapers. Also use quotation marks around the titles of short stories, essays, poems, and chapters from a larger work. Finally, use quotation marks around the titles of emails as given in the subject line.

- For works on a website, italicize the titles if the works are independent—that is, not part of a larger work. If the works are part of a larger work, use quotation marks instead.

- Include the medium of publication—print, Web, DVD, email, etc.

- For sources accessed electronically, give the date you accessed the source on the website.

Following are some examples of entries in a Works Cited list:

1. Book with one author

   Roberts, John. *Communications for Law Enforcement Professionals.* 3rd ed. Toronto: Emond Montgomery, 2010. Print.

2. Book with three authors

   Cryderman, Brian K., Christopher O'Toole, and Augie Fleras. *Police, Race and Ethnicity: A Guide for Police Services.* 3rd ed. Toronto: Butterworths, 1998. Print.

3. Book with more than three authors

   Shusta, Robert M., et al. *Multicultural Law Enforcement: Strategies for Peacekeeping in a Diverse Society.* Upper Saddle River: Pearson, 2005. Print.

4. Corporate author

   John Howard Society. *Youth Criminal Justice Manual.* Hamilton: John Howard Society, 2003. Print.

5. Edited book

   Green, L.C., and Olive Dickason, eds. *The Law of Nations and the New World.* Edmonton: U of Alberta, 1989. Print.

6. Government publication (print)

   Canada. Statistics Canada. *Market Research Handbook.* Cat. No. 63-224-XPB. 2006 ed. Ottawa: Statistics Canada, 2006. Print.

7. Government publication (Internet)

   Canada. Department of Justice Canada. "The Aboriginal Justice Strategy." *Department of Justice Canada,* n.d. Web. 15 Apr. 2010.

8. Article in a reference book

   Yerema, Richard W., ed. "Hamilton Police Service." *The Career Directory.* Toronto: Mediacorp Canada, 2005. Print.

9. Article in a magazine

   Hayes, Michael. "A Clean Case for Security." *Canadian Security* Aug.-Sept. 2002: S4-S6. Print.

10. Article in a newspaper

   Dunphy, Bill. "Finger-Pointing Begins as Toronto Police Close Ranks." *Hamilton Spectator* 22 Jan. 2004: A12. Print.

11. Article in a scholarly journal

    Bala, Nicholas, and Sanjeev Anand. "The First Months under the Youth Criminal Justice Act: A Survey and Analysis of Case Law." *Canadian Journal of Criminology & Criminal Justice* 46 (2004): 251-72. Print.

12. DVD

    High Risk Offender. Dir. Barry Greenwald. National Film Board, 1998. DVD.

13. Interview that you conducted

    Wu, Cst. Peter. Personal interview. 15 Mar. 2006.

14. Website

    Canadian Security Intelligence Service. Canadian Security Intelligence Service. Web. 16 Apr. 2010.

15. Work on a website

    Procter, Margaret. "How Not to Plagiarize." *Writing at the University of Toronto.* University of Toronto, 11 May 2004. Web. 16 Apr. 2010.

16. Email message to you

    Prazeres, Jessica. "Re: Communications Course." Message to the author. 17 Feb. 2006. Email.

Below is an example of a Works Cited list. To save space, the following Works Cited list contains only a sample of the entries listed above and is not double-spaced.

Works Cited

Canada. Statistics Canada. *Market Research Handbook.* Cat. No. 63-224-XPB. 2006 ed. Ottawa: Statistics Canada, 2006. Print.

Canadian Security Intelligence Service. Canadian Security Intelligence Service. Web. 16 Apr. 2010.

Dunphy, Bill. "Finger-Pointing Begins as Toronto Police Close Ranks." *Hamilton Spectator* 22 Jan. 2004: A12. Print.

Hayes, Michael. "A Clean Case for Security." *Canadian Security* Aug.-Sept. 2002: S4-S6. Print.

High Risk Offender. Dir. Barry Greenwald. National Film Board, 1998. DVD.

John Howard Society. *Youth Criminal Justice Manual.* Hamilton: John Howard Society, 2003. Print.

Prazeres, Jessica. "Re: Communications Course." Message to the author. 17 Feb. 2006. Email.

Roberts, John. *Communications for Law Enforcement Professionals.* 3rd ed. Toronto: Emond Montgomery, 2010. Print.

Shusta, Robert M., et al. *Multicultural Law Enforcement: Strategies for Peacekeeping in a Diverse Society.* Upper Saddle River: Pearson, 2005. Print.

Wu, Cst. Peter. Personal interview. 15 Mar. 2006.

Yerema, Richard W., ed. "Hamilton Police Service." *The Career Directory.* Toronto: Mediacorp Canada, 2005. Print.

APA (American Psychological Association) Documentation Style

The APA style of documentation is generally used in the social sciences. In an assignment, whenever you use someone else's ideas or information, either by quoting directly or by restating or rephrasing the material in your own words (that is, quoting indirectly), you must acknowledge and identify the source. If you're following APA style, this is done in two places:

1. Briefly, in the body of the assignment, where you insert a quotation or rephrase an idea at the point where you refer to it. This is known as a *text citation*.

2. At the end of the assignment, in a *list of References*, where you provide complete publication information about the source.

The following are guidelines for recording text citations in the APA style:

1. When you use a quotation, or summarize or paraphrase an idea in the body of your assignment, the identification of your source must include the surname(s) of the author(s), and year of publication. This can be done in a number of ways.

   According to Edson (2006), private security agencies ...

   Charters and Dean (2005) found that private security agencies ...

   A recent study (Saunders & Dean, 2006) found that private security agencies ...

   The basis for this assumption is provided by a study of private security agencies (Peters, Aikens, Abell, & Ford, 2003).

2. When a work has two, three, four, or five authors, cite all authors. Use a comma between each name. Use the word "and" to connect authors' names when used in your own text, but use an ampersand in the parenthetical citation. Where a work has six or more authors, use only the last name of the first author followed by the term "et al." ("and others").

   In 2004, Sherman et al. conducted a study of private security agencies ... [six or more authors]

3. If you use the author's exact words, you must put the words of the quotation in quotation marks, and you must include the author's name and the year of publication as well as the specific page number(s) on which the quoted words appear. Use *p.* (e.g., "p. 308") to indicate one page and *pp.* (e.g., "pp. 307-308") to indicate multiple pages.

   A study by Saunders and Dean (2006) concluded that "private security agencies offer significant future career opportunities" (p. 76).

4. Quotations of fewer than 40 words become part of the text, as in the previous example.

5. Quotations of 40 words or more are indented in a freestanding block. Quotation marks are not used. Start this block quotation on a new line, indented 5 spaces from the left margin. The reference source follows the last line of the quotation as part of the block, and is placed outside the final period in the quotation.

Klein (2005) notes that summer students working as border guards during peak periods of summer travel present certain problems:

> **Students are often not properly trained to handle the rush that accompanies long lines of cars at border crossings, and tend to overlook important procedures in order to keep things moving. With many experienced supervisors on vacation, assistance and advice aren't always readily available. (pp. 107-108)**

6. There must be an exact correlation between the text citations and the entries in the list of References, with two exceptions. Personal communications (conversations, memos, emails, interviews) and references to classical works, such as the Bible, are referenced in the body of the text, but not in the References list. For personal communications, you should provide the name of the source (initials and surname) and the date of the communication:

In a telephone conversation with the author, on March 15, 2006, J. Sherrif, Head of the Brant Intensive Care Unit, reported that there have been no occurrences of patients with gunshot wounds at Joseph Brant Hospital in Burlington.

GUIDELINES FOR PREPARING A LIST OF REFERENCES

A list of References is

- composed of a list of resources you have specifically referred to in the body of your assignment;

- arranged alphabetically by the last name of the first author (or editor), or by the title (ignoring the articles "a," "an," or "the") in cases where there is no author;

- placed on a separate page, entitled "References," at the end of the assignment.

The basic rules for preparing a References list are as follows:

- Double-space within and between entries.

- Begin each entry at the left margin. If an entry runs more than one line, indent subsequent lines 5 spaces.

- In titles of books and articles, capitalize only the first word, the first word after a colon, and proper nouns. All nouns in a journal name are capitalized.

- Italicize titles of books, and the volume number of journals, magazines, and newsletters.

- When a journal is paged consecutively from the first issue in a year to the last, only give the page of the article (that is, do not include the issue number). When each issue within a year starts paging from page 1, give the issue number as well.

■ When there are more than six authors, record the first six followed by "et al." This applies to books, magazines, and journals.

■ In general, treat electronic sources as you would print sources, adding any necessary additional information that will help others locate the source.

In many cases, the additional information will consist of either a URL or a digital object identifier (DOI). A DOI is a character string assigned by a publisher that provides a persistent link to an article's location online. DOIs are used mainly in scholarly or scientific materials. Record the DOI if one has been assigned by the publisher, or the URL if one has not. In general, provide the home page URL for periodicals, books, and reports, and the full URL for works that are difficult to find from the publisher's home page. Do not include a retrieval date unless you think the source material may change over time—as in the case of a Wikipedia article. (For a detailed discussion of APA electronic reference style, see the *Publication Manual of the American Psychological Association*, 6th edition.)

Following are some examples of entries in a References list:

1. Journal/magazine article

   Palk, G.R.M., Davey, J.D., & Freeman, J.E. (2010). The impact of a lockout policy on levels of alcohol-related incidents in and around licensed premises. *Police Practice and Research*, *11*(1), 5-15. doi:10.1080/15614260802586392.

2. Book (one author)

   Roberts, J.A. (2010). *Communications for law enforcement professionals* (3rd ed.). Toronto: Emond Montgomery.

3. Edited book

   Green, L.C., & Dickason, O. (Eds.). (1989). *The law of nations and the new world*. Edmonton: University of Alberta Press.

4. Article in a magazine

   Hayes, M. (2002, August/September). A clean case for security. *Canadian Security*, S4-S6.

5. Article in a journal

   Ouimet, M. (2002). Explaining the American and Canadian crime "drop" in the 1990s. *Canadian Journal of Criminology, 44*(1), 33-47.

6. Article in a newspaper

   Tyler, T. (2002, November 1). Talks blow dust off Criminal Code. *The Toronto Star*, p. A1.

7. DVD

   Barry Greenwald Inc., National Film Board of Canada. (Producer). (1998). *High risk offender* [DVD]. Available from http://www.onf-nfb.gc.ca/eng/home .php.

8. Government publication (print)

   Canada, Statistics Canada. (2006). *Market research handbook* (Catalogue No. 63-224-XPB). Ottawa: Statistics Canada.

9. Article on the Web

   National Crime Prevention Council. (2010, March 16). *Anti-bullying programs are working.* Retrieved from http://www.ncpc.org/.

EXERCISE 9

WRITING ESSAYS

1. Select a topic of local or national interest for law enforcement students and write a 500-word essay on it. Use an outline, an introductory paragraph, a closing paragraph, and support paragraphs. This essay should be an opinion-based one that does not contain research.

2. Turn the essay you have written into a research paper in which you include facts from outside sources to support your thesis. You should attempt to have at least three types of sources (e.g., a book, a newspaper, and a journal). Cite your sources in your text, and compile a bibliography or References list.

3. Conduct an employment search. Research employment opportunities available with each of the following:

   a. your local police service

   b. a police service outside your locality, a provincial police service, or the RCMP

   c. Corrections Canada

   d. Canada Border Services Agency

   e. a local private security firm.

4. Compile your findings in a research paper, quoting all relevant sources. You may write an essay covering all the law enforcement services mentioned above, or you may write a paper covering one of the services in greater depth, depending on your career interest.

Summary

The essay is the basic form of writing task in colleges, and to produce a well-constructed essay you must exercise organization, grammar, and spelling skills. Every essay is composed of a number of paragraphs: an introductory paragraph that contains a topic and a thesis statement; supporting paragraphs; and a concluding paragraph. Transitions form a link between paragraphs and the main points of the essay. Research is properly documented using either the MLA or the APA style.

ESSAY-WRITING CHECKLIST

FORMAT

- ❏ Have you provided enough background information for your reader to
  - ▪ recognize your thesis?
  - ▪ understand what follows?
  - ▪ want to read further?
- ❏ Do the ideas that you introduced in the beginning follow a continuous line of thought that moves from an introduction, to a discussion, to a conclusion?
- ❏ Have you used appropriate transitions?
- ❏ Is all of your discussion relevant to the topic and thesis?
- ❏ Are your time sequences logical and consistent?
- ❏ Does the last paragraph properly conclude the essay rather than simply restate information?

GRAMMAR*

- ❏ Have you eliminated sentence fragments?
- ❏ Have you eliminated run-on sentences?
- ❏ Have you checked for parallel construction within sentences and between sentences?
- ❏ Have you checked for misplaced and dangling modifiers?
- ❏ Are the elements of each sentence clearly and logically related?
  - ▪ Do subjects agree with verbs?
  - ▪ Do pronouns agree with their antecedents and with each other in person and number?
  - ▪ Is the relationship between nouns and pronouns clear?
  - ▪ Are verb tenses consistent?

STYLE*

- ❏ Are the beginnings of your sentences varied? Do some start with the subject, some with an introductory phrase or clause?
- ❏ Have you mixed your sentence lengths effectively?
- ❏ Have you varied the structure of your sentences, making some simple, some compound, some complex, some compound-complex?

WORDING

- ❏ Have you used vocabulary suitable to your reader?
- ❏ Have you used active verbs wherever possible?

* For further definitions of terms of grammar and style, see Chapter 3.

❑ Have you used appropriate adjectives and adverbs?

❑ Can you explain the reason for your choice of every word, and justify its location within the sentence?

❑ Have you used any words whose spelling or meaning you are not entirely sure about?

❑ Have you eliminated clichés, jargon, idiomatic expressions, and acronyms that will be unclear to your reader?

PUNCTUATION

❑ Have you used periods at the ends of sentences and after abbreviations?

❑ Are question marks used after interrogative sentences?

❑ Have you used exclamation marks very sparingly, only for very special emphasis?

❑ Have you used quotation marks for direct speech, direct quotations from sources, and titles of short works?

❑ Have you used—but not overused—commas to separate internal parts of your sentences and to clarify ambiguities?

❑ Are semicolons used to separate parts of a sentence that are grammatically distinct but logically related?

SPELLING

❑ Have you checked the spelling of difficult words?

❑ Have you checked *ie* combinations, spelling changes caused by suffixes, and consonants that must be doubled?

❑ Have you used capital letters for titles, names, countries, and months of the year?

❑ Have you used apostrophes for possessive nouns, indefinite pronouns, and shortened forms of words?

MANUSCRIPT FORM

❑ Has your source material been documented correctly and cited?

❑ Have you used the correct form (MLA or APA) of documentation?

❑ Have you used the proper format conventions for the piece you are writing: essay, research paper, report?

SPELLING AND DEFINITIONS

Be able to spell the following words:

aboard	cooperate	tranquil
backward	disease	transcript
cafeteria	misspell	utilities
calculate	opponent	whiplash
cemetery	surely	
communication	temperature	

Be able to spell and define the following words:

assimilate	negotiation	transpose
bystander	physiological	tribunal
detriment	punitive	
distraction	quota	

MINI-PUZZLE

Complete the following crossword using the definitions given below it. The words are taken from the Spelling and Definitions list for this chapter.

Across

2. Intended as punishment; very severe or harsh.
7. Relating to the body.
8. To become like people of a country, race, or group.
9. A person close to, but not taking part in, an action or event.
10. A talk with another person or group that is meant to bring about a settlement.

Down

1. Something that briefly turns a person's attention from another matter.
3. A court of people specifically appointed to deal with special matters.
4. To reverse the position or order of two things or more.
5. The condition of suffering harm or damage.
6. A number or amount that has been fixed as someone's share.

WORD SEARCH

Below the puzzle is a list of words taken from the Spelling and Definitions list. Find these words in the puzzle and circle them.

```
N  V  K  D  X  K  T  C  D  F  W  J  A  N  R  V  W  M  R  X  B  K  Q  O  V
P  O  W  M  U  U  M  I  V  L  Y  Q  E  E  M  X  S  F  U  G  T  G  A  T  X
T  F  I  L  R  X  S  H  C  M  I  Y  C  Y  R  C  H  P  A  H  S  N  C  S  A
P  Q  Z  T  N  E  G  O  T  I  A  T  I  O  N  U  H  Y  D  P  O  N  A  S  I
I  Z  M  P  A  P  T  R  I  B  U  N  A  L  T  X  T  R  N  I  Q  S  L  H  R
R  X  W  S  Z  C  K  X  B  Z  S  H  K  I  P  R  A  A  T  T  B  V  C  Y  E
C  Y  E  H  N  E  I  I  Q  D  X  N  J  O  W  O  A  C  R  I  O  N  U  Z  T
S  T  C  Q  I  S  Z  N  Y  F  M  R  V  K  B  Z  A  N  C  E  T  M  L  H  E
N  L  T  O  T  P  V  A  U  P  M  I  I  A  B  R  Z  F  S  E  P  J  A  A  F
A  M  I  E  O  T  L  F  M  M  A  K  S  J  T  Z  Q  T  A  P  C  M  T  C  A
R  D  J  U  A  P  N  A  Q  Q  M  G  Y  S  B  V  G  Z  P  H  O  P  E  B  C
T  F  D  W  Q  C  E  E  S  J  A  O  I  N  P  Q  N  K  I  E  T  S  D  T  S
G  N  P  B  X  N  I  R  N  H  M  D  C  E  L  E  P  C  E  M  E  T  E  R  Y
B  E  V  L  G  R  A  K  A  O  O  F  B  Q  O  K  L  D  F  G  T  P  U  J  L
C  V  W  D  X  S  V  R  W  T  P  Y  V  J  A  N  I  L  W  K  K  L  S  A  X
Y  Y  N  Y  T  Y  O  A  T  L  E  P  E  T  A  L  I  M  I  S  S  A  X  F  C
F  G  Q  B  W  C  M  O  B  N  O  H  O  Q  X  C  T  C  U  A  T  R  X  H  W
```

ABOARD	ASSIMILATE	CAFETERIA
CALCULATE	CEMETERY	COMMUNICATION
COOPERATE	DISEASE	DISTRACTION
MISSPELL	NEGOTIATION	OPPONENT
TEMPERATURE	TRANQUIL	TRANSCRIPT
TRANSPOSE	TRIBUNAL	WHIPLASH

CHAPTER 6

Speaking Effectively

Learning Objectives

After reading this chapter, you should be able to:

- Speak effectively in front of an audience.
- Select a topic for an oral presentation.
- Organize an oral presentation.
- Understand the mechanics of oral presentations.
- Handle question-and-answer periods.
- Avoid nervousness and distracting gestures.
- Use audiovisual aids to enhance presentations.
- Understand non-verbal communication methods.
- Use influential language.
- Understand the SIR method of impromptu speaking.

◻ Introduction

Effective speaking skills improve interpersonal communications and are an occupational necessity for all law enforcement officers. Whether you are interviewing witnesses, questioning people, or testifying in court, effective speaking skills will enhance your effectiveness as a law enforcement officer. One way to improve oral communication skills is to prepare and deliver an oral presentation. Many of the skills that you learn and refine by giving oral presentations can be used in all com-

145

munications situations, personal as well as professional. You should also learn about non-verbal communication skills, so that you can use them yourself and recognize their use by others.

Have you ever noticed that whenever certain people speak, no matter what they say, it hardly seems worth the effort to listen? Other people speak with such authority that whatever they say seems to be worth listening to. Speaking in such a way as to be heard, to be influential, and to command respect depends on three factors:

1. your words

2. your delivery and tone

3. your appearance.

In other words, your message is made up of what you say, how you say it, and how you look when you say it. For a spoken message to be effective, all three must concur. Learning to prepare an oral presentation will help you develop skills that will be of permanent value in your professional and personal life.

Effective Oral Presentations

PURPOSE

An effective oral presentation can enable you to sway a group of people toward your point of view or merely to inform people about something that you think is important. You must ask yourself what you are trying to accomplish through any particular oral presentation. Initially, of course, you are attempting to obtain a good grade from your instructor. However, beyond this, you must decide whether you are trying to inform (through exposition), to persuade, or to tell a story (through narration). Decide on the subject of your presentation, and ask yourself what you expect from your audience after your presentation.

For example, do you want your audience to

- recognize the role of the customs officer,
- realize that our jails are overcrowded,
- understand the *Youth Criminal Justice Act*, or
- create a Community Watch program?

Whatever your purpose, select and develop a topic that suits your interests and those of your audience.

SELECTING A TOPIC

You may be in a position to select a topic that is of particular interest to you, or you may be assigned a topic by your instructor. Selecting your own topic can become one of the most difficult parts of the oral presentation. It is not easy to come up with a topic that is both interesting and manageable in the time allotted for your presentation. If you have the freedom to select your own topic, there are a few guidelines that might be useful:

1. Draw on your own interests, experiences, and opinions.

2. Consider your audience.

3. Select a topic that is timely and of which your audience might already be aware.

A student who is interested in the legal field and is giving a presentation to a class of law enforcement students has a wide range of topics to draw from that meet the criteria outlined above. Look in your local newspaper for ideas: stories relating to the field of law are usually well covered. If a topic is covered in the local newspaper, it is usually timely and of sufficient importance that most of your audience will be aware of it.

EXERCISE 1

ORAL PRESENTATION: STARTING RESEARCH

In your school library, look in local and national newspapers and find between five and ten stories likely to interest people in the legal profession. List the titles of these articles and briefly summarize them. Be sure that each summary contains the article's thesis and main supporting points. For each article, determine the following:

1. Who is the intended audience for the article?

2. What do you yourself know about the topic covered in the article?

3. Do you hold any strong opinions about the topic?

4. What more would you like to know about the topic?

5. How would you obtain additional information about the topic?

NARROWING THE TOPIC

Once you have selected a topic, you don't just start writing out your presentation. Now is the time to give even more thought to your topic and your presentation. Consider the following matters:

1. How much time is available for your presentation?

2. How many ideas can you cover in that time?

3. What are the most important parts of the topic, and how many of them can be covered in the given time?

4. Which ideas will be of most interest to your audience?

EXERCISE 2

ORAL PRESENTATION: GATHERING INFORMATION

Using the articles you have selected for Exercise 1, choose the one that you feel would be most interesting to an audience of law enforcement professionals. Assume that you have been assigned a five-minute oral presentation on the topic covered in this article. Within the time allotted to prepare your presentation, determine the following:

1. What is the purpose of your presentation (e.g., to inform, to teach, to entertain)?

2. What points to support your purpose can you cover within the allotted time? (Assume that the average speaker can deliver between 115 and 120 words per minute.)

3. What are some secondary issues you might want to cover—are there issues related to the main topic that would help your audience understand your main point?

4. How much research on the topic will you need to do in order to make an effective presentation?

5. What is a thesis statement that effectively defines the purpose of your presentation?

6. What is an appropriate title for your presentation?

RESEARCH

Having decided on your topic, you must begin researching it, compiling as much information as you can within the time you have. Summarize any information you find, noting the main points found in your sources. Be sure to keep a full bibliographic record of each source so that you can find the source again if necessary. You may find it useful to record the following information on notecards:

1. a full citation of your source

2. a summary of the article's contents

3. the main points in the article

4. any direct quotations you'll be using

5. a paraphrased version of the ideas you'll be using

6. any additional references, indicated in your source, that might provide you with further information about your topic.

This research method will likely require more than one card for each source, but you can organize the cards by putting the name of the source, along with the category of information, at the top of each card, as shown here:

```
Jones, Source Citation                                    Card 1

Summary



Main Points
```

```
Jones, Direct Quotations                                  Card 2

p. 3

p. 13

p. 16
```

```
Jones, Ideas                                              Card 3

p. 12

p. 34

p. 123
```

Cite evidence accurately; avoid distorting data or taking it out of context. Credit your source for any information and ideas you've used, even when you have paraphrased the material. Edit your cards, eliminating unnecessary material or material that won't fit into your allotted time.

PREPARATION

An oral presentation must be prepared, and prepared well. In this way, it is like any of the written material discussed in this book. Whether speaking to a colleague, making a presentation to a superior, or delivering a classroom presentation, you must be prepared. Some things to remember when preparing your oral presentation are set out below.

1. *Prepare an outline.* Include a topic and thesis statement, as you would for an essay or a paragraph. The topic is what you are speaking about; the thesis statement is your point of view, usually expressed at the beginning of your discussion.

2. *List your main points.*

3. *Revise your list.* Review your points, and omit those that are unnecessary.

4. *Arrange your remaining points in logical order.* Use the procedure you would use for writing an essay.

5. *Write your opening sentence.*

6. *Write your introduction and conclusion.*

7. *Prepare your final draft.* Do not write it out or memorize it. Put your topic, thesis, opening sentence, main points, and conclusion on cue cards. You should know your topic well enough that you need the cue cards only to jog your memory. If you have audiovisual material, you should indicate on the cue cards where the audiovisual material is to be used.

There are various strategies for beginning an oral presentation, and they are similar to those described in Chapter 5, "From Words to Essay." Some of the more common ones are as follows:

- Tell a story or an anecdote.

  My only previous contact with the legal system occurred when I was finishing high school. I was arrested on my graduation night. A couple of friends insisted that we go out for a few drinks. No sooner had I sat down in the local pub and had a few sips of beer than an undercover police officer came up and asked me for identification. I was taken to the police station. After what I saw that night, I resolved to do what I could to help those who can't afford legal assistance. I saw a lot of unfortunate people that night.

- Read a quotation.

  As I read in a recent newspaper report, "Judges in this country never cease to amaze me." I have the greatest respect for the Canadian judicial system and for the people who sit behind the bench. However, I want to tell you about some questionable, and humorous, decisions that have recently been reached in our courts.

- Use a gimmick.

  I'm holding in this plastic bag a small amount of marijuana—no, it's not really marijuana, just some common grass clippings from my front lawn. Look at how small the amount of grass is in this bag. If it was marijuana, and I was caught, I'd be risking a jail term. Our marijuana possession laws have to change.

- Reveal an interesting fact.

  The legal aid system in Ontario is in turmoil. Too few lawyers want to take legal aid cases, because it is too expensive for them within the legal aid guidelines legislated by the province. At the same time, the number of people needing legal aid is exploding, and the system is not able to handle these people.

- Relate a new fact about the subject.

  The federal Cabinet will be looking at new legislation that would give police and security agencies the right to intercept personal emails and text messages, and monitor password-secure websites without explicit court approval.

The conclusion of an oral presentation, like the introduction, may be approached in various ways, but try to ensure that you accomplish at least one of the following:

- Restate your main topic.

  As I said at the beginning of this discussion, the legal aid system is in turmoil, and I have pointed out only a few examples to prove my point.

- Summarize your main points.

  Law and Security programs are now found in almost every provincial community college, as well as in private training institutions. The need to coordinate these programs becomes essential if students are to graduate with acceptable minimum requirements acknowledged by all law enforcement agencies. Possibly the provincial government should step in.

- End with whatever method you used to begin.

  So, I guess the only thing I'll be holding in this little plastic bag is my grass clippings—at least until the law changes. I don't want to go to jail.

- Leave the audience with a challenge.

  As citizens of this country, we must stand up and speak out against this contemplated invasion of our privacy.

- Set an example for the audience to follow.

  Talk is cheap. Here's what I intend to do.

EXERCISE 3

ORAL PRESENTATION: MAKING AN OUTLINE

Prepare an outline that is appropriate for the topic you have selected. In point form, list the following:

1. topic

2. thesis

3. method of beginning (e.g., anecdote, interesting fact)

4. the main points you wish to cover.

After creating this broad outline, list any subpoints you wish to cover.

ORGANIZATION

Many experts recommend a three-step method of organizing an oral presentation:

1. Tell the audience what you're going to say.

2. Say what you have to say.

3. Tell the audience what you've said.

These steps can be expanded into the "Six Ps" of public speaking:

1. *Preface.* What in your background qualifies you to speak on the chosen topic?

2. *Position.* What is your thesis—the position you take on the topic?

3. *Problem.* Define the problem and give some background to the topic, including relevant issues and any terminology that the audience might need to know.

4. *Possibilities.* Be sure to explore all sides of the issue, and be respectful toward points of view different from your own.

5. *Proposal.* Once you've explored an issue, suggest some possible solutions. Are all solutions workable?

6. *Postscript.* Restate the issue you've discussed, pointing out that you have proven something, solved a dilemma, or in some other way accomplished what you set out to do in your introduction.

A presentation that lasts from five to ten minutes can easily be organized along these lines.

EXERCISE 4

ORGANIZING AN ORAL PRESENTATION

Using the principles of organizing an oral presentation, prepare an outline for one of the following topics, or a topic of your choice:

- smokers' (or non-smokers') rights
- cats make better (or worse) pets than dogs
- students should have longer (or shorter) weekends
- conjugal visits should (or should not) be allowed in prisons.

Write a sentence for each of the Six Ps.

MECHANICS

When the organizational part of your oral presentation is complete, you should begin working on the mechanics of it, including the following:

1. *Volume.* Speak to people at the back of the room. If they can hear you, everyone can hear you.

2. *Rate.* People speak at the rate of 115 to 120 words a minute. Practise this. Nervous speakers speak too quickly.

3. *Pause.* Pause between main ideas, and even slightly after sentences. This will give your audience time to consider what you've said.

4. *Stance.* Don't slouch; project confidence. If you use a lectern, stand behind it with your hands to either side of the lectern; don't lean on it for support. If you don't use a lectern, keep your hands out of your pockets, and do not jiggle your change. Use your hands to express yourself. If you can't think of anything else to do with your hands, leave them at your sides.

5. *Personality.* Be sincere, and smile. Show your audience that you care about the topic you're presenting.

▶ DO'S AND DON'TS

1. Give your audience what it wants to hear: be relevant.

2. Know your audience.

3. Realize that humour can work for or against you.

4. Dress appropriately.

5. Don't read your presentation.

6. Don't exceed your time limit.

7. Use visual aids.

8. Rehearse.

9. Be aware of the level of your vocabulary.

ANSWERING QUESTIONS

You may have a question-and-answer period after your presentation to allow your audience to gain additional information about your topic. Prepare for this beforehand, during the planning phase, by anticipating any questions that might be asked. Know your topic well enough that you can expand on certain points if asked. Prepare potential answers ahead of time.

There are three common categories of questions that might be asked:

1. *Open.* Open questions ask for your opinion about something.

2. *Closed.* Closed questions require a specific "yes" or "no" answer.

3. *Clarification.* Questions seeking clarification invite you to expand on a point.

Here are some general guidelines for responding to questions:

1. *Listen and respond.* Listen to the entire question, and think before you answer. Be objective in your response.

2. *Restate and respond.* Restate the question to the person who asked it. This will give you time to think. Restating the question also ensures that you have understood it.

3. *Categorize and respond.* Be aware of the category of the question, and respond accordingly. Don't give an opinion if a factual answer is requested.

4. *Retain your point of view.* Don't change your point of view from the position you adopted in your presentation.

If you don't know the answer to a question, admit it. You can ask your audience for help, or refer the questioner to a source where the answer may be found, but don't try to fake an answer. This ruins the effectiveness of your presentation.

NERVOUSNESS

Many people are nervous about speaking in front of an audience, but there are ways to overcome this anxiety:

1. *Observe others.* Watch other speakers and pick up on their strengths.

2. *Lower your blood pressure.* Run cold water over your wrists before you begin your presentation; this lowers your blood pressure.

3. *Try to relax.* Loosen tense muscles through stretching and self-massage.

4. *Move your body.* Relax by moving your body unhurriedly and deliberately when you present.

5. *Suck on a candy.* Suck on a small, hard candy before your presentation; this eliminates a dry mouth.

6. *Breathe.* Take deep, regular breaths.

EXERCISE 5

EXPLORING PHOBIA

Fear of speaking in front of an audience is a common phobia. What is a phobia, and why do so many people have this particular phobia? Suggest some ways, apart from the techniques described above, that people might overcome their fear of public speaking.

VISUAL AIDS

Visual aids, when used effectively, can enhance any presentation. There are a few things that must be kept in mind, however, when considering the use of visual aids.

1. *Use visuals to clarify or enhance.* Visual aids should be used judiciously. They should not be used excessively or without a specific reason.

2. *Keep visuals simple.* You don't want to give your audience so much information visually that they're too distracted to listen to your words.

3. *Make visuals large.* Visuals should be large and visible enough that all members of your audience can see them.

4. *Provide time to absorb the visuals.* After displaying a visual, give the audience a moment to absorb the information before you paraphrase it and incorporate it into your presentation.

5. *Practise using visuals.* Don't ignore your visuals when you practise your presentation. Be sure they go where they're supposed to go and work when they're supposed to work.

Visual aids help an audience to understand your presentation and to remember what you have said. It is important that you use appropriate visuals for your presentation. Each kind of visual has particular advantages.

1. *Overhead transparencies.* Overhead transparencies are the most common type of visual. They are easy to prepare and use, and they allow the speaker to maintain contact with the audience during the presentation.

2. *Computerized visuals.* Computerized visuals, such as PowerPoint, have become widely used. They create professional results, can offer sound, movement, and colour, and can be used with a television or computer monitor. Slides and transparencies can be created with the computer. Most computerized visuals are easy to use and inexpensive.

3. *Flip charts.* Flip charts are becoming old-fashioned, but they are easy to prepare and use, are portable, and allow the speaker freedom to create new visuals while the presentation is in progress.

4. *Videos.* Videos can be effective if they are properly prepared in advance. It is very distracting to have to search for the right spot in a video during a presentation, or to find an alternative if the equipment isn't available.

5. *Slides.* Slides are old standbys, but they need a darkened room, a projector, and a great deal of preparation. There are costs involved if the slides need to be created.

6. *Handouts.* Handouts are still common in presentations, and can be as effective as other visuals. The audience often likes these souvenirs, and they do help retention, but you have to avoid having your audience focus on them rather than on what you are saying. Provide handouts *after* you've made your points.

EXERCISE 6

SPEAKING SKILLS FOR LAW ENFORCEMENT STUDENTS

1. As a class, discuss ways in which effective oral presentation skills are valuable in law enforcement. Be specific: what situations can law enforcement officers (police, customs, corrections, security) encounter where effective oral communication skills are valuable?

2. Select a topic found in a newspaper or magazine article that deals with a law enforcement matter, and prepare a brief oral presentation on that topic. Do your presentation one-on-one for another member of your class. Submit your topic, thesis, and conclusion to your instructor.

Non-Verbal Communication

"Actions speak louder than words." This statement is certainly true in oral communication. Body language reveals a great deal about both the communicator and the person receiving the communication. Understanding non-verbal communication is essential for effective communication, for interpreting others' behaviour, and, in many cases, for discovering the truth.

Approximately 65 percent of our face-to-face communication is non-verbal; many of our messages are transmitted through facial expressions, gestures, eye movements, and tone of voice. Many speakers are unaware of the non-verbal dimensions of their communications, and therefore send unintended messages. Frequently glancing at the clock while someone is speaking, for example, is clearly sending the message that you're impatient or bored or that you consider the speaker's words to be unimportant.

Non-verbal communication can be divided into *visual* elements, *vocal* elements, and *spatial* elements.

VISUAL ELEMENTS

Eye Contact

People who fail to make or to maintain effective eye contact are not good communicators, since they are allowing others to take control of a situation or are indicating that they have something to hide, are embarrassed, anxious, dishonest, or ashamed of something. A law enforcement officer should quickly take note of a resistance to eye contact in a person being questioned; it usually indicates that something is wrong or that something is being hidden.

Facial Expression

Your facial expression, which is the key to non-verbal communication, must match your message in order for you to be taken seriously. Scowling throughout your oral presentation will give the impression that you want to be anywhere else but in front of the class. And a sea of bored faces in a classroom sends an effective message to the teacher regardless of the verbal communication taking place.

Gestures and Posture

Using your hands during an oral presentation can be very effective. Generally speaking, your gestures and posture can contribute to your message. On the other hand, they can detract from it. Fidgeting, nervous hand movements, shuffling from foot to foot: all of these may signal that a speaker is nervous or insincere. Exaggerated gestures, such as excessive use of the hands, extreme body movements, or stabbing with the fingers to make a point, often indicate a lack of confidence on the speaker's part. If the "speaker" is someone being questioned in a law enforcement matter, the officer should look out for these signs of anxiousness or dissembling.

Body Orientation

The position in which a person places his or her body during a conversation or confrontation tells a great deal about that person's approach to the situation. If a person faces you head-on, with squared shoulders and feet and other indicators of aggression, a physical confrontation may follow. If this body attitude is taken within your personal distance, it demands the response, "Back off!" You might want to take a step or two backward, although such a retreat may suggest a lack of control on your part and may encourage the other person to follow you into your space.

VOCAL ELEMENTS

Loudness

A loud voice can indicate that you have control over a situation, but it can also convey aggression toward the other party and provoke loudness and aggression in response.

"Please step out of the car," said in a firm, normal speaking voice asks for cooperation. A shouted command of "Step out of the car!" might indicate that you're expecting, indeed looking for, an aggressive response. The use of the word "please" indicates a desire for cooperation.

Rate

Rapid speaking indicates nervousness. There is also the fact that, if you speak quickly, the other person may not understand you. Combine rapid speaking with a loud voice and an aggressive tone and body language, and you have a potential confrontation.

Emphasis

A sentence can have different implications depending on whether and how you emphasize certain words. Consider how differing emphasis in the following sentences changes the meaning:

"Step out of the car, please." [*Get out slowly.*]

"Step *out* of the car, please." [*Get out before I drag you out.*]

"Step out of the car, *please*." [*This is the last time I'll tell you.*]

EXERCISE 7

PRACTISING VERBAL AND NON-VERBAL COMMUNICATION

Role-play in a number of different situations involving both verbal and non-verbal communication. Imagine that you are a law enforcement officer dealing with

- a 12-year-old shoplifter
- a striker on a picket line
- a tourist at the border returning to Canada
- an impaired driver
- a speeding motorist.

Have someone in the class play the role of the person you're dealing with. Attempt to question the person, who should respond using different types of verbal and non-verbal communication. Afterward, discuss how you coped with the different communication styles.

SPATIAL ELEMENTS

Most people "need their own space"—that area surrounding a person that others aren't allowed to enter or are allowed to enter only under certain circumstances. Someone who "gets in your face" is aggressively asserting himself or herself. There are different types of space or distance.

1. *Personal distance.* Usually between 1½ and 4 feet (roughly ½ to 1¼ metres) from one's body, this "arm's-length" distance is where we allow friends and acquaintances. It is not an intimate distance.

2. *Social distance.* Usually between 4 and 12 feet (roughly 1¼ to 3½ metres) from one's body, this is the distance at which most of our social interactions occur.

3. *Public distance.* Usually 12 feet (roughly 3½ metres) or more, this is the preferred distance for meetings, classroom teaching, and interviews.

Cultural differences are a factor in personal space preferences. Where North Americans usually prefer to communicate at arm's length, people from Asian cultures prefer a greater distance. On the other hand, some cultures from the Middle East or Latin America traditionally communicate at much closer quarters, in some cases toe to toe. When speaking to a client, try to establish a distance that is comfortable for both of you.

Impromptu Speaking: Say What You Mean, SIR

Your supervisor requests a report for an upcoming court hearing, but you don't have it ready yet. Don't give way to the stress of the moment and offer excuses in a hesitant or garbled manner. Instead, muster your resources, collect your thoughts, and offer an organized, cohesive response. This skill can be learned by following a simple formula whose initials form the acronym SIR. The letters stand for *statement, information, restatement.*

According to the SIR principle, you would answer your supervisor as follows:

1. *Statement:* "I can't complete the report you asked for because I'm still waiting for some information."

2. *Information:* (a) "The witness hasn't been cooperative." (b) "Information from one of the social service agencies involved has been late because of vacation schedules." (c) "I'm waiting for the detective involved in the case to clarify one of her statements."

3. *Restatement:* "Although I still expect to complete the report in time for the hearing, I wanted you to know why it's not ready yet."

The impression this message creates is of an organized, well-thought-out position. A closer look at the structure of the message reveals the following:

1. Your initial *statement* is your basic position. Take a moment to decide on this main point, then express it simply and clearly.

2. The *information* comes next. One of the key factors in this formula is providing three pieces of information. Human beings like things expressed in threes. So, figure out a way to follow your initial statement with three pieces of information. You may have more than one sentence for each, but you should clearly enumerate the three points.

3. When you make your *restatement*, take the opportunity to add something. In our example, the supervisor is reassured that the report will be ready. This indicates that the situation is under control.

The ability to think on your feet and convey a message succinctly with little or no preparation is a highly regarded skill, and one worth cultivating for the sake of your career.

IMPROMPTU SPEAKING

1. Use the SIR method to answer the following questions:

    a. Why were you late for work today?

    b. You didn't return my call. Were you ill?

    c. Where have you been? I've been trying to phone you all morning.

2. Work with a classmate to perfect the SIR technique. Throw questions at each other concerning a variety of topics, and work on coming up with appropriate answers, giving three pieces of information with every answer.

A Last Word About Oral Presentations: Don't Read

It is one thing to review a cue card for directions; it is fine to glance down and check a statistic; it is even acceptable to read out a quotation you've copied from your notes. However, it is not acceptable to read a report and pretend that it is an oral presentation. Without eye contact, gesture, and enthusiasm, without visuals and audience involvement, there is no oral presentation—only a reading. Watching someone read is a miserable experience. When someone stands up and reads a presentation, the audience becomes distracted and loses interest. In other words, *the presentation is a failure.* Do not read your report!

Don't read. Don't read.

One-on-One Communication

Law enforcement personnel often have to deal with difficult people who are severely stressed at finding themselves in a legal situation—in the unwanted position of accused, victim, or witness.

DEALING WITH A DIFFICULT PERSON

In any confrontational or challenging situation, the most important thing you can do is be professional. Remember that you are dealing with an emotional person and that your best approach is to defuse the emotion and conduct the conversation on a practical level.

There are numerous ways of accomplishing this, many of which have been discussed in Chapter 1 under the heading "Nine Rules for Effective Listening." Keep the following in mind:

1. Adjust the behaviour. Emotional or difficult people react in a certain way for a reason—they may be angry or fearful; they may feel threatened, or feel that they have been used unjustly. Instead of responding to the emotion, attempt to determine what is making the person react in a difficult or emotional manner, and then remove whatever is triggering that reaction. In other words, get to the root of the person's behaviour, and then use the principles of active listening to adjust it.

2. Be tolerant. Remember that the person's difficult behaviour is justified in his or her mind. Perhaps it has helped the person deal with problems in the past. Defensiveness or reticence in a victim, for example, may stem from long-standing mistrust of outsiders, and even though you're there to help, you are still seen as an outsider—someone who, ultimately, won't be affected by the victim's plight. You will get paid or keep your job regardless of what happens to the victim.

3. Reward non-defensive behaviour on a person's part by mirroring it when it occurs. Keep the pace of your conversation slow, do not exhibit negative non-verbal communication, listen carefully, and bring a calming manner to the situation.

4. Show that you are on the person's side and want to help by using phrases such as "I see what you mean," "I understand what you are saying," or "I think that I can help you." But don't make promises that you can't keep.

5. Give difficult people options and let them make decisions that will allow them to feel in control of their own lives. People often react negatively when they feel that their lives are entirely in the hands of a law enforcement professional.

6. Reassure the person with empathetic statements like, "After all you've been through, I can understand why you are angry."

7. Don't make the person feel anonymous by saying things like, "Every witness has to fill out these forms." It is embarrassing for a witness to be deprived of individuality this way.

8. If the person is abusive or non-responsive, look for any part of his or her conversation that is appropriate and constructive, and reward it with attention and gratitude. Be forgiving.

Victim: All you ever do is talk! I'm being threatened and all you can do is talk!

Officer: I do talk a lot.

Victim: If you were paying attention to what I've been saying, you might have some answers for me. That's why I'm talking to you!

Officer: That may be true. I could be paying more attention.

Victim: You're just like all of the other cops. You use me and use a lot of language that I don't understand, and I still have to face the consequences!

Officer: So far there are no consequences. I talk a lot and ask questions because I'm trying to find the best way to help you.

In *Impact: A Guide to Business Communication*, Margot Northey discusses ways to deal with aggressive behaviour:

> Sometimes emotions run high and, if left unchecked, they can create hostility. You can help by encouraging participants to stick to the facts, so that their comments don't become a personal attack. ... Try to remain neutral rather than taking sides. ... Create a constructive atmosphere where ideas are built up and developed (Northey, 1998).

In the end, you can maintain your professionalism with difficult people by simply maintaining good listening habits, responding when appropriate, and offering constructive advice.

CONFERENCING WITH PEERS

Small conferences and workshops and discussions with your peers must be structured in much the same way as formal presentations. A presentation to our peers is more than a conversation, and the fact that you might be seated does not allow you to be offhand or casual. Your approach should be based on the following questions:

1. What is the purpose of your presentation?

2. Who is the audience, and how much do they know about your topic?

3. How much time will be allotted to your talk?

4. Will there be a question period?

5. Are other speakers involved?

After answering these questions, begin to prepare by

- brushing up on your topic,

- planning a general outline,

- gathering key facts and statistics, and

- preparing visual aids, diagrams, or handouts if necessary.

Following these suggestions and practising good speaking skills should allow you to make an effective presentation.

EXERCISE 9

PRESENTING TO SMALL GROUPS OF PEERS

Form the class into small groups and have the instructor assign topics to each member of each group. These topics will either be related to something taught in the course or be something of which the participants have knowledge. Each class member will be responsible for making a presentation to his or her small group.

Applications of Speaking Techniques

TESTIFYING IN COURT

Most law enforcement officers eventually must testify in court. In addition to applying the principles of effective oral presentations discussed above (and testifying in court is simply another type of oral presentation), remember to do the following:

1. Tell the truth.

2. Don't guess. If you don't know, say so.

3. Be sure you understand any questions put to you.

4. Take your time.

5. Give clear answers.

6. If you are estimating, say so.

7. Be courteous.

8. Avoid humour.

Remember, the purpose of testifying in court is to assist the court in getting at the truth. If your testimony is properly prepared, you will not have any problems.

EXERCISE 10

THE DEBATE

Having a debate involves making arguments for and against a particular statement or point of view. A debate is a contest in which different speakers take affirmative and negative sides of an issue. For this exercise, you will need to divide yourselves into even-numbered groups, and then settle on a topic for debate. You might consider the following questions: Should private security officers be given expanded police powers? Should restorative justice be instituted in Canada? Your debate might take the following format.

Resolved: That restorative justice be instituted in Canada

Affirmative (Speaker 1):   Opening statement

Negative (Speaker 1):   Opening statement

Affirmative (Speaker 2):   Expand on a specific point from the affirmative side's opening statement

Rebut points from the negative side's opening statement

Negative (Speaker 2):   Expand on a specific point from the negative side's opening statement

Rebut points from the affirmative side's opening statement

When all members except one from each side have spoken in the manner outlined above, proceed to your closing statements:

Affirmative (Final speaker):   Closing statement, or summary

Negative (Final speaker):   Closing statement, or summary

In the debate, keep the following in mind:

1. When you prepare the debate, keep in mind that the opposing side will attempt to undermine your argument. Consider the opposition's point of view, and attempt to anticipate and counter any arguments that the opposition might make.

2. The strongest arguments for your position should appear in the opening statement.

3. Be persuasive; the opposition will be a hostile audience.

4. In your rebuttals, emphasize your opposition to the main points made by the opposing side.

5. Use the summary to repeat your side's main points, to repeat your rebuttals to the opposition's major points, and to re-emphasize your own side's strongest points.

Keep in mind that a code of conduct applies to debates. The following rules should be observed:

1. Stay with the subject in question.

2. Do not speak out of order.

3. No personal attacks—deal with the issues.

4. Stand while speaking.

5. Address the chair or moderator rather than the other participants.

6. Limit your discussion or rebuttal to a maximum of three minutes.

The debate format outlined above might be done differently, depending on the nature of the topic and the time available. After the debate, the moderator or chair can decide which side won. Or the audience can decide through a show of hands or a secret ballot.

EXERCISE 11

THE MOCK TRIAL

Conducting a mock trial will help to improve the oral presentation skills of everyone involved, and it will give you a taste of courtroom behaviour. The focus is not, however, on courtroom protocol. What is important is the way participants conduct themselves and communicate the facts. The number of people involved will depend on the size of the class. At a minimum, you will need students to play the following parts:

- a judge (the instructor might assume this role)

- a Crown attorney

- a defence lawyer

- a complainant

- an accused.

The prosecution will present its case, and the defence will attempt to refute it. Then the judge (in a non-jury trial) or the jury will decide whether the accused is guilty. The trial procedure for a jury trial is as follows.

Opening Statements

1. The Crown attorney summarizes the prosecution's case.

2. The defence lawyer summarizes the defence's case.

Presentation of Evidence

1. The prosecution presents its case.

   a. The prosecution calls witnesses and questions them one by one.

   b. The defence can cross-examine each witness called by the prosecution.

   c. The prosecution can re-examine witnesses to clarify points.

   d. The prosecution rests its case.

2. The defence presents its case.

    a. The defence calls witnesses and questions them one by one.

    b. The prosecution can cross-examine each witness called by the defence.

    c. The defence can re-examine witnesses to clarify points.

    d. The defence rests its case.

Closing Statements

Each side points out the strengths of its case and the weaknesses of the case for the opposing side.

Deliberations by the Jury

The 12 members of the jury attempt to come to a unanimous decision; if they cannot reach a verdict, the case ends with a "hung jury," and a retrial is ordered.

However, the verdict is not important; what is important is how the participants conduct themselves and how the principles of effective oral presentations are applied.

The number of participants can be increased to include most members of the class. In addition to the roles listed above, the trial could include

- a bailiff (responsible for the conduct of the court)
- an assistant Crown attorney
- an assistant defence lawyer
- 4 witnesses (Blunt, Lynden, Caron, and Mayville: see the hypothetical situation that follows)
- a victim (Yaworsky)
- a police officer
- character witnesses (as many as required)
- expert witnesses (such as doctors and forensic experts)
- a stenographer.

The following account involves a hypothetical hit-and-run incident. The accused has been arrested and brought to trial. It is the prosecution's job to convict the accused and the defence team's job to defend him. No critical evidence other than that contained in the scenario can be generated, although evidence can be expanded upon. For example, a twin brother can't miraculously appear at the trial and confess to the crime. However, certain things will need to be added. If you are going to call character witnesses, for example, these witnesses will have testimony not mentioned in the scenario, although it can't be contrary to the facts presented. For example, it is an established fact that the accused was the driver of the vehicle; therefore, you can't suddenly claim that he was having dinner with his mother when the crime occurred.

Decide among yourselves who is going to play each of the roles, and use class time to prepare the prosecution and defence and to conduct the trial. Regardless of the roles they are playing, class members can contribute to either the defence or the prosecution. The trial itself can take anywhere from one to six hours, depending on the depth of evidence presented.

If there are problems with points of law or objections from those assuming the roles of the lawyers, the judge can reserve his or her decision and consult with the instructor. The judge's decision on all matters is final and will not be subject to further objections or appeals. Remember, it is the effort put into the trial that is important, not the outcome.

Facts for the Mock Trial

You are a constable employed by the Brantford Police Service, Badge #372. On 21 August of this year you are working the night shift in the downtown division from 1900 to 0700 the following day. The weather is clear and the roads are dry. At 2125 on 21 August, you are dispatched by radio to 198 Queen St., Brantford, ON to respond to a hit-and-run accident. You arrive on the scene at 2130 and find a male sitting on the curb bleeding heavily from a cut on the forehead and suffering from a possible broken left arm. A female is administering first aid. An ambulance was dispatched to the scene at the same time you received the call, and it arrives at 2136. You speak with the victim briefly before he is transported to General Hospital, 1223 Festival St., by District Ambulance Services, at 2140. The victim's basic identity is as follows:

Victim:	Charles Yaworsky
Address:	21 Bold St., Brantford, ON N4C 1T1
DOB:	30 May 1946
SIN:	471 832 136
Telephone:	519-555-1212

After identifying himself, Yaworsky tells you that just before the accident he was walking southbound along the west side of Queen St. He decided to cross the street to the east side near the intersection of Queen St. and King St. at approximately 2120. He was looking at a couple who appeared to be having an argument in a laundromat on the east side of King St. at the corner of Queen St. when he was sideswiped by a vehicle that didn't appear to have its headlights on. Yaworsky didn't see the vehicle, but he heard a loud blast of music just before he was hit. He doesn't remember anything else because he was rendered momentarily unconscious after being struck and thrown to the sidewalk.

You tell Yaworsky that you will be at the hospital as soon as you have gathered evidence and interviewed witnesses. By this time, a crowd of about 20 people has gathered at the scene. Two people come forward as witnesses. Following are the basic facts about one of them:

Witness:	Mary Blunt
Address:	202 Queen St., Brantford, ON N8P 3S7
DOB:	16 July 1977
SIN:	411 756 027
Telephone:	519-555-2222

Mary Blunt is a registered nurse. She was sitting in her living room watching television at approximately 2120 when she heard a loud thud and a scream. She ran out of her home to find a man lying on the sidewalk on the west side of the street in front of 198 Queen St. He was unconscious and bleeding from a cut on the forehead. His left arm looked as if it had been broken. Blunt called 911 on her cellphone. While she was tending to the victim's cut, he regained consciousness. He was groaning, but he didn't say anything. Blunt did not see the accident or speak to the victim or to anyone who saw the accident.

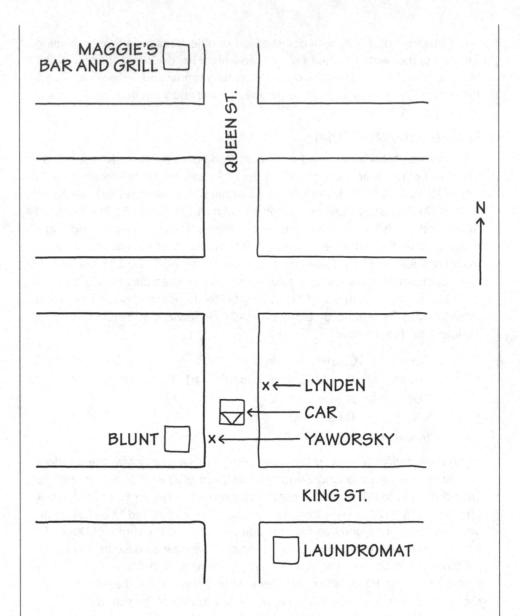

You call dispatch for an incident number (03-1350), write it on your business card, and give it to Blunt, asking her to call the police station if she thinks of anything else. Then you speak to the second witness, whose basic identity is as follows:

Witness:	George Lynden
Address:	71 Duke St., Brantford, ON N7B 3W2
DOB:	15 September 1971
SIN:	400 351 058
Telephone:	519-555-3333

George Lynden was walking his dog southbound on the east side of Queen St. sometime after 2100 on 21 August. He didn't know what time it was because he didn't have a watch. As Lynden was walking opposite Maggie's Bar and Grill at 130 Queen St., about two blocks north of King St., he saw a man leave the bar. Lynden noticed him because the man was very unsteady on his feet. Lynden described the man as "middle aged, wearing a green shirt and dark pants." Lynden didn't notice anything else about him. The description matches the clothing worn by the victim. As the man walked southbound on Queen St., he fell several times and occasionally wandered onto the street from the sidewalk. As the man approached the intersection of Queen St. and King St., he attempted to cross from the west side to the east side. Lynden is aware that there is a laundromat on the southeast corner of the intersection, but didn't hear any noise of an argument coming from there.

As the victim was nearing the centre of Queen St., a vehicle going southbound approached at high speed. Lynden had the impression that the vehicle had no headlights on, although he was seeing it from behind. He did get a partial licence plate number. Like the victim, Lynden said that the vehicle's radio was playing very loudly. Lynden said that the right side of the vehicle, near the passenger door, hit the victim. The driver, whom Lynden didn't see, didn't apply the brakes and kept going after impact. Even though Queen St. is lit by streetlights on the east side, Lynden didn't get a good look at the vehicle because the accident happened so quickly. Lynden didn't assist Blunt, whom he saw running to help the victim, nor did he speak with her.

Lynden described the vehicle involved as a mid- to late-1990s model, possibly a General Motors product, silver or grey, four-door, with an Ontario licence plate whose first two letters are "AJ." There was no visible damage to the car.

You give Lynden the incident number and ask him to call if he thinks of anything else.

You leave the scene at 2230, proceed to General Hospital, and interview Yaworsky. He is conscious and admits to having had "three or four" beers at Maggie's Bar and Grill in the hour or so he was there. He says he wasn't intoxicated. The attending physician reports that Yaworsky needed five stitches to close the gash on his head, that his left arm is bruised but not broken, and that he has other minor cuts and scrapes possibly caused by his being thrown to the sidewalk.

You leave the hospital at 2300 after broadcasting a description of the car allegedly involved in the incident, and resume general patrol.

At 2320, you receive a call from dispatch directing you to see Maurice Small at 575 Oak St., who is complaining that his 18-year-old son took the family car without his permission. You arrive at 575 Oak St. at 2325 and interview Small. The basic facts about Small are as follows:

Complainant:	Maurice Small
Address:	575 Oak St., Brantford, ON N3T 5V2
DOB:	15 October 1958
SIN:	428 716 276
Telephone:	519-555-3022
Driver's Lic:	S6018-40715-81015 (ON) G
Employer:	Dade Enterprises, 22 Main St., Brantford, ON
	Telephone: 519-732-4177

Small reports that earlier in the evening, his son Brent told him that he was going out with some friends. At approximately 2100, Small noticed that his car was missing from the driveway. The basic facts about this vehicle are as follows:

Vehicle:	Saturn SL-1
Year:	1997
Colour:	Silver
Plate:	AJXW 846 Ontario
Valtag:	1148131

VIN:	1G8LM5281RS293176
Insured by:	Boyson Insurance Brokers
Policy #:	NY93BC1176

Small didn't report the vehicle missing at the time because he suspected that his son, despite not having a driver's licence, might have taken it. This had happened before. His son hadn't arrived home by 2300, so Small decided to call the police, fearing that there had been an accident. Brent and his friends returned with the car at 2315, but Small decided not to report that the car was returned because he felt that his son needed to be taught a lesson. The son's identity is as follows:

Accused:	Brent Maurice Small
Address:	575 Oak St., Brantford, ON N3T 5V2
DOB:	30 August 1988
SIN:	486 756 027
Telephone:	519-555-3022
Employment Status:	Unemployed
Physical Description:	Brown hair, hazel eyes, no facial hair, no glasses
	No outstanding features
	Medium build, fair complexion
	Height—180 cm
	Weight—73 kg

You interview Brent Small on 22 August, beginning at 0012. Brent admits that he took his father's car and went joyriding with a couple of friends. They were driving on Queen St. at about 2130, when they noticed a police car parked in front of a house. Brent turned off the lights on his father's car and sped up, then turned on the lights again when he felt he was in the clear. He didn't want to get stopped without a licence. He says that the car's radio was quite loud.

When you tell him about the hit and run, Brent claims that he had nothing to do with it. He had noticed a man staggering along Queen St., but the man was on the sidewalk. You examine the car and find a large scratch on the passenger door, but Small states that this could have happened previously. Small doesn't want to press charges against his son for taking the car. You arrest Brent at 0025, 22 August, for leaving the scene of an accident and for driving without a licence. You read him his rights. Brent Small is transported to the Downtown Division.

The two people who were in the car with Brent are as follows:

Passenger 1:	Melissa Caron
Address:	923 Oak St., Brantford, ON N3T 4X6
DOB:	18 September 1981
SIN:	416 275 572
Telephone:	519-555-7777

Passenger 2:	Sandra Mayville
Address:	76 Harper St., Burford, ON N6L 9H6
DOB:	28 April 1982
SIN:	492 512 560
Telephone:	519-555-1256

You interview Melissa Caron and she provides the following witness statement:

I was in the car with Brent Small last night. Sandra was staying at my place overnight, and Brent called and said that he had his father's car, and he'd stop by to pick us up. I guess he came around 9 o'clock, or maybe a bit after. We had the radio on kind of loud, and we drove around a bit. When we got on Queen St., Brent turned out the lights on the car. I asked him what he was doing, because it was getting dark and I couldn't see very much, and he told me that he saw a police car parked by the curb, and he didn't want to be stopped because he didn't have a licence. I didn't know that he didn't have a licence, and I told him that he'd better take us home because I didn't want to get in trouble. My parents would kill me if they knew I was driving around with a guy without a licence. I guess I kind of freaked out, because I was upset and I was mad at Brent for not telling us. Brent was going pretty fast by this time, and he turned on the lights. I didn't see Brent hit anybody, but I wasn't really paying attention, because I was sitting in the front seat and I was yelling kind of loud at Brent and looking at him, so I wasn't watching the street. Brent took us home about 10 o'clock. I didn't hear anything more until you came to interview me.

You then interview Sandra Mayville and she provides the following witness statement:

My father says I should have a lawyer, but I didn't do anything, so I guess I'll talk to you. I spent the night at Melissa's house in Brantford. My parents said it was OK. She has this friend Brent Small who called to say he wanted to come over and take us for a ride. We weren't doing anything else, so she said it was OK. I don't know the town too well, but one time he was driving and all of a sudden turned off the headlights. He said he didn't want the cops to see him because he didn't have a driver's licence, but it seems to me that turning off the lights was the quickest way for somebody to notice him. Brent and Melissa were having a big argument about Brent not having a licence, and the radio was real loud, so I just sat there and looked out the window. I can remember seeing somebody walking down the street. It looked like he was drunk—you know, staggering a lot and I even saw him fall down once, but Brent still didn't have the lights turned on in the car, so I couldn't see too good. I don't know if Brent hit somebody. I didn't see anything, but there was so much going on in the car that I wasn't paying much attention to what was going on outside.

Brent pleads not guilty to the charge of leaving the scene of an accident, and the case goes to trial.

COMMUNICATING EFFECTIVELY TO MAKE A GOOD IMPRESSION

After the class puts on the mock trial, try this scenario:

Imagine the Brent Small trial ended in a mistrial because of a hung jury. Two weeks ago, you were asked to evaluate your effectiveness in the trial, suggest ways you could improve in the upcoming retrial, and write a report. You've completed most of the report, but now you must finish the "Specifics" section.

Specifics

Obviously, the first impressions of witnesses, lawyers, and other parties in the courtroom are what start the credibility process. How individuals carry themselves, how they relate to those they question or answer, how they respond under pressure, whether they speak with confidence, their knowledge of the facts, their ability to get their ideas across clearly, the expression on their face, their general body language—all contribute to first impressions. And once that first impression is made, the individual's only challenge is to do nothing that will call into question the legitimacy of their word.

Analyze your impact on the trial and make suggestions about how you can improve your effectiveness in the upcoming retrial by completing the paragraphs below.

In the Small trial, I would evaluate my effectiveness as follows …

In the upcoming retrial, I can improve my effectiveness in the following ways …

Summary

In order to communicate effectively, a law enforcement officer must understand and practise oral communication skills. One way to improve such skills is to prepare and present an oral presentation. Many of the skills you'll develop this way can later be applied to questioning people or to testifying in court. Non-verbal communication skills must also be mastered, both for improving the effectiveness of your own communications and for identifying the significance of non-verbal communication in others.

SPELLING AND DEFINITIONS

Be able to spell and define the following words:

acquaintance	auxiliary	obstacle	transfer
adamant	circumvent	perusal	transpire
alienate	classification	pigment	trivial
amenable	convenience	recourse	unilateral
apt	equity	sustain	witness
authentic	imminent	tournament	wounded
authoritative	location	trafficking	wrist

MINI-PUZZLE

Complete the following crossword puzzle using the definitions given below it. The words are taken from the Spelling and Definitions list for this chapter.

Across

5. Fairness; justice; even-handedness.

7. A particular place or position.

8. A group, division, class, or category into which something is placed.

9. That which is going to happen very soon.

10. Carrying on a trade in illegal goods.

Down

1. The natural colouring of plants, animals, or humans.

2. Exactly suitable.

3. Read through carefully.

4. Done by or having an effect on only one side.

6. Supplementary; kept in reserve.

WORD SEARCH

Below the puzzle is a list of words taken from the Spelling and Definitions list. Find these words in the puzzle and circle them.

```
W  R  I  S  T  N  Y  E  G  F  E  C  N  A  T  N  I  A  U  Q  C  A  E  W  U
M  O  W  M  T  J  M  Q  C  N  H  O  S  P  R  M  D  D  E  G  K  M  Q  N  C
U  L  J  L  N  N  L  A  Z  N  I  F  K  S  R  M  R  I  L  X  C  E  I  V  I
L  T  Q  A  A  B  L  O  U  T  E  K  A  A  E  H  C  S  X  M  L  L  Z  O  R
B  L  R  X  M  U  I  A  A  X  Q  I  C  K  Y  N  D  K  T  S  A  C  A  A  C
S  C  E  A  A  Z  Z  C  P  M  I  X  N  I  D  U  T  S  K  T  S  A  F  U  U
G  I  F  F  D  J  O  J  I  T  E  L  C  E  F  J  M  I  E  U  S  T  E  T  M
I  T  S  S  A  L  O  C  O  X  I  S  I  H  V  F  V  R  W  I  I  S  E  H  V
E  N  N  F  A  C  F  Z  M  Y  Z  Q  R  A  X  N  A  W  B  M  F  B  V  O  E
R  E  A  E  R  M  K  P  G  E  L  W  N  U  R  L  O  R  B  M  I  O  I  R  N
I  H  R  S  M  B  E  M  R  M  J  X  N  M  O  Y  F  C  T  I  C  H  T  I  T
P  T  T  Z  D  A  B  N  W  O  U  N  D  E  D  C  F  S  O  N  A  N  C  T  X
S  U  S  O  D  X  N  V  A  L  A  I  V  I  R  T  E  R  T  E  T  I  E  A  I
N  A  X  G  E  X  T  R  P  B  D  K  W  G  S  Q  I  R  A  N  I  F  F  T  V
A  L  X  U  A  J  J  L  U  Z  L  S  U  S  T  A  I  N  E  T  O  A  F  I  M
R  N  S  E  P  U  J  G  S  O  N  E  F  P  G  H  F  H  S  B  N  J  E  V  S
T  A  L  I  E  N  A  T  E  T  T  G  E  E  X  T  R  O  V  E  R  T  N  E  G
```

ACQUAINTANCE	ADAMANT	ALIENATE
AMENABLE	APT	AUTHENTIC
AUTHORITATIVE	AUXILIARY	CIRCUMVENT
CLASSIFICATION	CONVENIENCE	EFFECTIVE
EXTROVERT	IMMINENT	LOCATION
OBSTACLE	RECOURSE	SUSTAIN
TOURNAMENT	TRAFFICKING	TRANSFER
TRANSPIRE	TRIVIAL	UNILATERAL
WITNESS	WOUNDED	WRIST

CHAPTER 7

The Memo Book

Learning Objectives

After completing this chapter, you should be able to:

- Make accurate and complete entries in a law enforcement memo book.
- Understand the rules for writing in memo books.
- Understand what kinds of information are recorded in memo books.
- See how the memo book functions as a legal document.
- Understand the relationship between the memo book and the report.
- Use the memo book when testifying in court.

Introduction

A law enforcement officer's memo book, like a carpenter's hammer, is one of the most essential tools of the trade. Unaided, the conscious mind can recall only 10 to 30 percent of the impressions it has received during an event. However, with the help of notes taken during the event, the conscious mind can recall about 75 percent of the information received.

During any tour of duty, an officer will have reason to interrogate various persons and investigate different incidents. In most cases, reports are required. Since accuracy in reporting is essential, officers should maintain comprehensive notes, recording in chronological order and in detail all significant matters that come to their attention during their tour of duty.

Apart from containing information needed for reports, memo books are a legally sanctioned means for officers to refresh their memories while giving evidence in court.

To some degree, an officer's ability, efficiency, and character are reflected in his or her memo book. The officer who consistently makes complete, clear, and concise notes when dealing with trivial matters will do the same when recording data related to more serious occurrences.

Prosecutions and other matters related to law enforcement are dependent, in large measure, on reports. Unless they are accurate, these reports are of little value—hence the need for notes that are legible, understandable, and meaningful.

Questioning to Obtain Information

The information recorded in an officer's memo book will be drawn from every useful quarter. In 1912, judges of the King's Bench Division in England prepared a set of rules for police officers investigating crimes. These rules constitute excellent guidelines for proper investigative procedure. Rule 1 is as follows:

> When a police officer is endeavouring to discover the author of a crime, there is no objection to his putting questions in respect thereof, to any person or persons whether suspected or not, from whom he thinks useful information may be obtained.

The effectiveness of this extensive questioning will depend on the law enforcement officer's verbal and non-verbal skills.

EFFECTIVE QUESTIONING

Effective notes depend on effective questioning. Effective queries will elicit clear answers and, ultimately, more information for the questioner. Ask questions of the speaker that

- increase your understanding
- help the speaker to relate his or her experiences
- build trust between you and the speaker.

Don't ask questions that

- merely satisfy your curiosity
- allow the speaker to merely show off his or her knowledge
- criticize
- offer your opinions.

There are two types of questions: *open-ended questions* and *closed-ended questions*. The previous chapter of this book discussed the different types of questions, but a brief review is in order here.

An open-ended question invites the speaker to say more about a topic; it does not impose limits on the answer. Open-ended questions tend to draw the speaker out and encourage him or her to speak. Following are some examples of open-ended questions:

> Can you tell me what happened?
>
> Could you say more about that?
>
> Can you help me understand what happened?
>
> What did you do next?
>
> What do you think was going on?

Closed-ended questions invite "yes" or "no" answers. They tend to shut down communication and can make a speaker feel defensive. Some examples of this type of question follow:

> Do you think you overreacted?
>
> Did you overhear the conversation?
>
> Did you see the accident?

HOW TO ASK QUESTIONS

The memo books issued to police officers usually contain a section on how to ask questions. The following suggestions are based on some that appear in a memo book issued by Armour Dial Inc.:

1. Don't use the "third degree." Ask questions that help the other person think. Don't pry or degrade the other person in your role as questioner.

2. Remember the "Five Ws and an H." Questions that ask *who? what? where? when? why?* and *how?* are the key to eliciting facts and information. "Who was with you at the time of the incident?" "What happened next?" "Where was the other car when you were approaching the intersection?" "When did you enter the United States?" "Why?" "How?"

3. Ask questions that produce in-depth answers, not superficial ones. Ask for evidence, explanations, or examples to discover the reasons or motivation behind actions.

4. Ask "suppose" questions. Introduce a new idea or bring up an overlooked point to break a deadlock. Preface your question with the phrase "Suppose we …"

5. If you are asked a question, avoid committing yourself to a position or opinion. Try turning the question back on the questioner or referring it to another qualified person. You might say, for example, "Why do *you* think the accident occurred?" Or, "My sergeant will have to answer that question." Or, "That's a matter for the courts to decide."

6. Ask questions that solicit agreement. Offer likely answers in the form of questions. For example, "Don't you think that the car was on the wrong side of the road?" "You should have been aware of how much alcohol you could legally bring into Canada before you left, don't you think?"

EXERCISE 1

EFFECTIVE QUESTIONING

Mary Blunt was one of the witnesses in the alleged hit-and-run accident in the mock-trial scenario for Exercise 11 of the previous chapter. The basic information about Mary Blunt was as follows:

Witness:	Mary Blunt
Address:	202 Queen St., Brantford, ON N8P 3S7
DOB:	16 July 1977
SIN:	411 756 027
Telephone:	519-555-2222

Mary Blunt is a registered nurse. She was sitting in her living room watching television at approximately 2120 when she heard a loud thud and a scream. She ran out of her home to find a man lying on the sidewalk on the west side of the street in front of 198 Queen St. He was unconscious and bleeding from a cut on the forehead. His left arm looked as if it had been broken. Blunt called 911 on her cellphone. While she was tending to the victim's cut, he regained consciousness. He was groaning, but he didn't say anything. Blunt did not see the accident or speak to the victim or to anyone who saw the accident.

Prepare a series of questions for Mary Blunt that will assist the investigating officer in obtaining information. Some sample questions follow, along with the rationale for asking them:

- "Can you describe your duties at the hospital where you work?" (To obtain Mary's qualifications and competence to give adequate first aid to the victim.)

- "You said that you heard a loud thud and a scream. Can you tell me what you mean by a 'thud'?" (To determine whether or not the thud was made by a car hitting the victim, from the victim falling, or from some other source.)

- "Would you tell me more about the victim's injuries?" (To determine whether the victim was injured from a fall or from contact with a vehicle.)

Note Taking

Keeping good notes is essential, so it is important to look at some strategies for effective note taking. In the first place, make sure that irrelevant material is not included in your notes. There *is* such a thing as taking too many notes. You want only facts. Any information that is not factual is irrelevant and cannot be used in a court of law. Material that is not factual includes rumour, innuendo, and second-hand information. The following, for example, would qualify as irrelevant inclusions in an officer's notes.

> All teenagers are disrespectful.
> I wasn't there, but I know he did it.
> That family has a bad reputation.
> I've heard about her, and I don't like her.
> The victim was having a cup of coffee before the robbery.
> Banks deserve to be robbed because their fees are outrageous.
> That's a horrible colour for a car.
> She must have done it; you know what those people are like.
> My friend told me that her friend is a smuggler.

Such statements should not go into your notebook.

EXERCISE 2

DELETING IRRELEVANT MATERIAL

Eliminate the irrelevant material from the following statement:

I was walking down Oak Street approaching the intersection of Elm Street about 1:30 in the afternoon when I heard a loud crash. There were a lot of people just standing around looking at the scene of the accident. Don't these people have jobs? A blue Ford Fairlane was in the middle of the intersection facing north, while a silver Pontiac Capri had mounted the curb in front of 223 Oak Street. A yellow Hummer was parked near the intersection. I've always wanted one of those. I know the drivers of the two cars: June Southern, who was driving the Ford, and Julie Ying, who was driving the Pontiac. Julie's husband teaches at the college. Ying had a cut on her arm, while Southern looked like she had just come from a food fight. She told me she was eating her lunch while she was driving. I have to remember to call home after we leave here to see if I need to pick anything up for dinner. Ying told me that she couldn't find her cellphone. That's when the police arrived.

TIPS ON NOTE TAKING

Following are some guidelines for taking effective notes:

1. Pay attention to the speaker's tone of voice and body language. Many speakers give as many non-verbal clues as verbal clues about what they really think.

2. Use common abbreviations for long or frequently used words, as long as they can be understood by anyone using your notes.

3. Stay alert and focused. Avoid distractions. For example, don't stop taking notes to give directions to a passerby while you are interviewing a witness.

4. Take careful notes on anything that is technical or complicated, even if you find it boring.

5. Ask questions about anything you don't understand.

6. Make complete notes. The "Memo Book Checklist" at the end of this chapter indicates the amount of detail needed. For example, you need at least the following information about a witness:

   - complete name with any nicknames
   - date of birth
   - address, including postal code
   - home and business telephone numbers
   - email address
   - CPIC results (that is, the results from running the person's name through the Canadian Police Information Centre system, which will indicate whether he or she is wanted for something).

The "Memo Book Checklist" would be followed to the letter in the case of an accused or a missing person.

USE OF NOTES IN COURT

When a law enforcement officer is testifying in court, the memo book becomes a valuable aid to his or her recollection of events. The following principles apply to the use of notes in court:

- Whether the court permits the officer to use the notes in court depends on when they were made. Permission may be denied if the notes were made a significant time after the event in question.

- When testifying, an officer should not read directly from notes unless quoting distances, measurements, or statements where details must be exact.

- The officer should thoroughly review his or her notes before testifying.

- There should be no discrepancy between information in the memo book and information in the report based on notes in the memo book.

- Notes may have to be physically presented in court. For example, a judge may order an officer's notes to be produced if a defence lawyer requests it, and these notes may be entered as an exhibit in the case.

- A witness who gave a statement to a law enforcement officer may refer to that statement while testifying, provided that the statement was recorded in the officer's memo book, and the witness has read the statement and signed it.

- At the scene of an incident, two or more law enforcement officers may be involved in questioning witnesses and taking statements. It may not be convenient or possible for all officers present to take notes. In these situations, it is acceptable if one officer takes notes that the other officers review and sign. All officers may refer to this single set of notes in court.

DIAGRAMS IN NOTES

Clear, complete diagrams are an integral part of good notes, and assist you and others in interpreting a situation. A good diagram can also help the investigating officer recall events at a later date and will help others to understand what the officer observed. Diagrams can be transferred from the memo book to the report, and there must be consistency between the notebook and report versions of the diagram. Don't make changes to the diagram at a later date.

Some elements that could be included in the diagram are

- directions (north, south, east, west)

- dimensions (the measurements from fixed objects at the scene of the incident)

- people's positioning (in relation to other objects or persons at the time of the incident)

- street names

- positioning of vehicles (point of impact in a traffic accident, location of other vehicles involved)

- road markings

- intersection markings

- stationary objects relevant to the incident in question

- a legend describing symbols you use.

You don't need to draw everything in the area, just those things relevant to the incident in question.

Use a black pen and a ruler to make diagrams, and use symbols that can be readily understood as representing, for example,

- an automobile

- a transport truck

- a stoplight

- a stop sign
- a crosswalk
- railway tracks
- a building with street number
- a hospital
- a church
- road markings (one-way street, two-lane street)
- intersections.

There are variations you can use, but be consistent and clear (see Figure 7.1). You don't have to be an artist to draw an understandable diagram.

FIGURE 7.1   COMMON SYMBOLS FOR MEMO BOOK DIAGRAMS

Automobile*

Stoplight

Stop sign

Crosswalk

Railway tracks

Building with street number

Hospital

Church

One-way street

Intersection

* Automobile #1, identified in your legend, showing direction of movement.

In Figure 7.2 you see a generic diagram of the following traffic accident: Cyril Jones was driving westbound along William St. and approached the intersection of Crabbe Lane, where he applied his brakes to stop at a red light. Because the roads were slippery, Jones slid into the intersection despite the brakes, where he struck a southbound car, driven by Lonny Smith, that had entered the intersection on a green light.

FIGURE 7.2   DIAGRAM OF A TRAFFIC ACCIDENT

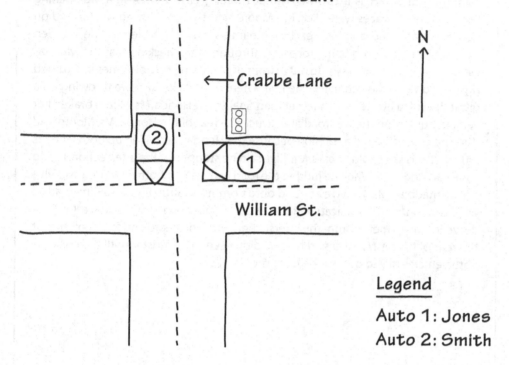

Legend

Auto 1: Jones
Auto 2: Smith

DIAGRAMMING A MOTOR VEHICLE ACCIDENT

Draw a diagram of the motor vehicle accident described below:

The collision occurred on Communication Rd., and it involved a 2003 Honda Odyssey EX driven by Dale Silva and a 2002 Ford Windstar driven by Sarah Moore. Communication Rd. is a two-way street running east and west. It was raining heavily. Road surfaces were slick. Ms. Moore said she was driving westbound on Communication Rd. and had reached the intersection at Adrien St. She stopped at this intersection and then proceeded through after checking that the way was clear. Suddenly a Honda swung out in front of her, taking up both lanes as it turned right onto Communication Rd. The rear wheels of the Honda were throwing up a great deal of rainwater from the wet road. Seeing the Honda, Ms. Moore braked her vehicle but slid on the wet road and struck the rear of the Honda. Ms. Moore said that she couldn't avoid a collision because the Honda was taking up both lanes as it turned and she couldn't pass. Mr. Silva said he stopped at the intersection, facing south on Adrien St. When he judged the road was clear in both directions, Mr. Silva slowly made a right turn westbound onto Communication Rd. He said he made a wide turn onto Communication Rd. to avoid slipping on the wet surface. Mr. Silva drove about 15 metres from the intersection when he heard and felt a collision at the rear of his car. Mr. Silva said that he didn't see the Windstar until the collision. Both vehicles pulled over to the right shoulder.

Guidelines for Memo Book Entries

Following are guidelines for making entries in your memo book.

1. Begin with your rank, name, and badge number.

	PC Maria Gonzales #1298

- Use a black ballpoint pen for writing in the memo book.

2. Record the date on the next line.

	PC Maria Gonzales #1298
	Thursday 09/05/04

- Don't leave blank spaces between lines. If you do so accidentally, put a line through the blank space and initial it, as in the example below.

	PC Maria Gonzales #1298	
	————————————————————————	*MG*
	Thursday 09/05/04	

- Be consistent in the manner in which the date is recorded. No particular format is required; however, on most forms, such as the incident report, the date is written as year/month/day. Fewer mistakes occur if the date format in the memo book is the same as the one used for reports.

- Don't tear any pages out of the memo book.

- Write on every page. If a page is missed, make a diagonal line through the page that was missed and initial the line. It is not necessary to cross out and initial every line on the page; one diagonal line for the entire page will do.

3. Record the weather and road conditions on the next two lines.

	PC Maria Gonzales #1298
	Thursday 09/05/04
	-2C, Overcast
	Roads ~~dry~~ dry MG

- If a spelling error or some other mistake is made, put a single line through the mistake and initial it.

- Don't use correction fluid or correction tape to cover up a mistake.

- Don't scribble over the mistake.

- No information of a personal nature is to be written in the memo book.

- If rough notes need to be made, make them on the back of the page, and clearly label them as rough notes.

4. Record the time you arrive for duty, the time of roll call, and any special circumstances, then record the time you go on duty (0800 in the example below).

	PC Maria Gonzales #1298
	Thursday 09/05/04
	–2, overcast
	Roads dry
0730	Arrive downtown division
0745	Roll call
	Assigned #3 patrol area, car 506, portable radio 3
	Partner: Don McAdams
	Special attention: 76 Lock St., ongoing vandalism
	Missing person: Tammy Kuhn
	128 Prosper St., North Bay, Ont.
	DOB 14 March 1956
	Last seen vicinity of King St. and Main St. bus station 1145,
	11/29
	Contact regarding urgent family matter
	Stolen vehicles: 1. 1999 red Honda Civic ABFS 334 (ON)
	2. 2001 green Chrysler Newport 766 NHT (ON)
0800	10-8 General patrol

- Record items such as lunch breaks, followups from previous shifts, and warrants to be issued.

5. Begin to note events of the day, in chronological order. Wherever possible, write in complete sentences free from errors in spelling and grammar.

0810	Dispatched to 45 Elm St. regarding break and enter
0817	10-7 at 45 Elm St.
	Homeowner: Thuy Nguyen
	DOB 31 May 1944 10-60
	Ms. Nguyen reports that she and her husband were in

	Niagara Falls overnight and that they returned home about
	0730 this morning. When Ms. Nguyen entered the house, she
	found that furniture had been overturned and drawers
	cleaned out. The back door of the house had been forced open.
	Ms. Nguyen states that she and her husband left the house
	sometime after 2000 last night, so the break-in must
	have occurred after that. She states that she didn't see anyone
	suspicious in the neighbourhood last night, but she says,
	"There have been a lot of kids hanging around the
	neighbourhood lately. It was probably one of them, after
	money for drugs. Why don't they get a job?"
	Ms. Nguyen does not have an alarm system on the house.
	I entered the house and found that the living room had been
	ransacked. Glass items and dishes were taken from the china
	cabinet and thrown onto the floor. Cushions were taken from
	the couch and chairs and cut open with a sharp object. Books
	and magazines were scattered across the floor. Ms. Nguyen
	says that nothing seems to be missing from the living room.
	The bedroom was also ransacked. A jewellery box was on the
	floor, and two diamond rings, valued at approximately
	$2,000 each, were missing.
	The mattress on the bed was overturned. Ms. Nguyen said
	that she usually keeps $100 in cash under the mattress for
	emergencies, and this was missing.
	Clothing from closets was strewn on the floor.
	Nothing else seemed to be missing.
	I checked the back door and found marks to indicate that the
	lock had been forced, likely with a crowbar or large screwdriver.
0840	I radio Identification Branch and ask for an identification
	officer to attend.
	While waiting for ID, I question neighbours about any
	suspicious activity in the neighbourhood. No one reports
	anything suspicious.

0910	PC Joe Falls, identification officer, on scene
	Incident no. 02-335602
0920	10-8 from 45 Elm St. I inform dispatch that I will be parked
	in the Ryerson Public School parking lot on Robinson St. for
	paperwork on the break-in.
1000	Coffee break
1020	10-8 general patrol
1033	10-7 near 216 Progress St. for traffic violation
	Edward James Wall, DOB 16 November 1956 10-60
	37 Cumberland Dr., Hamilton, ON L9K 2C4
	905-383-5776
	2000 blue Mercury Sable ACDH 990 (ON)
	Mr. Wall was stopped for failing to signal a left-hand turn
	from Foss St. onto Turner St. Driver released with warning.
1040	10-8 general patrol
1110	Dispatched to Highway 403 westbound at Garner Rd. 10-50

6. Record the end of your shift.

1545	10-7 downtown division
1600	Off duty

- You must sign your memo book at the end of each shift. It is suggested that you indicate the end of a shift by drawing a line through the space following your signature at the bottom of the page.

EXERCISE 4

KEEPING A MEMO BOOK

1. Keep a memo book that records your daily activities in this course, beginning with your first class of the day. Note weather and road conditions, the time you start your first class, the topic for the class, any breaks, the end of class, and any assignments or homework you're given. Record the grades you receive for assignments or tests, announcements, seminars, workshops, and anything out of the ordinary that happens. Do this for every class. Your "shift" is over when your last class ends.

2. Make necessary corrections to the following memo book entries:

	Wednesday, 13 May
1630	Report for duty
1700	10-8
1735	Phone home to find out what my daughter wants for her birthday
1740	Pull over a red Chevrolet and writ a ticket to the driver for not wearing her seat belt
1800	Coffee break
1830	Resume general patrol
1845	Dispatched to 10-50 at Wilson St. Welcome St.

Summary

The memo book is used to record information for future reference, and to refresh an officer's memory if an incident comes to trial. There are many rules covering the use of memo books, and these rules must be followed. Most important, the memo book must be complete and free of errors. The most useful written statements are accurate records of people's spoken words.

MEMO BOOK CHECKLIST

1. Upon beginning your shift, have you included the standard information? This would include

    a. your rank, name, and badge number

    b. the date (year/month/day)

    c. the weather conditions

    d. the road conditions

    e. the patrol area assigned

    f. your partner(s)

    g. matters requiring special attention (e.g., persons wanted, stolen cars, liquor checks).

2. Have you included all relevant times? These include

    a. time on duty

    b. time in service

    c. time out of service

    d. time you received a call or were dispatched

    e. time you arrived at the scene of an incident

    f. time the incident occurred

    g. time a statement was begun

    h. time a statement was finished

    i. time that other emergency personnel arrived

    j. time of arrest

    k. time a prisoner or suspect was transported

    l. time a search was begun

    m. time a search ended

    n. time a Breathalyzer demand was made

    o. time a Breathalyzer test was administered

3. Have you obtained all relevant information about persons connected with an incident? This information includes

    a. name (surname, first given name, second given name)

    b. nickname or alias

    c. race

    d. sex

    e. date of birth (day/month/year)

    f. marital status

    g. condition (whether sober, intoxicated, high on drugs, aggressive)

    h. home address

    i. home phone number

    j. occupation

    k. business address

    l. business telephone number

    m. social insurance number

    n. driver's licence number

    o. other identification

    p. relationship to victim or complainant.

4. Have you obtained sufficient information regarding physical identification? This includes

    a. height (in centimetres)

    b. weight (in kilograms)

    c. hair (colour, moustache, beard, wig, bald, partly bald, short, long, straight, wavy, bushy, unkempt)

    d. eyes (colour, glasses, contacts)

    e. build (slender, medium, heavy)

    f. complexion (sallow, light, fair, ruddy, freckled, dark, swarthy, pock-marked)

    g. teeth (good, irregular, false, gold, stained, decayed, missing)

    h. physical condition (diseases, deformities)

    i. mental condition (suicidal, depressed, violent)

CHAPTER 7   The Memo Book   193

j.   scars

k.   marks

l.   tattoos (type, location)

m.   other outstanding features (disabled, juvenile)

n.   description of clothing.

5. Have you obtained the necessary information about vehicles concerned with the incident? This includes

   a.   type (automobile, truck, motorcycle, snow-mobile, trailer)

   b.   make (Pontiac, Jaguar)

   c.   model (Sunbird, Newport, Corolla)

   d.   style (convertible, station wagon, four-door)

   e.   vehicle year

   f.   colour

   g.   licence number (with province or state of issue and year of issue)

   h.   vehicle identification number

   i.   Valtag number

   j.   special features (special equipment, damage)

   k.   owner (with address, driver's licence number, and category/restrictions)

   l.   insurance information (broker, insurance company, policy number).

6. Have you inquired about the value and storage status of the property (excluding guns) concerned in the incident? This includes property such as

   a.   appliances

   b.   bicycles and tricycles

   c.   electronic equipment (radios, televisions, DVD players, cellphones)

   d.   household articles

   e.   jewellery

   f.   machinery and tools

   g.   musical instruments

   h.   office machines

   i.   personal accessories

   j.   photographic equipment

   k.   scientific devices

   l.   sporting goods

   m.   weapons.

7. Have you inquired about the types of guns involved? The different types include

   a.   air gun

   b.   bolt action

   c.   breech or muzzle loader

   d.   flare or tear gas

   e.   fully automatic

   f.   multi-barrel

   g.   pump action

   h.   restricted

   i.   revolver

   j.   rifle

   k.   semi-automatic

   l.   shotgun

   m.   single shot.

8. Have you obtained relevant information about arrests in connection with the incident? This information would include

   a.   charges

   b.   dates and times of offences

   c.   locations of offences

   d.   dates and times of arrests

   e.   locations of arrests

   f.   arresting officers

   g.   times of transport.

9. Upon ending your shift, have you included

   a.   the time

   b.   your signature?

AN EXPANDED LIST OF 10-CODES

Many law enforcement agencies have slightly different 10-codes from those found in the back of your memo book. Below is an expanded list of 10-codes:

10-1:	Transmitting poorly
10-2:	Transmitting well
10-3:	Stop transmitting
10-4:	Acknowledge/everything okay
10-5:	Relay message
10-6:	Busy
10-7:	Out of service
10-8:	In service
10-9:	Repeat
10-10:	Call home
10-16:	Pick up prisoner at
10-19:	Return to station
10-20:	What is your location?
10-21:	Call by telephone
10-22:	Talk car-to-car
10-23:	Permission to meet with another car
10-26:	Detaining suspect
10-28:	Vehicle registration information
10-29:	Checking for wanted
10-38:	Checking something
10-43:	Break
10-45:	Fatality
10-50:	Accident
10-51:	Need tow truck
10-52:	Need ambulance
10-60:	Suspect has no record
10-61:	Suspect has record, suspect not wanted
10-62:	Suspect possibly wanted
10-63:	Suspect wanted
10-64:	Proceed with caution
10-65:	Assist with 10-63
10-66:	Suspect under observation
10-67:	Suspect is parolee
10-68:	Suspect charged
10-78:	Officer needs assistance
10-90:	Alarm
10-92:	Prisoner in custody
10-93:	Set up roadblock
10-100:	Bomb threat

CHAPTER 8

Reports

Learning Objectives

After completing this chapter, you should be able to:

- Write reports from information recorded in a memo book.

- Understand the level of detail required in law enforcement reports.

- Eliminate errors from reports.

- Write reports that are complete and accurate.

- Establish the facts in issue.

- Understand the Crown brief.

Introduction

Many of the writing skills you have learned from this book will be used to write reports. You will need to summarize as well as to write clearly and accurately, with excellent spelling and grammar. In short, you will need to use everything you've learned thus far to produce reports of the quality required by law enforcement agencies, courts, lawyers, and insurance companies.

It was pointed out in Chapter 5 that writers seek to *inform*, to *explain*, to *persuade*, or to *put something on record*, and to do so as efficiently as possible. In writing for law enforcement, the last aim—to put something on record—is essential. Yet, to some degree, all four of these objectives apply to law enforcement writing. If you are writing a report about a traffic accident, for example, you might need the record for

- your supervisors

- the insurance companies

- the courts

- lawyers

- the person charged in the incident

- the victim

- anyone else who might need the information you gather.

With such a diverse audience, you need to *inform* your readers about what happened, and *explain* the situation using the *who? what? where? when? why?* and *how?* approach essential to all good reports. The information that you *put on the record* should clearly explain the background to the situation, the facts of the situation, and the outcome. Who are you trying to *persuade* in your report? There is an underlying element of persuasion involved in justifying the charge you may have laid against a motorist involved in an accident. You must "persuade" the motorist who was charged, your sergeant, and, if the matter comes to court, the judge, possibly a jury, and lawyers, that your information is correct, that the situation is properly explained in your report, and that any fault you have assigned in connection with the incident is substantiated clearly and factually.

Parts of the Report

Reports are made up of two basic parts: the *summary* (discussed on page 199) and the *details*. The details of a report follow the sequence "Five Ws and an H":

- *who?*

- *what?*

- *where?*

- *when?*

- *why?*

- *how?*

When writing a report, remember the "Four Cs." Be

- clear

- concise

- complete

- correct.

EXERCISE 1

IDENTIFYING PARTS OF THE REPORT

In the following scenario, identify the parts of the scenario under the headings Who?, What?, Where?, and When?

Mr. Fred Quick stated that on Tuesday, 4 April 2009, he was driving eastbound on Robinson St. in his 1997 silver Saturn SL-1, licence AJXW 846, at a speed of approximately 55 km/h in the 50 km/h zone. At approximately 1529 a child's ball rolled in front of Mr. Quick's car, causing him to apply his brakes hard. As soon as Mr. Quick put on his brakes, he heard the screeching of tires behind his car. The rear of his car was then struck by a grey Mercury Sable, licence AYWN 202.

Ms. Joan Hamilton was the driver of the grey Mercury Sable. She stated that she was travelling eastbound on Robinson St. at approximately 50 km/h when she noticed Mr. Quick's brake lights come on. She stated that she immediately applied her brakes but failed to avoid a collision.

Mr. Quick identified himself by means of a valid Ontario driver's licence. His date of birth is 30 May 1970, and he lives at 314 Peach Lane in Paris, ON. Ms. Hamilton identified herself verbally and stated that she lived at 444 Bales Rd., Kitchener, ON. Her date of birth is 22 April 1989.

The Saturn SL-1 has a bent rear bumper for an estimated damage of $700. The Mercury Sable received extensive damage to the front bumper and right headlight, for an estimated damage of $2,000. Neither driver was hurt.

Who?	What?	Where?	When?
____	____	____	____
____	____	____	____
____	____	____	____
____	____	____	____
____	____	____	____

General Rules for Report Writing

The following are some general guidelines for writing reports:

1. *Start at the beginning, and describe events in chronological order.* This sequential format clarifies the cause-and-effect element of events and is essential to law enforcement reports.

2. *Write in the past tense.* The past tense reflects the fact that the report was written after the events being described.

3. *Use common words.* Some words mean different things to different people. Use words that all readers will understand in the same way.

4. *Write in the first person.* Use "I" instead of "the officer" when referring to yourself as the writer. You should write, for example, "I arrived on the scene at 0930."

5. *Write in the third person when referring to other people.* Write, for example, "The victim said that he was not injured."

6. *Use complete sentences, unless a list is called for.* In the following example, which involves a catalogue of features, the list format is appropriate.

   The witness described the suspect as
   - approx. 185 cm tall
   - approx. 80 kg
   - having shoulder length brown hair
   - wearing a blue jacket and dark pants.

7. *Follow the rules of grammar and spelling.*

8. *Avoid using parentheses (brackets) in report writing.* Parenthetical asides are distracting and rarely necessary. The parentheses in the following sentence, for example, are unnecessary: "She was motionless (I thought she might have been unconscious) until someone spoke to her."

9. *Quote exactly what was said, and put quotation marks around direct quotations.* You should write, for example, "The driver said, 'I didn't see the stop sign.'"

10. *Don't use personalized abbreviations.*

11. *Keep sentences under 20 words.*

Organization for Writing Reports

Organizing a report from your memo book is difficult. Once you have taken statements from several people, you'll have a number of different statements about the same incident. In the case of a traffic accident, for example, you will have statements from drivers, passengers, witnesses, and others, including emergency personnel. All of these must be grouped into a logical sequence, such as the Five Ws and an H sequence, and then organized chronologically. Witness statements may be contradictory and contain irrelevant information. One driver involved in an accident may have seen things differently from another driver involved, especially if one of them is facing a charge under the *Highway Traffic Act*. To organize the information, use the following procedure:

1. Gather information.

2. Jot down topic headings in outline form (background, facts, conclusions).

3. Delete irrelevant information.

4. Group related topics.

5. Arrange topics chronologically.

EXERCISE 2

CHRONOLOGICAL REPORTING

Arrange the following scenario in chronological order.

A blue Jeep was on the other side of the street from the Mazda. It is June 13. Ms. Helen Elogar parked her car facing west at 1020. When she returned to her car, Ms. Elogar found the paint on her driver's door had been scratched. The owner of a grey Chevette had parked his car at 1030. A blue Jeep was parked, facing east. Most of the parking spaces were blocked by craft displays. There was a shopping cart overturned in the street, beside a grey Chevette. There was a large community sale being conducted in front of the stores. A red Mazda was parked in front of the pharmacy. The police were notified of the damage at 1052. A Chevette was parked in front of the Mazda. Traffic was detouring around a shopping cart that was blocking the people on the sidewalk. There were only three vehicles parked along the street. There was red paint evident on the front right corner of the shopping cart. The owner of the grey Chevette said he had parked in front of the red Mazda, and that he had taken the last available parking spot. He stated that the shopping cart was not there when he pulled in. The weather was warm and dry but very windy.

REPORT OUTLINE

It can be helpful to put information down in outline form before beginning to compose your report. Produce an outline by following the steps below:

1. Write an introductory sentence or paragraph that indicates in a general way the events that occurred. Indicate weather and road conditions if applicable. This section will become your summary.

2. List in the correct order the points to be considered:

   a. Background (What led up to the event, what people and vehicles were involved)

   b. Facts (What happened)

   c. Conclusions (Results of the events, such as damages, injuries, charges laid).

3. In point form, fill in the details from point 2 above.

COMPOSING THE REPORT

The best reports are derived from the spoken word (a good reason to keep accurate memo books). A simple report appears in Figure 8.1 below, with an explanation of the sections, based on the report outline above, included in square brackets. Any law enforcement report follows this basic format.

FIGURE 8.1   A SIMPLE REPORT

A two-vehicle accident at the corner of King St. and Queen St. resulted in severe damage to one vehicle and the hospitalization of the driver of the second vehicle. A charge of impaired driving was laid. It had been raining and the roads were slippery. [*Summary*: This section provides a brief overview of the incident, and usually includes weather and road conditions.]

On 12 March 2009, a 2009 Chevrolet Caprice was travelling westbound on Queen St. at 2150 approaching King St. A 2005 Plymouth Fury travelling southbound on King St. approached the intersection of King and Queen streets and stopped for a red light. [*Background*: This section gives details of events leading up to the incident. It usually includes names of drivers, any additional information about the vehicles, measurements if necessary, and any other relevant information. Background information sets the scene. Usually written in the past tense, this section describes how the event began and answers the questions who?, why?, where?, and when?]

The light at the intersection turned green for southbound traffic. The driver of the Plymouth proceeded into the intersection with the green light. The westbound Chevrolet went through the red light and struck the Plymouth. [*Facts*: This section tells what happened, and gives relevant details. Written in the past tense, this section answers the questions what? and how?]

The driver of the Plymouth sustained serious injuries and was transported to General Hospital by ambulance. The driver of the Chevrolet, who was not injured, smelled of alcohol and was unsteady on his feet. He was given a roadside Breathalyzer test and was subsequently arrested for impaired driving. Saadia Boffim was transported by Metro Emergency Services ambulance to General Hospital at 1115. Pedro Cidade witnessed the incident and gave a statement. Recommend additional checks at 257 Harbour St. for liquor violations. Case turned over to Cst. R. Smith of CIB. [*Conclusions*: This section details the aftermath of the incident and describes anything that remains to be done. It can include information about medical attention given at the scene, about the time emergency services arrived and the time of the Breathalyzer test and results, about any statements given by persons involved, about names of witnesses, and so on.]

EXERCISE 3

IDENTIFYING PARTS OF THE REPORT

Identify the summary, background, facts, and conclusions portions of the following scenario.

At 1110 on 4 May 2009, a single vehicle accident occurred in the westbound lane of Highway 403 approaching Garner Rd. in Ancaster, Ontario. A half-ton "Hauler" truck overturned in the median between the eastbound and westbound lanes of Highway 403.

When you arrived at the scene at 1116, a number of containers from the truck were strewn around the median, although none were on the highway. Traffic had slowed in both directions, and a number of cars had stopped, with people attempting to assist a female who appeared to be the driver of the truck. She was sitting in the median near the overturned truck.

Fire and ambulance crews arrived simultaneously at 1123, determined that the driver wasn't injured, and that there were no fuel spills to be cleaned up. A tow truck arrived at 1127.

Based on her own words, on a valid Ontario driver's licence, ownership papers for the truck, and an insurance card, the driver was identified as Muriel Wainman of Oakville, Ontario. The vehicle was a half-ton Chevrolet "Hauler" truck. Wainman stated that she was not injured. She was wearing her seat belt at the time of the accident. The weather was warm and dry, and the roads were clear.

Wainman stated that she was driving westbound on Highway 403 after picking up a dozen cartons of electrical supplies in Hamilton, to be delivered to Brantford, Ontario. She was driving in the right-hand lane of the highway at approximately 100 kilometres per hour, approaching the Garner Rd. exit, when a blue mid-sized car travelling in the passing lane suddenly swerved in front of her to exit at Garner Rd. Anticipating a collision, Wainman turned the wheel hard to the left. The truck veered across the passing lane and onto the median, where it overturned, spilling some of the truck's contents onto the median.

No other vehicles were involved.

Wainman didn't get a description of the blue car or its licence number. She estimates the damage to the cartons at $1,500, and you estimate the damage to the truck at $4,000.

Cartons were placed back on the truck by representatives of Provincial Haulage, who were contacted by Wainman by cellphone. Wainman also called a tow truck. At 1142, Wainman's truck was towed by Towable Towing Co. to the Provincial Haulage offices in Oakville.

No charges were laid.

Summary	Background	Facts	Conclusions

■ Facts in Issue

Any report of an incident that could lead to a charge must include the facts in issue. The facts in issue are the components of an offence that the Crown must prove in order to get a conviction. In other words, they are the building blocks to or support structure for a conviction (see Figure 8.2). There are two types of facts in issue: *general* and *specific*. General facts include the *who? what? where? when? why?* and *how?* of a situation. These facts are general because they apply to every offence. Specific facts relate to the statute that defines the offence. For example, in order to lay a charge of trespass by night, the *Criminal Code* requires that the following specific facts be present:

- the trespasser must be on the property without lawful excuse;
- the trespasser must loiter upon the property of another;
- the event must occur near a dwelling; and
- the event must occur at night.

And in order to lay a charge of assault, the *Criminal Code* requires that the following facts be present: physical force must be applied

- without consent,
- directly or indirectly.

Whether the assault qualifies as level 1, 2, or 3 depends on the nature of the injuries.

FIGURE 8.2 FACTS IN ISSUE

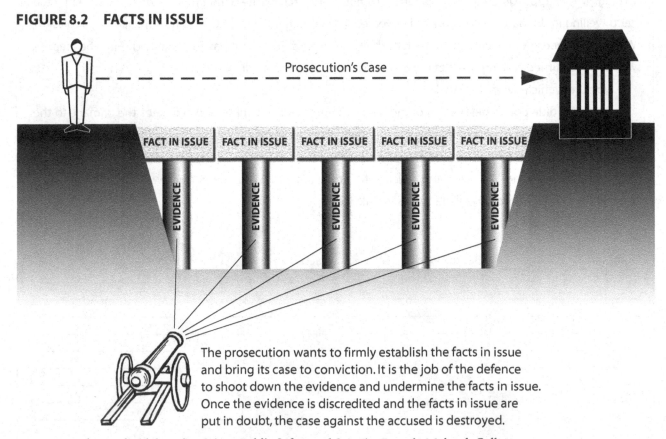

The prosecution wants to firmly establish the facts in issue and bring its case to conviction. It is the job of the defence to shoot down the evidence and undermine the facts in issue. Once the evidence is discredited and the facts in issue are put in doubt, the case against the accused is destroyed.

Source: Based on a sketch by John Grime, Public Safety and Security Branch, Mohawk College.

EXERCISE 4

FACTS IN ISSUE

Are all of the necessary facts in issue present in the following scenario for a charge of trespass by night to be laid?

Sophia Robertson reports that she saw her neighbour, John Levine, walking around the Robertson residence at 2330, peering into the windows. Her husband was out of town on business, so Sophia called police, who questioned Levine at his residence. Levine admitted that he was on the Robertson property at the time stated, but said that he told Mr. Robertson that he'd keep an eye on the Robertson property while Robertson was away. Mr. Robertson had replied, "That's not a bad idea," although Mr. Robertson, according to his wife, assumed that Levine would merely watch the house, not actually go on the property.

Common Errors in Report Writing

Common errors in report writing include the following:

- omitting information, such as names and addresses of witnesses
- omitting details, such as information from the "Memo Book Checklist" on pages 192-193
- writing illegibly, which results in unclear and ambiguous details that are difficult to decipher at a later date
- using poor grammar, which causes confusion regarding the meaning of sentences and details
- showing a lack of objectivity, which suggests a bias in recording information and favouritism shown to persons involved in an incident.

From Memo Book to Report

Notes from your memo book must be transferred to a report blank so that the officer can generate a report. The most common form of report blank is the general incident report, consisting of the cover page, which gives the details of the incident, and the supplementary report, where the narrative or story of the incident is told. This is the form you'll write on most often. The other forms you might encounter are

- arrest reports
- fraudulent document reports
- homicide/sudden death reports
- vehicle reports
- missing person/escapee reports
- property reports.

These reports vary somewhat from one law enforcement agency to another, but they all contain the same basic components, and they all need accurate detail recorded. The facts will come from your memo book. Keep in mind that *facts* consist of what you personally see or hear; anything else is *hearsay* (second-hand information, such as that offered by a witness) or *opinion* (conjecture, either yours or someone else's). For example, if you, as a police officer, see a break and enter in progress, your account of the break and enter is a *fact.* If a witness sees a break and enter, your report of the witness's account is *hearsay.* If a witness tells you that he thinks the kid down the street committed a crime because she looks like the type, the witness is offering you an *opinion.* Your account of the witness's opinion is *hearsay.*

Notice that all the information included in these reports (see, e.g., Figures 8.3 and 8.4) answers the questions posed by the Five Ws and an H: *who? what? where? when? why?* and *how?* If you don't have the information requested in the form, put a diagonal line through the box or line where the information should appear. Remember to sign the document.

INCIDENT REPORT (COVER PAGE)

The incident report is often called the cover page, as it is the first document that appears in your package of documents. The incident report records the details surrounding the offence or situation, and must be filled in completely. If certain information is not available, such as the hair colour of a suspect, a line must be put through the space supplied for that information, which indicates that the information is unavailable. Information for this report is taken from your memo book.

SUPPLEMENTARY REPORT

The supplementary report, often simply called "the supplementary," is the narrative or story about the incident or situation, written by the officer from the officer's point of view. Usually, it is strictly factual, confined to information the officer actually witnessed. If it includes other types of information, such as testimony from a witness, this material must be clearly identified.

The supplementary usually begins with a brief summary of the situation, including road and weather conditions if relevant. After the summary come sections containing information on the background and the facts, and then a conclusion that indicates whether any charges are being laid, along with the reason for the charges.

The supplementary must contain the facts in issue, but can be more general than the incident report. For example, if a vehicle used by a suspect in a robbery is detailed in the incident report, the details need not be repeated here.

Sample Incident Report and Supplementary

In the previous chapter, you learned how to make complete and accurate notes in your memo book. The memo book entries of PC Maria Gonzales were used as an example. Recall that on page 190 Maria was dispatched to Highway 403 westbound at Garner Rd. at 1110. Assume that she was being called to the scene of a motor vehicle accident involving Muriel Wainman and that she made the following entries in her memo book.

	Thursday, 09/05/04
1110	Dispatched to Highway 403 westbound at Garner Rd.
	Fire and ambulance dispatched
1116	10-7 Highway 403 and Garner Rd. Incident #02-9846
	Truck overturned in median
	Female being assisted by passersby—no injuries
	Driver: Muriel Wainman
	12 Forest Lane
	Oakville, ON L9H 4S3 Phone 905-555-4121
	DOB 31 May 1964
	Ontario licence W6018-40716-40564
	10-60
	Vehicle: 1999 half-ton Chevrolet "Hauler" truck
	VIN 1H8ZH5282VZ2294022
	Valtag 2409127, Licence plate RH6103 Ontario 2009
	Registered to Provincial Haulage
	578 Crane St.
	Oakville, ON L8D 5A6 Phone 905-555-1793
	Insured by Market Insurance
	Policy LN84DD1061
1123	Fire and ambulance on scene
1125	Interview with Wainman begins

	Wainman states: "I'm not hurt, and I was wearing my seat belt.
	I was driving westbound along Highway 403 after picking up a
	dozen cartons of electrical supplies in Hamilton. I was delivering
	them to Brantford. I was driving in the right-hand lane of the
	highway at the speed limit. When I got close to the Garner Rd.
	exit, suddenly a blue mid-sized car swerved out of the passing
	lane in front of me to get off at Garner Rd. I turned the steering
	wheel hard to the left because I thought we were going to crash.
	My truck skidded across the passing lane and onto the median.
	It rolled over, and cartons spilled onto the median. People stopped
	to help me get out of the truck. No other vehicles were involved.
	I phoned the police. I can't describe the blue car, and I didn't get
	the licence number. I think the damage to the cartons is about
	$1,500."
	I estimate the damage to the truck at $4,000.
	Wainman phoned for a tow truck from Towable Towing Co.
1127	Tow truck arrives on scene.
	Cartons placed back on truck by representatives of Provincial
	Haulage, who were contacted by Wainman by cellphone.
1142	Truck towed to the Provincial Haulage offices in Oakville.
	No charges laid.
1146	MTO contacted by dispatch for cleanup in the area.
1152	10-8

The sample incident report and supplementary in Figures 8.3 and 8.4 are written from Maria's memo book information. The process for completing these forms is described below.

SAMPLE INCIDENT REPORT

There must be an entry made on every space of the incident report; leave nothing blank. If the information needed is not supplied in the exercise, put a diagonal line through the space. Do not make any assumptions; don't add information to the report that does not appear in the exercise.

As noted above, this incident is a continuation of Maria's memo book entries on page 190. Therefore, use "Downtown" for the division and "#3" for the patrol area. (See Figure 8.3.) The date of the incident is given (09/05/04) but the time of the incident is not given. The fact that the officer was dispatched at 1110 means that the incident occurred sometime before this time. The incident number is given

FIGURE 8.3 SAMPLE INCIDENT REPORT

MITCHELL'S BAY POLICE SERVICE
INCIDENT REPORT

No. of supplementary reports _1_

Division _Downtown_   Patrol area _#3_   Date/time of incident _09/05/04_

Type of incident _MVA_   Incident no. _02-9846_

Location of incident _Hwy 403 and Garner Rd._

How incident committed _Truck cut off by auto_

Victim/complainant

Surname _Wainman_   Given (1) _Muriel_   Given (2)

Address _12 Forest Lane, Oakville, ON L9H 4S3_

Sex _F_   DOB (Y/M/D) _64/05/31_   Marital status   Home phone _905-555-4121_

Employer _Provincial Haulage_   Business phone _905-555-1793_

Reported by

Surname _SAME_   Given (1)   Given (2)

Address

Sex   DOB (Y/M/D)   Relationship to victim   Home phone

Employer   Business phone

Vehicle used

Type _auto_ Licence no.   Licence year   Province

Style _mid-size_   Colour _blue_   VIN

Owner surname   Given (1)   Given (2)

Outstanding features

Accused/suspect

Surname   Given (1)   Given (2)

Nicknames/alias

Address   Home phone

Sex   DOB (Y/M/D)   Height   Weight   Race

Hair colour   Moustache/beard/wig   Eye colour   Glasses

Build (slender/medium/heavy)   Complexion

Description of clothing

Victim/accused relationship

Physical/mental condition, marks, scars, tattoos, outstanding features

Employer   Business phone

Reporting officer

Rank/name/no. _PC Maria Gonzales #1298_   Date/time report taken _09/05/04_

Other officers attending

Case reassigned to

(02-9846), the location of the incident is given (Highway 403 and Garner Rd.), the type of incident is known ("MVA" or "motor vehicle accident" or "10-50" or "hit and run"), and how the incident was committed can be derived from the complainant's statement (truck cut off by automobile).

Victim/complainant. The victim or complainant is Muriel Wainman. The memo book entry states that she phoned in the accident, and we are told that she was the driver.

Reported by. Wainman reported the accident. Rather than repeating all of the same information found in the previous section, write "Wainman" or "victim" or "SAME" in the area where the surname is required, and put a diagonal line through the rest of the section.

Vehicle used. The vehicle used in this case is not Wainman's truck, but the other vehicle. This is the car that police will be looking for in relation to the accident. Not much is known about it—it's an automobile, it's mid-sized, and it's blue. Insert those three entries in their proper places on the incident report, and put a diagonal line through the other spaces, since the information required is not available.

Accused/suspect. There is no accused or suspect, since Wainman didn't see the driver. One diagonal line through the entire section will suffice.

Reporting officer. PC Maria Gonzales is the reporting officer. No other officers were involved in the preparation of this report, so put a diagonal line through the appropriate space.

SAMPLE SUPPLEMENTARY

Keep in mind four things:

1. All relevant information from the memo book must appear in the report, either in the incident report or the supplementary.

2. Information doesn't have to be repeated in the supplementary if it's already in the incident report.

3. Each section of the supplementary will be of a different length, depending on the amount of information provided. You can have more than one paragraph in each section.

4. The supplementary usually contains four sections: summary, background, facts, and conclusions as discussed above.

First, fill out the information at the top of the supplementary form. (See Figure 8.4.) The report concerns Muriel Wainman, whose name is entered in full. Wainman is the victim (circle "victim"). Give her full address, including postal code. The type of incident is "MVA" or "motor vehicle accident" or "10-50" or "hit and run," and the incident number is 02-9846.

The first paragraph is a brief summary of the incident, and should contain brief information from the background, facts, and conclusions of the report. Weather conditions also appear in this paragraph, and in the Wainman case are found in the first part of the memo book on page 188.

The next section contains the background to the report, the information leading up to the accident. Everything that happened before the accident should be stated here. Also included in this section will be information about the driver that you don't have in the incident report.

FIGURE 8.4   SAMPLE SUPPLEMENTARY REPORT

MITCHELL'S BAY POLICE SERVICE
SUPPLEMENTARY REPORT

Name   *Muriel Wainman*   (Victim)/accused

Address   *12 Forest Lane, Oakville, ON L9H 4S3*

Type of incident   *MVA*   Incident no.   *02-9846*

A single vehicle accident occurred at the intersection of Highway 403 and Garner Rd. A truck was cut off by a car and the truck rolled over in the median. There were no injuries, but some property damage. Weather was warm and dry, roads clear.

I was dispatched to Hwy 403 westbound at Garner Rd. Fire and ambulance were also dispatched. I was on scene at 1116. I found that a truck had overturned in the median, and the female driver was being assisted by a passerby. There were no injuries. Fire and ambulance were on scene at 1123.

The driver of the truck, Muriel Wainman, identified herself with Ontario licence W6018-40716-40564. She is 10-60. She was driving a 1999 half-ton Chevrolet "Hauler" truck

> *– VIN   1H8ZH5282VZ2294022*
> *– Valtag   2409127*
> *– Licence plate RH6103 Ontario 2009*
> *– Registered to Provincial Haulage*
>   *578 Crane St.*
>   *Oakville, ON L8D 5A6*
>   *905-555-1793*
> *– Insured by Market Insurance*
>   *Policy LN84DD1061*

I began an interview with Wainman at 1125. She stated:
"I'm not hurt, and I was wearing my seat belt. I was driving westbound along Highway 403 after picking up a dozen cartons of electrical supplies in Hamilton. I was delivering them to Brantford. I was driving in the right-hand lane of the highway at the speed limit. When I got close to the Garner Rd. exit, suddenly a blue mid-sized car swerved out of the passing lane in front of me to get off at Garner Rd. I turned the steering wheel hard to the left because I thought we were going to crash. My truck skidded across the passing lane and onto the median. It rolled over, and cartons spilled onto the median. People stopped to help me get out of the truck. No other vehicles were involved. I phoned the police. I can't describe the blue car, and I didn't get the licence number. I think the damage to the cartons is about $1,500."

Reporting officer

Rank/name/no.   *PC Maria Gonzales #1298*   Page no.   *1*

FIGURE 8.4   CONCLUDED

MITCHELL'S BAY POLICE SERVICE	STATEMENT CONTINUATION

Name   *Wainman*   Page no.   *2*

Wainman phoned for a tow truck from Towable Towing Co., which arrived on scene at 1127. The cartons were placed back on the truck by representatives of Provincial Haulage, who were contacted by Wainman by cellphone.

At 1142, the truck was towed to the Provincial Haulage offices in Oakville, and at 1146 MTO was contacted by dispatch for cleanup in the area.

No charges were laid.

I was 10-8 at 1152.

The third section contains the facts—the information about the accident. In the Wainman case, all of the information for this section comes from her interview, and since Wainman was speaking in the first person, and the information she gave was transcribed into the memo book exactly as she stated it, the quotation marks should remain.

The final section contains the conclusions—what happened as a result of the accident, or what is to happen. Damages and injuries can also be found in this section, since both are the result of the accident (there are no injuries in the Wainman incident). Specifically, as a result of the accident,

1. damage is estimated at $4,000,

2. Wainman phoned for a tow truck,

3. the tow truck arrived,

4. the cartons were placed back on the truck,

5. the truck was towed,

6. MTO was contacted,

7. no charges were laid (Wainman not responsible, the other driver not found), and

8. the officer returned to patrol duty.

Statement Forms

In the previous sections, we looked at two common statement forms: the incident report and the supplementary. However, there are some other forms you should be familiar with: the statement of a witness, statement from accused, and motor vehicle accident statement. Blank forms for each are reproduced in Figures 8.5 to 8.9. Refer to them as you read the sections below.

STATEMENT OF A WITNESS

This form can be used when interviewing witnesses. Ideally, a witness's statement will be a direct quotation. If the statement is not a direct quotation, be sure to indicate that. The information you obtain can initially be recorded in your memo book and transferred later, but it is preferable to fill out this form as the statement is being taken. Whether you record the statement on this form or in your memo book, always read the statement back to the witness, ask whether the statement is correct, and have the witness sign the statement. You may wish to refer back to the section entitled "How to Ask Questions" in Chapter 7. A complete statement depends on effective questioning.

There are two types of witness statements:

1. An exact statement of the witness's words, recorded either on a form or in the memo book, and signed by the witness.

2. The "will say" witness statement. This statement is written by the officer who, owing to circumstances, is unable to get a complete statement from

a witness. It is written in the officer's own words, and it occurs in cases where the witness is reliable and the facts are not disputable. For example, if a businessman witnesses a traffic accident but is too busy to give a formal statement, he might simply tell the officer what he saw, then leave. The officer would then produce a "will say" witness statement.

STATEMENT FROM ACCUSED

Once the statement from the accused is taken, it must be read back to him or her. The accused (that is, the person who is being charged with an offence) must then sign or at least initial the statement. If the accused refuses to do so, write "refused" in the appropriate space. You must quote the accused's words directly, enclosing them in quotation marks. While you can't put words into the mouth of an accused, there are effective questioning techniques that can help you elicit information. (Review the section entitled "How to Ask Questions" in Chapter 7.) If you make a mistake, put a single line through the mistake, and initial it. It is a good idea to have the accused initial the mistake as well.

MOTOR VEHICLE ACCIDENT STATEMENT

The motor vehicle accident statement is a shorter statement taken from those involved in a motor vehicle accident, including pedestrians and other witnesses. It is written in the same manner as other statements. Quote the participants directly if possible; use proper questioning techniques to acquire complete statements; use quotation marks around direct statements; use a single line to cross out errors, with yourself and the witness initialling errors; and have the witness sign the statement, attesting to its accuracy.

FIGURE 8.5   INCIDENT REPORT

MITCHELL'S BAY POLICE SERVICE
INCIDENT REPORT

No. of supplementary reports _____

Division   Patrol area   Date/time of incident

Type of incident   Incident no.

Location of incident

How incident committed

Victim/complainant

Surname   Given (1)   Given (2)

Address

Sex   DOB (Y/M/D)   Marital status   Home phone

Employer   Business phone

Reported by

Surname   Given (1)   Given (2)

Address

Sex   DOB (Y/M/D)   Relationship to victim   Home phone

Employer   Business phone

Vehicle used

Type   Licence no.   Licence year   Province

Style   Colour   VIN

Owner surname   Given (1)   Given (2)

Outstanding features

Accused/suspect

Surname   Given (1)   Given (2)

Nicknames/alias

Address   Home phone

Sex   DOB (Y/M/D)   Height   Weight   Race

Hair colour   Moustache/beard/wig   Eye colour   Glasses

Build (slender/medium/heavy)   Complexion

Description of clothing

Victim/accused relationship

Physical/mental condition, marks, scars, tattoos, outstanding features

Employer   Business phone

Reporting officer

Rank/name/no.   Date/time report taken

Other officers attending

Case reassigned to

FIGURE 8.6   SUPPLEMENTARY REPORT

MITCHELL'S BAY POLICE SERVICE
SUPPLEMENTARY REPORT

Name   Victim/accused

Address

Type of incident   Incident no.

Reporting officer

Rank/name/no.   Page no.

FIGURE 8.7 STATEMENT OF A WITNESS

MITCHELL'S BAY POLICE SERVICE
STATEMENT OF A WITNESS

Page no. _____

Name _____ Date of birth _____

Address _____ Phone no. _____

Business address _____

Occupation _____ Phone no. _____

Date _____ Time started _____ Time completed _____

Officer taking statement _____

_____

_____

_____

_____

_____

_____

_____

_____

_____

_____

_____

_____

_____

_____

_____

_____

_____

_____

_____

_____

_____

_____

_____

_____

_____

_____

(Continued on the next page.)

FIGURE 8.7   CONCLUDED

MITCHELL'S BAY POLICE SERVICE

STATEMENT CONTINUATION

Name _____

Page no. _____

FIGURE 8.8 STATEMENT FROM ACCUSED

(Continued on the next page.)

FIGURE 8.8   CONCLUDED

MITCHELL'S BAY POLICE SERVICE   STATEMENT CONTINUATION

Name _____   Page no. _____

_____

_____

_____

_____

_____

_____

_____

_____

_____

_____

_____

_____

_____

_____

_____

_____

_____

_____

_____

_____

_____

_____

_____

_____

_____

_____

_____

_____

_____

_____

_____

_____

_____

_____

_____

_____

_____

Signature _____   Witness _____

FIGURE 8.9   MOTOR VEHICLE ACCIDENT STATEMENT

MITCHELL'S BAY POLICE SERVICE
MOTOR VEHICLE ACCIDENT STATEMENT

No. of photos taken _____

Date _____   Time _____   Location _____

STATEMENTS

Driver 1

Name and address _____

Phone no. _____   Employer _____

Name of insurance agent _____

_____

_____

_____

_____

_____

_____

_____

_____

_____

_____   Signed _____

Driver 2 (or pedestrian)

Name and address _____

Phone no. _____   Employer _____

Name of insurance agent _____

_____

_____

_____

_____

_____

_____

_____

_____

_____

_____   Signed _____

REPORT WRITING

Before beginning this exercise, refer to the discussion of the incident report and supplementary report on pages 204-205 and the statement forms on pages 211-212. To complete the exercise, use the blank forms supplied above (Figures 8.5 to 8.9). Assume that you are a constable employed by the Brantford Police Service, Badge #372.

1. Write the incident report and supplementary for your interview with Brent Small. Use the information from Exercise 11 in Chapter 6 ("The Mock Trial").

2. Write an incident report for the hit-and-run accident described in Exercise 11 of Chapter 6 ("The Mock Trial"). Assume that Charles Yaworsky is the victim. In addition, write witness statements for Mary Blunt and George Lynden.

3. Write an incident report, a supplementary report, and witness statements, if necessary, for the following situation:

At 2230 on 12 June of this year, you were dispatched to Frank Rizzo's Bar at 125 Main St., Thorold, ON, to make a report on an assault.

You are 10-7 at 125 Main St. at 2240.

The owner of Frank Rizzo's Bar, Stephen Van Sickle, states that he was notified by bartender Irina Ossine, who called Van Sickle in his office at the back of the bar, that a fight had broken out on the dance floor. Irina had been informed by a bouncer, Peter Northwood, that the fight was in progress. Northwood and another bouncer, Ron Valentine, went to break up the fight. Ray Harewood, the victim, was dancing when he was pushed in the back by an unknown male. Harewood turned around on being pushed and was immediately struck in the face with a beer bottle, which did not break. He fell to the ground unconscious. Harewood regained consciousness several minutes later. A patron, Carlos Lopez, noticed a male running from the dance floor and exiting through a fire

exit. Lopez chased the man and followed the suspect to his motorcycle. The suspect left the parking lot on a Harley-Davidson motorcycle.

Stacy Cordiero, a friend of the victim, was standing beside the victim at the time of the assault. She corroborated Harewood's story. Earlier in the evening, the suspect had approached Cordiero and had made derogatory comments about her. Harewood had intervened, and Harewood and the suspect exchanged words. Harewood stated he had never seen the suspect before that evening.

Harewood declined medical attention.

You broadcast a description of the suspect and his vehicle. You are 10-8 at 2315 on routine patrol.

Witness:	Stacy Cordiero 10-61
DOB:	11 April 1975
Home address:	1566 Chrysler St., Thorold, ON
Phone:	905-555-1122
Witness:	Irina Ossine 10-60
DOB:	4 July 1979
Home address:	1569 Freeland Ave., Niagara Falls, ON
Phone:	905-555-6869
Witness:	Peter Northwood 10-61
DOB:	8 September 1961
Home address:	3 Queen St., Apt. 56, Thorold, ON
Phone:	905-555-7361
Witness:	Carlos Lopez 10-60
DOB:	24 January 1965
Home address:	29 Neo Rd., Thorold, ON
Phone:	905-555-8791
Witness:	Ron Valentine 10-60
DOB:	1 July 1977
Home address:	201 Oak St., Fonthill, ON
Phone:	905-555-5554

Victim: Ray Harewood 10-67
DOB: 28 February 1978
Home address: 1073 Mallard Blvd.,
                St. Catharines, ON
Phone: 905-555-9111

Suspect: Heavy build; weight 102 kilograms; height 188 centimetres; very short blond hair on top of head, long hair at back; Caucasian; black leather jacket, blue tapered jeans, brown cowboy boots, jacket had "O'Doole Rules" printed on back. Motorcycle: Black Harley-Davidson, Ontario plate, licence number possibly 3M536.

4. Write an incident report, a supplementary report, and witness statements for the following situation:

You were dispatched at 0215 on 25 June of this year to take a report about a hit-and-run accident.

You are 10-7 at 0223.

Catriona Hicks reports that she was driving northbound on Bay St. at approximately 0200 at the posted speed limit of 60 kilometres per hour. She proceeded through the intersection of Bay St. and Bloor St. on a green light. Hicks's car was then struck on the driver's side near the rear door by a car eastbound on Bloor St. Hicks's car was spun around and ended up facing south on Bay St. She could see that the car that hit her was speeding away eastbound on Bloor St. Hicks managed to get out of the car and onto the sidewalk. A witness, Ashras Baddar, assisted her and called an ambulance through 911. Hicks complained of neck and back pain.

Baddar stated, "I saw the Ford Focus enter the intersection as I was waiting to cross Bay St. at the light. The Ford was struck by a red Pontiac Sunfire that entered the intersection against the light. I ran over to the Ford to assist the driver. I could see that the driver of the Pontiac was a white male with short dark hair and a large tattoo on his neck, on the left side. The licence number of the Pontiac was AMAX 133, Ontario plate. I called 911. I sat with the driver until the ambulance arrived. I heard the ambulance attendant say that Hicks had a concussion and possible neck injuries."

You tell Baddar to call the police if he has additional information. Your interview of Baddar began at 0245 and ended at 0257.

You check the licence of the Pontiac on CPIC. Information comes back that the owner of the Pontiac is John McClure. You proceed to McClure's address and arrive at 0330.

You see a red Pontiac Sunfire in the driveway with significant damage to the front panel on the passenger's side. You knock on the door, and it is answered by a man with a large tattoo on the left side of his neck. The man identifies himself as the owner of the Pontiac. You arrest him and read him his rights at 0340.

Victim: Catriona Hicks 10-60
DOB: 12 July 1983
Address: 214 Charles Ave., Kenora, ON
Phone: 705-333-1050
Valid
driver's
licence: H4112-10728-35712 (ON)
Vehicle: 2000 silver Ford Focus, Ontario plate AJTZ 917, owned by Hicks
VIN: 2KFLA1545H831208
Insurer: Albany Insurance
Broker: Economical
Policy no.:   7024-Z-4G9

Witness: Ashras Baddar 10-60
DOB: 1 December 1957
Address: 455 Bay St., suite 602, Kenora, ON
Phone: 807-555-8874

Suspect: John McClure 10-60
DOB: 11 November 1980
Address: 193 Young St., Kenora, ON
Phone: None

Supply any information that might be needed to complete your report.

5. Write an incident report, with all of the required forms, for the following situation:

You are on duty at 2130 on 24 June of last year when you are dispatched to respond to a break-and-enter call at an abandoned warehouse at 4 Culver Road, Pickering, ON. You are 10-7 at 2135. Since the warehouse is in an industrial part of the city, you request backup. PC Amy Zhang #2587 is 10-7 on scene at 2137. You enter the unlit building together.

After a thorough search of the building, you find nothing out of place, except that a door on the east side of the building is unlocked and open. Since there is a strong wind that night, it is possible that the wind blew open the door. PC Zhang returns to her patrol area, and you begin to write a brief report in your cruiser.

Suddenly, you notice a person who appears to be hiding in the shadows on the south side of the building. You leave the cruiser and call to the person to come out into the light of an overhead light fixture on the building. The person does so, and identifies himself as the night watchman for the building. His birth certificate identifies him as James Donnelly.

Donnelly states that he was hired by the owner of the warehouse, whose name he forgets, to keep an eye on the place, especially since it's abandoned and there have been break-ins recently. Donnelly smells strongly of gasoline, so you put him in the back of the cruiser to interview him at length. In the meantime, you do an inspection of the outside of the warehouse, and find a full can of gasoline along the south wall of the building near to where you first saw Donnelly. Donnelly claims that the gasoline is not his, and that he found it sitting there. He says he picked up the container before leaving it where he had found it. A further search of Donnelly's person turns up a disposable lighter, but no cigarettes. You arrest Donnelly at 2215 on suspicion of attempted arson and transport him to the police station. You learn that Cameron Nolan is the owner of Getup Properties Inc. and the owner of the building. A phone call to Nolan confirms that he has no knowledge of Donnelly.

Incident report #05-01-2010.

Complainant:	Cameron Nolan 10-60
Home address:	1 Day Crescent, Pickering, ON L2A 5R5
Home phone:	905-555-7985
Business phone:	905-869-4127
DOB:	26 March 1978
Suspect:	James Donnelly 10-61
DOB:	2 January 1988
Home address:	905 Credit Union Lane, Whitby, ON L9T 3T5
Phone:	None

6. Write an incident report, with all of the required forms, for the following situation:

You are dispatched at 1832 on 24 February of this year to 8131 Book Lane, Your Town, to take a report of a missing child, Leanne Burgess. You arrive at 1840 and interview the mother of the missing child, Lisa Burgess.

Mrs. Burgess (she prefers to be known as "Mrs.") states that her daughter left the house at approximately 3 p.m. today to go to the playground and see if any of her friends were there. The playground is on the next block, on Wave St. near Hagen Blvd. Leanne was supposed to have been home at 4:30 p.m., and when she didn't arrive back by 5 p.m., Mrs. Burgess walked over to the playground to look for Leanne. She wasn't there, and one boy who was at the playground said that he hadn't seen anyone else at the playground. Mrs. Burgess says she hadn't seen the boy before today. Mrs. Burgess states that she phoned Leanne's friends, but none of them had seen her. She then phoned the police.

Mrs. Burgess tells you that she and her husband recently separated, and their relationship was not good. She hints that he might have had something to do with Leanne's disappearance, although she has no evidence to support this suspicion. Mrs. Burgess doesn't know where her husband is living, and doesn't have a telephone number for him. She tells you that his name is Roger Burgess, and that he was born 30 June 1975. The couple does not have a formal separation agreement, and Roger has been visiting his daughter regularly.

You interview neighbours, but no one is able to supply you with any additional information. You then drive to the playground, and find two boys there. You ask them if they know Leanne Burgess, and when both of them state that they go to school with Leanne, you ask them whether they had seen her earlier today at the playground. One the boys, James Wardley, tells you that he had seen Leanne at that playground earlier, and that he had seen her leave with a man who James thought was her father. The man had been driving a brown car, and Leanne got into the car without resisting, indicating that she knew the man. You phone Mrs. Burgess, and she confirms that her husband drives a brown 2008 Ford Focus. You run the name on CPIC. Information comes back confirming that the owner of the Focus is Roger Burgess.

You return to the Burgess residence at 1945 and enter the house to obtain a photo and description of Leanne Burgess when a brown Ford Focus pulls into the driveway. Mrs. Burgess runs to the window and yells, "That's him! That's my husband! And he's got Leanne with him! He's the one who kidnapped my daughter!"

Mr. Burgess enters the house with Leanne, who says, "Hi, Mommy. Daddy picked me up at the park and we went for a ride." She appears to be unhurt.

You interview Roger Burgess, who claims that he was driving past the playground on his way to the convenience store, saw Leanne, and stopped to take her with him. They drove around the city for a while because he wanted to spend some time with his daughter, and he lost track of time. When he realized how long they'd been gone, he hurried back to the house. He admits that he should at least have phoned Mrs. Burgess, but says that he didn't want to get into an argument, and besides, he never thought that she'd call the police.

Since there is no legal reason why Mr. Burgess could not take his daughter for a ride, no charges are laid. However, you remind Mr. Burgess that his inconsiderate attitude has cost a lot of your time that could have been useful elsewhere. You also tell him that you will submit a report on this incident. You are 10-8 at 2015.

Incident report #10-01-2010.

Complainant:	Lisa Burgess
DOB:	31 October 1976
Home address:	8131 Book Lane, Your Town
Phone:	705-582-0099
Missing child:	Leanne Burgess
DOB:	25 October 2000
Home address:	8131 Book Lane, Your Town (same as mother)
Phone:	705-582-0099 (same as mother)
Suspect:	Roger Burgess
DOB:	30 June 1975
Home address:	30 Fennel Ave., Your Town
Phone:	705-582-1028
Vehicle:	2008 brown Ford Focus, Ontario licence BJDW 878
VIN:	1G8LM5281RS293176
Witness:	James Wardley
DOB:	23 July 1999
Home address:	21 Calibri Ave., Your Town
Phone:	705-555-1234

The Crown Brief

The Crown brief is a package of documents that the prosecution needs to prove its case at trial against an accused person. Taken all together, the documents are structured in a specific manner and contain no unnecessary information. The Crown brief

- is prepared by the police officer primarily responsible for a case
- is passed on to the Crown Attorney to prepare the case against the accused
- is the police officer's primary method of presenting information and evidence against the accused
- is the prosecution's primary method of disclosing information against the accused to the defence
- is compiled and presented to the defence prior to the accused's first court appearance
- must be complete in every respect.

CONTENTS OF THE CROWN BRIEF

The Crown brief usually contains the following documents, although some of the documents, such as the title page, may not be required by all police services:

- title page or cover page
- introduction
- synopsis
- witness list
- summary
- witness statements.

These are the essential documents for the Crown brief. Other documents may be included as necessary, including

- officer's notes
- statement from accused
- exhibit list
- indictment
- appearance notice
- promise to appear
- criminal subpoena
- subpoena to a witness
- pre-sentence report
- victim impact statement
- consent from victim for release of medical records
- photos.

Use whatever documents are necessary to ensure full disclosure. Incomplete disclosure could violate the Charter rights of the accused and seriously harm the prosecution's case. If additional information is obtained after the Crown brief is prepared, this information must be added to the documentation.

The sample Crown brief shown in Figure 8.10 is concerned with the offence of assault causing bodily harm. Under the *Criminal Code* of Canada:

> 265.1(1) Assault—A person commits an assault when
>
> (a) without the consent of another person, he applies force intentionally to that other person, directly or indirectly;
>
> (b) he attempts or threatens, by an act or a gesture, to apply force to another person, if he has, or causes that other person to believe upon reasonable grounds that he has, present ability to effect his purpose; or
>
> (c) while openly wearing or carrying a weapon or imitation thereof, he accosts or impedes another person or begs.
>
> ...
>
> 267. Assault with a weapon or causing bodily harm—Every one who, in committing an assault,
>
> (a) carries, uses or threatens to use a weapon or imitation thereof, or
>
> (b) causes bodily harm to the complainant
>
> is guilty of an indictable offence ... .

Assault causing bodily harm is usually considered a level 2 assault, which means that injuries to the complainant are more than transient or trifling.

FIGURE 8.10   A CROWN BRIEF

Regina

v.

Eric Sanchez

(Continued on the next page.)

FIGURE 8.10 CONTINUED

[Introduction]

OFFENCE: ASSAULT CAUSING BODILY HARM

SECTION 267, CRIMINAL CODE OF CANADA

DATE: 24 DECEMBER 2009

VICTIM: ROBERT JAMES PIDZERNY

ACCUSED: ERIC SANCHEZ

2010 Conrad St. North

HAMILTON, ON

(d.o.b. 08 December 1954)

PLACE: CITY OF HAMILTON

OFFICER: CST. GINO POLARI #372

(Continued on the next page.)

FIGURE 8.10   CONTINUED

[Witness List]

	WITNESSES	SYNOPSIS
(1)	DAN DIBIACCO	• witness from home
	206 Mariah St.	• saw partial incident and suspect
	Hamilton, ON	
	or	
	c/o Founders Middle School	
	38 Robinson St.	
	Hamilton, ON	
(2)	RAN CAO	• witness driving past incident
	132 Dickens Ave.	• saw beginning of incident and suspect
	Toronto, ON	
	or	
	c/o Graphics Video	
	3 Drumm St.	
	Toronto, ON	

(Continued on the next page.)

FIGURE 8.10 CONTINUED

[Summary]

The charge of assault causing bodily harm in this matter arises from an incident that occurred in front of 206 Mariah St., Hamilton, ON, on December 24, 2009.

The person charged with assault causing bodily harm in this matter is:

Eric Sanchez, d.o.b. 54.12.08 of 2010 Conrad St. N., Hamilton, ON

The circumstances of the offence are as follows:

On Christmas Eve 2009, Robert PIDZERNY was driving to church. He left the parking lot behind his house at 344 Long St., Hamilton, ON, and turned left onto Mariah St. at approximately 5:45 p.m., and stopped at the corner of Mariah St. and Long St. to allow traffic on Long St. to clear before making a right-hand turn onto Long St., which is a one-way street southbound. It was dark, roads were snow-covered, and mounds of plowed snow at the corner of Long St. obscured PIDZERNY'S view of traffic on Long St. While he was stopped waiting for traffic to clear, PIDZERNY heard two loud bangs at the left front of his vehicle. He was at this moment looking to the right to check for pedestrian traffic.

PIDZERNY saw a male kicking the left front quarter panel of his vehicle. The male began to scream incoherently. PIDZERNY decided to leave the vehicle to speak to the male, who PIDZERNY thought may have been involved in an accident and needing assistance. PIDZERNY opened the door

(Continued on the next page.)

FIGURE 8.10   CONTINUED

of his vehicle, and as he put his left foot on the ground, the male grabbed the door of the vehicle and slammed it on PIDZERNY'S right leg, which was still partially in the vehicle. PIDZERNY'S left foot slipped on the ice, and as he slipped, the male punched PIDZERNY in the face, breaking his glasses and opening two cuts around PIDZERNY'S left eye, caused by the lens of his glasses breaking.

As he fell, PIDZERNY was kicked in the face by the male. The male continued to scream incoherently. The male then jumped on top of PIDZERNY, who was on the ground, and continued to beat PIDZERNY about the face. PIDZERNY was essentially defenceless at the time since his eyes were covered with blood. His left eye was swelling and he had lost his glasses.

When PIDZERNY lapsed into a state of semi-consciousness, the beating ceased. The man got up and walked away, saying, "That will teach you to run over pedestrians."

The incident was witnessed in part by Dan DIBIACCO, 206 Mariah St., Hamilton, ON, and Ran CAO, 132 Dickens Ave., Toronto, ON. DIBIACCO heard noise on the street, and when he went to investigate, he saw the incident occurring near his house. He called 911. CAO was driving past the incident and saw PIDZERNY lying on the side of the street and a male walking away.

PIDZERNY, DIBIACCO, and CAO described the male as Caucasian, approximately 55 years of age, medium build, 170 cm in height, with grey hair and a green jacket. The male walked southbound along Long St. after the incident.

(Continued on the next page.)

FIGURE 8.10   CONTINUED

Robert PIDZERNY   Page 3

PIDZERNY was transported by ambulance to Hamilton General Hospital, where he was reported to have been suffering from numerous facial cuts, most significantly a deep cut to the left of the left eye and a deep cut under the right eye. The left eye was swollen shut, and PIDZERNY had a broken left cheek bone under the left eye and a broken bone in the left eye socket. He also had cuts to his right leg from the vehicle door.

The area of the incident was searched. A male answering the assailant's description was seen walking southbound on Long St. near Rikley Dr. He was arrested at 6:12 p.m. on December 24, 2009. He was cautioned and informed of his right to counsel. He identified himself verbally as Eric SANCHEZ, 2010 Conrad St., Hamilton, ON, d.o.b. 54.12.08. He admitted to the arresting officer, Cst. Gino Polari #372, that he had been the assailant in the matter. SANCHEZ was transported to Central Division where he was held in custody pending a bail hearing.

(Continued on the next page.)

FIGURE 8.10   CONTINUED

[Witness Statements]

Name: Dan Dibiacco   **Date of Birth:** 58.03.27

Address: 206 Mariah St., Hamilton, ON L5T 1M1

Telephone: (905) 721-1864

Business Address: 38 Robinson St., Hamilton, ON

Occupation: Teacher   **Telephone:** (905) 721-0000

Date: December 24, 2009   **Time Started:** 6:35 p.m.

                                      Time Completed: 6:45 p.m.

Officer Taking Statement: G. Polari #372

<u>DAN DIBIACCO will say</u>

I am 46 years old. I live at 206 Mariah St., Hamilton, ON.
I am employed as a teacher at Founder's Middle School.

My house is at the corner of Mariah and Long streets.
Sometime before six in the evening of December 24, 2009, I
was sitting in my living room watching television, when I
heard shouting from the street. I looked out my window and
saw a car stopped at the intersection of Mariah and Long
streets facing east. The door on the driver's side of the
car was open and the motor was running. Two men were on
the ground on my property. One man was punching another in
the face. The man who was being punched was covered with
blood on his face, and the other man kept punching him in
the face. I could see both men reasonably well because
there is a street light on the corner. After what I would
say were 10 or 12 punches, the assailant stopped punching,

(Continued on the next page.)

FIGURE 8.10 CONTINUED

got up off the ground, and said something to the man on
the ground before walking away. He was walking southbound
on Long St. The man appeared to be in his mid-50s, was
150-160 lbs., medium build, and with salt and pepper hair.
He was wearing a green jacket.

I went to the phone and called 911, then went outside
to assist the man lying on the ground. He was nearly
unconscious, and didn't say anything until the police and
an ambulance arrived a short time later. Another man came
from one of the side streets to assist. I identified the
assailant verbally to the police. The victim was taken to
hospital by ambulance and I gave a statement to police.

Signed Dan Dibiacco

24 December 2009

6:45 p.m.

(Continued on the next page.)

FIGURE 8.10   CONTINUED

Name: Ran Cao   **Date of Birth**: 82.02.20

Address: 132 Dickens Ave., Toronto, ON M5T 1L3

Telephone: (416) 424-4171

Business Address: 3 Drumm St., Toronto, ON

Occupation: Video technician   **Telephone**: (416) 743-7196

Date: 09.12.24 **Time Started**: 6:25 p.m. **Time Completed**: 6:35 p.m.

Officer Taking Statement: G. Polari #372

<u>RAN CAO will say</u>

At approximately 5:50 p.m. on the evening of December 24, 2009, I was driving southbound on Long St., a one-way street. I came in from Toronto to spend Christmas with a friend in Hamilton. It was dark, but Long St. is well lit, and I could see the roadway clearly.

I noticed a commotion at the corner of Mariah St. A man was on the ground and another man was on top of him, punching him. I couldn't stop because I was in the left-hand lane, so I turned left onto Packard St. and went around the block. I parked at the corner of Mariah and Long streets and went across the road to see if I could help. By this time the man who was doing the punching had left the scene, but I could see him walking along Long St. I could see that he was middle aged, but he was slouching over, so I didn't see how tall he was. I did notice that he was wearing a lightweight green jacket, which didn't seem appropriate considering that it was quite cold. I think that I could identify the man if I saw him again.

(Continued on the next page.)

FIGURE 8.10 CONCLUDED

As I approached the man on the ground, another man ran from
one of the nearby houses and told me that he had called
the police and an ambulance. The man on the ground was
bleeding quite heavily from facial injuries, and was barely
conscious. We stayed with him until police and an ambulance
arrived a short time later.

Signed Ran Cao

24 December 2009

6:35 p.m.

FIGURE 8.11   STATEMENT FROM ACCUSED

Pg _1_ of _1_

ACCUSED STATEMENT

NAME *Eric Sanchez*   OCC# *05-31726*

ADDRESS *2010 Conrad St. North, Hamilton, ON L8P 4Z4*

DOB *54-12-08*   TELEPHONE *none*

OFFICER *Gino Polari*   BADGE# *372*

ARREST TIME *1812*

LOCATION OF ARREST *In front of 92 Long St., Hamilton, ON*

LOCATION OF INTERVIEW *In front of 92 Long St., Hamilton, ON*

START TIME *1815*   *09-12-24*   FINISH TIME *1820*   *09-12-24*

"People shouldn't run over pedestrians. I was walking along the street and this idiot in a van ran into me. I yelled at him and kicked the van a couple of times. When the driver got out of the van, I whacked him a couple of times to brighten him up. Then I just walked away. I think I taught him a good lesson. People like that shouldn't be allowed to drive."

SIGNATURE *Eric Sanchez*   WITNESS *Gino Polari #372*

FIGURE 8.12   PAGE FROM OFFICER'S MEMO BOOK

OFFICER'S NAME: Gino Polari

BADGE #:   372

DEPARTMENT: Traffic

1755	Dispatched to 206 Mariah St. by 911 dispatcher regarding assault
1759	10-7 206 Mariah St.
1800	Ambulance on scene
1802	I interviewed victim Robert Pidzerny, who told me that he had been assaulted by a Caucasian male approximately 55 years of age, medium build, 170 cm in height, with grey hair and a green jacket. The male had left the scene approximately ten minutes previously and was walking southbound along Long St.
	Two witnesses — Dan Dibiacco (58-03-27) and Ran Cao (82-02-20). I asked witnesses to remain on scene while I searched for assailant. I searched along Long St. and saw a male answering the description of the accused. He identified himself as Eric Sanchez (54-12-08) and admitted that he committed the assault.
1812	Sanchez cautioned and arrested
1815	Sanchez transported to Central Division
1825	Returned to scene to interview witnesses

Pg   1

EXERCISE 6

ASSESSING THE CROWN BRIEF

1. Does the Pidzerny case meet the definition of assault causing bodily harm as defined by section 267 of the *Criminal Code*? What elements in this case meet the definition, or what more information would be needed in order to meet the definition?

2. Does the summary of the Pidzerny case list all of the necessary facts in issue required to secure a conviction in this case? What are the facts in issue in this case?

3. Does the summary follow the report-writing format—discussed earlier in this chapter—of summary, background, facts, and conclusions? Define which details in the summary of the Pidzerny case fall into each of these categories.

4. Do the witness statements deal with the facts in issue of the case? For each witness statement, what are the facts in issue that are dealt with? Describe how each witness statement supports the facts in issue of the summary.

ADDITIONAL FORMS FOR THE CROWN BRIEF

When the Crown brief is assembled, other forms may be necessary, such as a disclosure certificate, a Breathalyzer Analysis Technician (BAT) certificate, a vehicle registration, a probation order, or a pre-sentence report.

NIAGARA REGIONAL POLICE SERVICE REPORTS

The following pages contain report blanks used by the Niagara Regional Police Service. These forms are reproduced with the permission of the Niagara Regional Police Service.

Summary

Reports are made up of a summary and details. They must answer the questions *who? what? where? when? why?* and *how?* They must be clear, concise, correct, and complete. Details of the report can be divided into summary, background, facts, and conclusions. Reports are based on facts that have been recorded in the memo book. The general incident report is the most common type of report used in law enforcement; it consists of the cover page and the supplementary report.

NIAGARA REGIONAL POLICE SERVICE

General Incident ☐   **Arrest Report** ☐

Request for Summons ☐   Young Offender ☐

No. OF SUPPLEMENTARY REPORTS

DESCR. OF PROPERTIES / INJURIES (INC SER #)   VALUE   DAMAGED   RECOVERED

INJURIES: MAJOR ☐   MINOR ☐   NONE ☐

VICTIM SERVICES OFFERED?   YES ☐   NO ☐

SPECIFY ON SUPPLEMENTARY: TYPE OF INJURIES SUSTAINED, TYPE OF FORC USED, SUFFICIENT DETAILS FOR PLEA OF GUILTY, CO-ACCUSED, PREVIOUS ADDRESS OF ACCUSED, ETC.

FOR NARRATIVE COMPLETE SUPPLEMENTARY REPORT

DATE AND TIME OF ARREST   ARRESTING OFFICER   BADGE #

LOCATION OF ARREST?   HAZARD ☐

CHARGES: (IF WARRANT EXECUTED, STATE TYPE)

CHARGES

NOTIFICATIONS: Y.O.A. - NOTICE TO PARENT SERVED?   YES ☐   NO ☐

OTHERS: SPOUSE ☐   GUARDIAN ☐   OTHER - NAME

   PARENT ☐   NEXT OF KIN ☐

ADDRESS   HOME PHONE

ARRESTED FOR OTHER DEPT. (SPECIFY)   WHO NOTIFIED?   TIME

RELEASED TO (RANK / NAME / No.)   TIME   HRS   YEAR   MONTH   DAY

FINGERPRINT DATE   FORM OF RELEASE   BAIL HEARING?   YES ☐   NO ☐

BAIL AND RELEASE RECOMMENDATIONS   STATEMENT TAKEN   YES ☐   NO ☐

CNI / CPIC QUERIED? RESULTS:

RELEASED BY OFFICER   BADGE #   NAME OF JUSTICE

DATE & TIME OF RELEASE   COURT LOCATION   COURT DATE AND TIME

HAZARD REMARKS (must be completed if any hazard is checked)

STATS CANADA CLEARED BY		INCIDENT CLASS	ADULTS		JUVENILES		INF.	DATA RECEIVED	DATE CLEARED
CHARGE	OTHER	UNF		M	F	M	F		

OFFICE ONLY	DATE ENTRY	DATA VERIF.	DATA VERIF		

DIVISION   PATROL AREA   INCIDENT CLASS   INCIDENT No.   YR   MO   DAY

TYPE OF INCIDENT   DATE AND TIME OF INCIDENT (OR TIME BETWEEN)   HAZARD ☐

LOCATION OF INCIDENT

HOW INCIDENT COMMITTED   MEANS (WEAPONS, TOOLS USED)

VICTIM / COMPLAINANT

SURNAME   GIVEN (1)   GIVEN (2)   RACE: WHITE ☐ NON-WHITE ☐

ADDRESS   HOME PHONE   HAZARD ☐

SEX   DOB   YR   MO   DAY   MAR. ST.   OCCUPATION   CONDITION: SOBER ☐ HBD ☐ INTOX ☐ DRUGS ☐

PLACE OF EMPLOYMENT / EMPLOYER   BUSINESS PHONE   EXT./LOCAL

REPORTED BY

SURNAME   GIVEN (1)   GIVEN (2)   GIVEN (3)

ADDRESS   HOME PHONE   HAZARD ☐

SEX   DOB   YR   MO   DAY   RELATIONSHIP TO VICTIM/COMPLAINANT   CONDITION: SOBER ☐ HBD ☐ INTOX ☐ DRUGS ☐

PLACE OF EMPLOYMENT / EMPLOYER   BUSINESS PHONE   EXT./LOCAL

VEHICLE USED

TYPE   LICENCE No.   LIC.YEAR   LIC.PROV.   VEH.YEAR   MAKE   MODEL

STYLE   COLOUR   VIN

OWNER   SAME ☐   SURNAME: GIVEN (1)   ADDRESS

OUTSTANDING FEATURES

ACCUSED / SUSPECT

SURNAME   GIVEN (1)   GIVEN (2)   NICKNAMES   ALIAS ☐ NEE ☐

ADDRESS   HOME PHONE   HAZARD ☐

SEX   DOB   YR   MO   DAY   AGE   MAR. ST.   MHT (HT)   MASS (WT)   RACE: WHITE ☐ NON-WHITE ☐

HAIR COLOUR   EYES-COLOUR   CONTACT LENSES ☐ GLASSES ☐   DESCRIPTION OF CLOTHING

BUILD: SLENDER ☐ MEDIUM ☐ HEAVY ☐

HAIR TYPE: BALD ☐ PART BALD ☐ SHORT ☐ LONG ☐ STRAIGHT ☐   MOUSTACHE ☐ BEARD ☐ WIG ☐   CURLY/WAVY ☐ WELL DRESSED ☐ UNKEMPT ☐ BUSHY ☐

COMPLEXION: SALLOW ☐ LIGHT/FAIR ☐ RUDDY ☐ FRECKLED ☐ DARK/SWARTHY ☐ POCK-MARKED ☐

TEETH: GOOD ☐ IRREGULAR ☐ FALSE ☐ VISIBLE GOLD ☐ STAINED ☐ PROTRUD. UPPERS ☐ PROTRUD. LOWERS ☐ VISIBLE DECAY ☐ VISIBLE MISSING ☐

VICTIM / ACCUSED RELATIONSHIP   DRIVERS LICENSE No.   PROV.   NRP No.

PHYSICAL / MENTAL CONDITION, MARKS, SCARS, TATTOOS, OUTSTANDING FEATURES   FPS No.

CNI CAUTIONS: V ☐ E ☐ A ☐ M ☐ S ☐ C ☐   CONDITION: SOBER ☐ INTOX ☐ HBD ☐ DRUGS ☐   OCCUPATION

PLACE OF EMPLOYMENT / EMPLOYER / SCHOOL AND GRADE   BUSINESS PHONE (EXT./LOCAL)

REPORTING OFFICER: (FULL NAME / RANK / No.)   DATE / TIME / REPORT TAKEN   YEAR / MONTH / DAY / TIME   HRS

OTHER OFFICER(S) ATTENDING   IDENT OFFICER RESPONDING

REPORT CHECKED BY (FULL NAME / RANK / No.)   CASE REASSIGNED TO   BY   DATE

REPORT CHECKED BY (FULL NAME / RANK / No.)   INCIDENT STATUS (IF INVEST. COMPLETE CHECK SOLVED OR UNSOLVED): INIT. / DATE   INVEST. COMP ☐ SOLVED ☐ INVEST CONT'D ☐ UNSOLVED ☐

ALL SHADED AREAS MUST BE COMPLETED **1**

-- ORIGINAL COPY --

NIAGARA REGIONAL POLICE SERVICE
Supplementary Report

CHECK APPROPRIATE BOX

☐ ORIGINAL   ☐ MISSING PERSON / ELOPEE
☐ ARREST   ☐ FRAUDULENT DOCUMENT
☐ INCIDENT   ☐ HOMICIDE / SUDDEN DEATH
☐ VEHICLE   ☐ OTHER

SURNAME: (OR NAME & TYPE OF BUSINESS)

DIVISION: PATROL AREA / ZONE: INCIDENT CLASS   INCIDENT NUMBER

TYPE OF INCIDENT: REFERENCE: POLICE INFORMATION:
☐ ACCUSED
☐ VICTIM / COMPLAINANT   (EXT./LOCAL)

DATE OF ORIGINAL REPORT   BUSINESS TELEPHONE: HOME TELEPHONE
(EXT./LOCAL)

ADDRESS   ☐ HAZARD

HAZARD REMARKS   (MUST BE COMPLETED IF HAZARD CHECKED)

STATS CAN CLEARED BY	CHG.	OTHER	UNF.	INCIDENT CLASS	ADULTS M F	JUVENILE M F	INF.
OFFICE ONLY	DATA ENTRY		DATA VERIF.	DATE RECEIVED IN RECORDS	DATE CLEARED		

REPORTING OFFICER: (FULL NAME/RANK/No.)   DATE/TIME OF THIS REPORT   YR   MO   DAY   TIME   PAGE No.

OTHER OFFICER(S) ATTENDING   I.D. OFFICER REPORTING

CASE REASSIGNED TO   BY   DATE

REPORT CHECKED BY (FULL NAME/RANK/No.)   INCIDENT STATUS (IF INVEST. COMP.: CHECK SOLVED OR UNSOLVED)
REPORT CHECKED BY (FULL NAME/RANK/No.)   INVEST: CONT. ☐ INVEST: COMP. ☐ SOLVED ☐ UNSOLVED ☐   INIT./DATE

ALL SHADED AREAS MUST BE COMPLETED   **1**

-- ORIGINAL COPY --

NIAGARA REGIONAL POLICE SERVICE

STATEMENT OF A WITNESS

NAME:	DATE OF BIRTH:
ADDRESS:	TELEPHONE NO.:

BUSINESS ADDRESS:

OCCUPATION:	TELEPHONE NO.:

DATE:	TIME STARTED:	TIME COMPLETED:

OFFICER TAKING STATEMENT:

NIAGARA REGIONAL POLICE FORCE

STATEMENT CONTINUATION

NAME:	PAGE NO.

CHAPTER 9

The Written Communication Test*

Learning Objectives

After completing this chapter, you should be able to:

- Understand the instructions to the Written Communication Test (WCT).

- Construct a fact sheet for the WCT.

- Write a well-organized essay based on the fact sheet using correct spelling and grammar.

Introduction

After you complete your studies, you may decide to apply for a position with a police service, or you may wish to enter the fields of private security, customs, or corrections. In most cases, you will be required to write the Written Communication Test (WCT) before you apply. The WCT tests your ability to sort out facts and to write an essay based on those facts.

The WCT is divided into two parts and includes detailed instructions. In the first part, you are given a scenario, usually concerning (but not necessarily) a traffic accident. The facts in this scenario are jumbled, and some are unnecessary to the final essay. Your task is to

1. eliminate unnecessary information, and

2. enter the facts of the scenario on a fact sheet under the headings *Who*, *When*, *Where*, and *What*.

In the second part, you are asked to use your fact sheet to write an essay. The essay must relate the facts of the scenario in chronological order.

---

* Permission acknowledged from Jo-Anne Procter, Associate Dean, Brantford Campus, to use material in this chapter that was originally generated for Mohawk College.

◻ The Instructions

The instructions for the WCT are usually handed to applicants with the WCT scenario (see Figure 9.1). It is important that you read them carefully. There are a few things to note:

1. A sample grading sheet has been included with this material. There are various methods of marking the WCT, but one method is to mark the WCT out of 25 marks, with Information Provided worth 10 marks, Organization worth 5 marks, Conclusion worth 5 marks, and Writing Clarity worth 5 marks (see Figure 9.2).

2. You cannot achieve a passing grade on the WCT without a passing grade of 60 percent in each of the four sections. For example, an overall score of 19/25 on the test with a grade of 2/5 in the Information Provided section will result in a failure on the entire test.

3. Be sure to take the time to read the instructions carefully. One of the factors that influences a good grade on this test is your ability to follow instructions.

4. Use the information provided. Use the words, spelling, and grammar of the scenario whenever possible. This is not a creative writing exercise, and you won't be charged with plagiarism for using the wording of the original. In fact, using the wording from the scenario will help you avoid spelling and grammar errors.

5. Don't make assumptions. All the information you need is in the scenario. Don't add anything just because you feel that something is incomplete.

6. Irrelevant information is anything that doesn't contribute to the resolution of the scenario. There are usually only one or two irrelevant facts in any one scenario.

7. The conclusion, stating who or what was at fault in the scenario, is usually short and doesn't require the student to have a knowledge of the *Highway Traffic Act*. For example, it is sufficient to say something like, "Mr. Smith was at fault in this scenario. He was travelling too fast for the road conditions and lost control of his car."

8. If your handwriting is poor, print your answers. The material can't be graded if it can't be read. There should be plenty of time to print if you need to.

9. An hour should be adequate time to finish the WCT. Pace yourself. For example, spend 20 minutes on the fact sheet, and 40 minutes on the essay. You'll get a better idea of your personal time requirements as you review the sample scenarios later in this chapter and complete Exercise 1.

10. Don't panic. Read the scenario at least twice before starting to rearrange sentences. Remember, the WCT is merely a scenario with the facts jumbled. All you need to do is to arrange the facts in chronological order. Chronological order (or logical order or cause and effect) simply means that something had to happen before something else happened. For example, you cannot have damage to a vehicle until after an accident occurs.

FIGURE 9.1   SAMPLE INSTRUCTIONS

INSTRUCTIONS

Your answer will be graded according to:

- Your fact sheet
- The organization of the essay
- Spelling and grammar
- Your ability to draw logical conclusions

Note: You must pass each of the 4 sections in order to pass the WCT.

Read all of the instructions carefully before proceeding. Part of your grade results from the ability to follow instructions, both verbal and written.

The Written Communication Test has two parts. Part 1 requires you to list the facts of a scenario in point form. Use the "4 Ws Fact Sheet" provided. Part 2 asks you to write an essay that describes what occurred in the scenario. Do not add new information that does not exist in the story. Do not change the facts or information. Use pen only. Don't forget to put your name and student number on the upper right-hand corner of each page.

1. Do not write or mark on the scenario page or this instruction page.

2. Examine the scenario carefully. In this scenario the information has not been organized. Some of the details are irrelevant.

3. On the "WCT Fact Sheet Guide" make a list of all of the relevant and important facts in the scenario. Important facts should include such things as time, date, location, witness statements, weather and road conditions, evidence, the chain of events in logical order as they occurred, assignment of responsibility for the incident. You must conclude who or what was at fault, based solely on the facts of the scenario.

4. Double space your essay. Print if your handwriting is not legible.

5. A separate sheet of paper may be used for notes and diagrams. Label this page "Rough Notes." Put your name at the upper right-hand corner of this page.

6. You have one hour to complete the WCT. You will not be able to leave the room once the test has started. You will be given a few minutes before the test starts to read these instructions and to ask questions. No questions will be answered once the test has started.

7. When you are finished, staple your pages together with the fact sheet first, followed by your essay, which should be followed by any rough notes. A stapler will be provided. Turn your paper upside down and leave it in the designated area, usually on a table at the front of the room. You will not be allowed to take any papers with you when you leave the room.

FIGURE 9.2   SAMPLE GRADING SHEET

Written Communication Test (WCT) Marking Guide

(NOTE: Students must score at least 60% in each of the four sub-sections to pass.)

STUDENT'S NAME: _____

Overall Grade:	A) *Information Provided*	/10
	B) *Organization*	/5
	C) *Conclusion*	/5
	D) *Writing Clarity*	/5

| | *Total* | /25 |

A: Information Provided: Fact Sheet & Essay   /10

Information ***must*** appear on both the fact sheet and the essay to earn credit.

1. All relevant times and dates.   /1___

2. Full names of all affected parties and witnesses.   /1___

3. Complete addresses of all parties and witnesses.   /1___

4. Precise locations, particularly house numbers,
   streets, intersections and other landmarks, sides of
   streets, lanes, NESW, etc.   /1___

5. Colour, year, make, model, and licence plates of all motor vehicles.   /1___

6. Damage and estimated cost of repair.   /1___

7. Injuries and action taken.   /1___

8. Visibility, weather, road conditions, etc.   /1___

9. All links in the chain of events start to finish.   /1___

10. Assignment of responsibility for the incident.   /1___

B: Organization: Fact Sheet & Essay   /5

Students must meet the following goals:

1. Followed instructions both oral and written, in all answers.   /1___

2. Organized the fact sheet using who, when, where, and what.   /1___

3. Provided a general introduction to the essay.   /1___

4. Organized the essay with a series of paragraphs.   /1___

5. Used logical order to establish the chain of events in the essay.   /1___

C: Conclusion: Essay Only   /5

The fact sheet should indicate and lead to a logical conclusion as to who was at fault, but only the essay must have a formal conclusion, which says *why* he/she was at fault:

1. Provided a formal conclusion.   /1___

2. Indicated who was at fault.   /1___

3. Supported the conclusion with information from the fact sheet.   /1___

4. Drew the correct conclusion regarding the fault.   /1___

5. Used appropriately objective language in assigned fault.   /1___

D: Writing Clarity: Fact Sheet & Essay   /5

Students must achieve clarity and accuracy in both the fact sheet and essay and avoid writing errors, which will affect their credibility as professional reporters:

1. Spelled names of all affected parties and witnesses correctly.   /1___

2. Made five or fewer spelling errors, including apostrophes.   /1___

3. Made two or fewer run-on sentences and sentence fragments.*   /1___

4. Avoided all other major grammar errors that affect clarity
   (agreement, verb tenses, verb formation, etc.).   /1___

5. Used professional, objective language throughout.   /1___

---

*   Please note: Point #3 does not apply to the fact sheet, which should be in point form.

The Fact Sheet

The blank fact sheet for the Written Communication Test is called the "WCT Fact Sheet Guide." Information from the scenario, minus irrelevant information, is written on this fact sheet in chronological order. In the end, *everything* in the scenario (minus irrelevant information) will be found somewhere on the fact sheet in point form. Everything on the fact sheet will be used to write the essay. A sample fact sheet is provided below in Figure 9.3.

FIGURE 9.3   SAMPLE WCT FACT SHEET GUIDE

WCT Fact Sheet Guide

W4 = who, when, where, and what

Use this sheet to help you organize the information as you read the scenario.

WHO

WHEN

WHERE

WHAT

Before beginning to make entries on the fact sheet, thoroughly read the scenario at least twice. You will have time for this. Reading the scenario, even though the facts are jumbled, helps to give you an overall picture of what happened. Then, eliminate irrelevant material. Since you can't write on the scenario, you'll have to either keep this irrelevant information in your head or write it on your Rough Notes sheet. A sample scenario has been provided in Figure 9.4.

FIGURE 9.4   SAMPLE SCENARIO

There was an amazingly wild ice storm and the roads were ice-covered and slippery. At approximately 1002 hours a green 2004 Ford Windstar, Ontario licence ANAP 277 was travelling southbound on Mainway St., Mississauga, ON, approaching the stop sign on Mainway St. The speed limit is 50 km/h on Gerrard St. East. On Wednesday, September 17, 2008, at approximately 0958 hours, a red 2008 Toyota Echo, Ontario licence ADGR 308, was travelling westbound on Gerrard St. East in the curb lane at approximately 40 km/h. At approximately 1002 hours the Ford slid into the side of the Toyota Echo in the intersection of Gerrard St. East and Mainway St., a T intersection. The driver of the Toyota was Jane Oliver of 56 Aylmer Blvd., Toronto, ON, d.o.b. August 8, 1984. Gerrard St. East is a four-lane highway, with two lanes each in the east-bound and westbound lanes. The weather was cold. Mr. Gulka couldn't stop at the stop sign due to the ice on the roadway. There were no leaves on the trees. Mainway St. is a two-lane roadway with one lane for southbound traffic and one lane for northbound traffic. There is a stop sign at Mainway St. and Gerrard St. East for traffic travelling southbound on Mainway St. The driver of the Ford was Shaun Gulka of 297 Front St., Brantford, ON. The Toyota received damage to the front passenger door for an estimated damage of $2,000. The Windstar was travelling at approximately 50 km/h approaching the T intersec-tion of Mainway St. and Gerrard St. East. Mr. Gulka's d.o.b. is March 23, 1983. Mr. Gulka started to apply his brakes when the Ford was approximately 5 metres from the stop sign. The drivers were not hurt. The Ford sustained damage to the front bumper and grill for an estimated damage of $600. The speed limit for Mainway St. is 50 km/h.

From this scenario, there are two irrelevant statements:

1. "There was an amazingly wild ice storm."
2. "There were no leaves on the trees."

Neither of these statements is relevant. The fact that there was an amazingly wild ice storm is irrelevant since the necessary information about road conditions, that the roads were ice-covered and slippery, is stated. Likewise, the absence of leaves on the trees is irrelevant because visibility was not a factor in the accident—the cause of the accident was Gulka's failure to adjust his speed to suit the icy conditions.

Now that you have read the scenario carefully, and have eliminated irrelevant material, you can fill out the fact sheet. To help you complete the fact sheet, ask yourself the following questions:

WHO

Who is the officer?

Who is the victim/complainant? (Include address, phone number, date of birth, etc.)

Who are the witnesses?

Who is the offender?

Who else assisted in the investigation? (Ambulance staff, fire department, coroner, youth bureau, etc.)

WHEN (include time and date, chronologically)

When did the event take place?

When was the officer dispatched, detailed, flagged down?

When did the officer arrive?

When were witnesses and/or victim(s) interviewed?

When was someone arrested?

WHERE

Where did the offence occur? (Address, general description of address, location of event within that address.)

WHAT

What were the road and weather conditions?

What type of occurrence was it? (For example, was it a motor vehicle accident or another type of occurrence?)

What happened? How did the occurrence take place?

What damage did the vehicles sustain? What injuries did the parties suffer?

What types of vehicles were involved? What were their licence numbers, etc.? What was the direction of travel?

What were the drivers doing leading up to the accident?

What emergency vehicles attended the scene? (For example, were there tow trucks, ambulances, Ministry of Transportation vehicles?)

One trick to putting information in the correct category is to fill in the *Who*, *When*, and *Where* categories first. The *Who* category will usually contain names, which are easy to pick out from the scenario. List the names in the order they appear in the scenario. The *When* category will contain the times and dates, in chronological order, when events occurred. Since times and dates are usually stated in the scenario, this category should also be easy to complete. Likewise, the *Where* category can be filled out by identifying the locations and addresses in the scenario. Anything not in these categories goes in the *What* category. Students are encouraged to draw a diagram on their Rough Notes sheet to assist in visualizing the accident scene and in putting events in chronological order.

Be sure that everything from the scenario, minus the irrelevant material, appears on the fact sheet (see Figure 9.5).

FIGURE 9.5 COMPLETED FACT SHEET

WCT Fact Sheet Guide

W4 = who, when, where, and what

Use this sheet to help you organize the information as you read the scenario.

WHO

– Jane Oliver, d.o.b. August 8, 1984, of 56 Aylmer Blvd., Toronto, ON, driver of the Toyota Echo.

– Shaun Gulka, d.o.b. March 23, 1983, of 297 Front St., Brantford, ON, driver of the Ford Windstar.

WHEN

0958   Toyota travelling westbound on Gerrard St. East.

1002   Ford travelling southbound on Mainway St.

1002   Ford approaching a stop sign.

1002   Collision occurred on Wednesday, September 17, 2008.

WHERE

– T intersection of Gerrard St. East and Mainway St., Mississauga, ON.

– Toyota travelling westbound on Gerrard St. East, Ford travelling southbound on Mainway St.

WHAT

– Motor vehicle accident involving property damage.

– Ice-covered roads, slippery, cold weather.

– Red Toyota Echo Ontario licence ADGR 308 travelling westbound on Gerrard St. E. in curb lane at approx. 40 km/h. Gerrard E. has 4 lanes, 2 each way eastbound and westbound. Speed limit is 50 km/h.

– Green Ford Windstar Ontario licence ANAP 277 travelling southbound on Mainway St. at approx. 50 km/h, approaching stop sign at T intersection of Mainway and Gerrard. Mainway is a 2-lane road, one lane each way northbound and southbound. Stop sign is for southbound traffic. Speed limit on Mainway is 50 km/h.

– When Gulka was about 5 m from the stop sign he applied his brakes but couldn't stop because of ice on the road. He ran into the side of the Toyota.

– No injuries. Damage to Toyota — front passenger door — estimated damage $2,000. Damage to Ford — front bumper and grill — estimated damage $600.

The Essay

When the fact sheet has been completed, usually in 20 minutes or less of the hour allowed for the test, the next step is to write the essay. Everything contained in the fact sheet (and therefore everything contained in the scenario, minus the irrelevant material) will be found in the essay.

The essay relates, in chronological order, the background, facts, and conclusions of the scenario. Like any essay, it is divided into paragraphs, with each paragraph dealing with a specific topic. Use as many paragraphs as you feel are necessary. The WCT usually is written as a five-paragraph essay, but five paragraphs are a minimum; there can be more, such as in Figure 9.7. A typical essay outline is provided below:

First paragraph. The first paragraph should provide a general summary of the incident, chronologically, including what type of incident occurred, when it occurred, and where it happened. You don't have to be specific here; the summary gives general descriptions and information, while the specifics are found later in the essay. The road conditions and weather should also be included in this paragraph.

Second paragraph. The second paragraph should identify the first person involved in the incident, how the person identified himself or herself, his or her address, what that person said and did, and any other pertinent information about that person. Usually, the first person is the first individual to be mentioned in the scenario.

Third paragraph. The third paragraph should identify subsequent persons involved in the incident and provide pertinent information about them.

Fourth paragraph. The fourth paragraph should include other relevant information (all information that didn't appear in the paragraphs above), such as estimated damage to vehicles, other property damage, injuries, and witnesses. If there's a lot of information, break it up into separate but related paragraphs.

Final paragraph. The final paragraph should state who was at fault and explain the reason for assigning fault. Your conclusions should be based on the facts provided in the scenario, including any statements made by the parties involved or by witnesses, and descriptions of evidence at the scene.

POINTS TO REMEMBER

1. Write in the *third person*.

2. Write in the *past tense*.

3. Write events in *chronological order*. Begin at the beginning, and then describe what happens after that.

4. Record *times* for everything.

5. Write in *complete, simple sentences*, using the wording of the scenario whenever possible.

6. State the *facts*; opinions are not a part of the essay.

7. Draw *conclusions* in the final paragraph on the basis of the *facts* presented in the scenario.

Two scenarios with sample essays are reproduced in Figures 9.6 and 9.7. Read both of them, noting how the essays demonstrate the essay format described above. After you have finished analyzing the essays, complete Exercise 1.

FIGURE 9.6   SCENARIO 1 AND SAMPLE ESSAY

Scenario 1

Miss Schwartz said the motorcycle tried to pass too close to her horse. Mrs. Marucci said she slowed down and moved well to the left to pass safely, but the horse had attacked her bike. Diamond Lil limped alone back to her stable. Stephanie Schwartz was on the gravel road directly north of the Chatham Horse Farm, 2478 Quarry Road, Chatham, ON L0R 1H3. Miss Schwartz was riding eastbound on Quarry Road on her black four-year-old quarterhorse mare, Diamond Lil. The Schwartz animal was valued at $2,500. Vet fees were $250. The collision at noon on May 1, 2008 resulted in the death of a valuable horse and damage to an expensive motorcycle. Marcella Marucci of RR #3, Jonesville, ON L8N 1J3, was riding her black 2007 Harley-Davidson. Mrs. Marucci was also eastbound on Quarry Road. Miss Schwartz was born on July 4, 1982. She lives at the Chatham Horse Farm, where her horse was stabled. Mrs. Marucci was born September 15, 1980. The road is marked with yellow and black signs warning the public of horse traffic. The personalized licence plate of the motorcycle is MI*HOG. Mrs. Marucci saw the horse and rider, slowed, and pulled into the centre of the road to pass. Later that day, Dr. Bill Davis of Chatham Animal Hospital examined the horse. He said her left hind leg was broken. He had to put her to sleep. As the motorcycle came by, the horse suddenly kicked wildly and struck the bike with its rear hooves. Mrs. Marucci lost control on the loose gravel. She and the bike slid 10 metres before coming to rest in the centre of the road. The Harley-Davidson had a broken windshield, damage to the front forks, and scratched paint. Mrs. Schwartz was also thrown to the ground. Neither person was hurt. Both identified themselves with Ontario driver's licences. Damage to the bike is estimated at $1,500. The weather was clear.

Sample Essay

A collision between a horse and a motorcycle occurred at noon on May 1, 2008 on a gravel road in Chatham, ON. The collision resulted in the death of the horse and damage to the motorcycle. The riders of the horse and the motorcycle were not injured. The weather was clear.

Stephanie Schwartz, d.o.b. July 4, 1982, was riding eastbound on her black four-year-old quarterhorse mare, Diamond Lil. She was on the gravel road directly north of the Chatham Horse Farm, 2478 Quarry Road, Chatham, ON, L0R 1H3, where the horse was stabled and Miss Schwartz lives. The road is marked with yellow and black signs warning the public of horse traffic.

Marcella Marucci of RR #3, Jonesville, ON, L8N 1J3, d.o.b. September 15, 1980, was riding her black 2007 Harley-Davidson motorcycle, licence MI*HOG. She was also heading eastbound on Quarry Road. She saw the horse and rider, slowed, and pulled into the centre of the road to pass.

As the motorcycle came by, the horse suddenly kicked wildly and struck the bike with its rear hooves. Mrs. Marucci lost control on the loose gravel.

She and the bike slid 10 metres before coming to rest in the centre of the road. Miss Schwartz was also thrown to the ground. Neither rider was hurt. Both women identified themselves with Ontario driver's licences. Diamond Lil limped alone back to her stable. Later that day, Dr. Bill Davis of Chatham Animal Hospital examined the horse. He said her left hind leg was broken. He had to put her to sleep. The Schwartz animal was valued at $2,500. Vet fees were $250. Mrs. Marucci's Harley-Davidson had a broken windshield, damage to the front forks, and scratched paint. Damage is estimated at $1,500. Miss Schwartz said the motorcycle tried to pass too close to her horse. Mrs. Marucci said she slowed down and moved well to the left to pass safely but the horse attacked her bike.

Mrs. Marucci was at fault for trying to pass too closely. Since the horse was able to reach the motorcycle with its hind legs, there was not enough room given to pass safely.

FIGURE 9.7   SCENARIO 2 AND SAMPLE ESSAY

Scenario 2

Damage to the Freestar exceeded $5,000. It will be sold for parts. Danielle Damphousse was driving eastbound about 8 metres behind the step van. The accident took place in front of Hamilton Financial Centre, 203 King St. West, Hamilton, ON. Financial centre employees came rushing out to assist. It was raining heavily and visibility was poor. When the step van suddenly stopped, Miss Damphousse lost control of her vehicle, which slid into the rear of the step van, and was partly lodged under the step/bumper. It was a 2005 Ford Freestar minivan. At that point, King St. has one lane eastbound, one westbound, and spaces for metered parking along both sides. The speed limit is 50 km/h. The collision between the minivan and the delivery vehicle occurred at 1603 on March 5, 2009 in the busy downtown shopping district of Hamilton, ON. Miss Damphousse escaped injury. Patrick O'Reilly, d.o.b. July 4, 1980, was driving eastbound on King Street in a white 2001 GMC step van. He has a good record with his employer, Mohawk Courier Services, which owns the vehicle. Damage to the van was limited to the rear step/bumper and is estimated at $500. Its Ontario licence plate is SCS 200. The Ford is red. Its Ontario licence plate is AJXW 846. Mr. O'Reilly lives at Apartment 1460, 400 Sixteenth St., Hamilton, ON L0R 1S0. Mr. O'Reilly said that at the time of the collision, he had to make an emergency stop because "an old Volkswagen Beetle" pulled out of a parking space on his right and cut in front of him. Miss Damphousse is a Capricorn and was born on January 8, 1979. Though Mr. O'Reilly barely stopped in time, the Volkswagen did not remain on the scene, and there were no independent witnesses. Miss Damphousse lives at 198 King St., Hamilton, ON L8N 1J3. Both drivers showed valid Ontario licences. Both said they were driving at about 40 km/h. O'Reilly was not injured.

Sample Essay

A collision between a delivery van and a Ford Freestar minivan occurred at 1603 on March 5, 2009, in the busy downtown shopping district of Hamilton, ON. It was raining heavily, and visibility was poor.

The accident took place in front of Hamilton Financial Centre, 203 King St. West, Hamilton. At that point, King St. has one lane eastbound, one westbound, and spaces for metered parking along both sides. The speed limit is 50 km/h.

Danielle Damphousse, d.o.b. January 8, 1979, lives at 198 King St., Hamilton, ON L8N 1J3. She was driving eastbound at about 40 km/h about 8 metres behind the step van in her red 2005 Ford Freestar van, Ontario licence AJXW 846. She identified herself with a valid Ontario driver's licence.

When the step van suddenly stopped, Ms. Damphousse lost control of her vehicle, which slid into the rear of the step van and partially lodged under the step/bumper. Miss Damphousse escaped injury.

Patrick O'Reilly, d.o.b. July 4, 1980, lives at Apartment 1460, 400 Sixteenth St., Hamilton, ON L0R 1S0. He was driving eastbound at about 40 km/h on King St. in a white 2001 GMC step van, Ontario licence SCS 200, owned by his employer, Mohawk Courier Services. He identified himself with a valid Ontario driver's licence.

Mr. O'Reilly said that at the time of the collision, he had to make an emergency stop because "an old Volkswagen Beetle" pulled out of a parking space on his right and cut in front of him. Though Mr. O'Reilly barely stopped in time, the Volkswagen did not remain on the scene, and there were no independent witnesses. Mr. O'Reilly was not injured.

Damage to the Freestar exceeded $5,000. It will be sold for parts. Damage to the GMC was limited to the rear step/bumper and is estimated at $500.

Miss Damphousse was at fault for following too closely. She should have allowed more space between her vehicle and the van because of the wet weather. Posted speed limits are only valid in clear, dry weather, and a driver must adjust to adverse weather conditions.

EXERCISE 1

WRITING A WCT ESSAY

Construct a fact sheet and essay based on the following scenario. (Use the blank "WCT Fact Sheet Guide" in Figure 9.3 to record your facts.)

Charlie Smith is employed as a delivery driver by Hampton Community Care. Damage to the front grill, hood, and windshield of the Mustang was extensive and is estimated to be $4,500. Mr. Smith said he did not see the Mustang until after the collision. Both drivers identified themselves with Ontario driver's licences. Mr. Shumaker said the van was a dangerous obstruction. He said it was barely moving and, although he braked hard, he had no time to avoid a collision. Mr. Shumaker said he is fed up with jokes linking him to the famous race car drivers. He says he travelled eastbound at the posted speed limit through the S bend in his red 2000 Mustang GT, Ontario licence 299 PFS. The collision between the delivery van and the automobile occurred at 1001 on May 26, 2010. Mr. Smith was born on January 8, 1944. He was driving the charity's white 2006 Ford panel van carrying a full load of donated furniture. Peter Shumaker lives at Apartment 904, Queen Apartments, 4300 Queen St., Southam, ON L8N 2S3. Mr. Shumaker says, as he exited the S bend, he saw the panel van. Mr. Smith lives at RR #3, Jonesville, ON L0R 1J3. The van's Ontario licence is AAKN 201. Damage to the van's loading door and bumper was estimated at $1,100. Mr. Smith acknowledged that his fully loaded vehicle was travelling slowly up an incline. He said that, before the collision, he was travelling northbound on Twenty Road, stopped at the intersection with Regional Road 18, and checked the road in each direction. At the time of the collision, both vehicles were travelling eastbound on Regional Road 18, Hampton, ON, 20 metres east of the intersection with Twenty Road. Mr. Smith has an excellent employment record. He said it is not possible to see more than 30 metres west on Regional Road 18 from the intersection with Twenty Road, because of a blind S bend, a house, and trees. There were no injuries. The weather was clear. The speed limit through the S bend is 50 km/h. The car destroyed a sign posting a speed limit change to 70 km/h. Peter Shumaker was born February 5, 1980. When Mr. Smith was satisfied that the road was clear, he turned right, accelerating slowly up the incline in the eastbound lane of Regional Road 18. Replacement of the speed limit sign is estimated at $500. The front of the Mustang came into contact with the right rear of the Ford van. The car then slid into the ditch.

Summary

The Written Communication Test is required for many positions in law enforcement. The WCT presents a scenario in which the facts are jumbled. You must eliminate irrelevant facts, arrange the remaining facts in chronological order on a fact sheet, and then write an essay based on those facts.

APPENDIX A
Memos

Introduction

The memorandum ("memo" for short) is an informal written statement, usually brief, that is used for communicating within an organization and may be consulted in the future or used as a memory aid.

General Purposes

The memo can be used for a variety of purposes:

- to convey messages to large groups,
- to convey messages to individuals,
- to convey complicated information, or
- to create a permanent record.

Regardless of its original purpose, a memo should always be written with the expectation that it may later be used as a source of information. Much like the memo book, the memo can be an important record of past events and circumstances.

Specific Uses

You can use a memo to

- announce meetings;
- discuss meeting agendas;
- describe organizational policies or changes in policies;
- announce changes to external policies, such as amendments to the *Criminal Code*;
- announce changes in organizational structure;
- announce social functions; or
- convey any other information that employees need to know.

IS A MEMO NECESSARY?

Before composing a memo, consider whether it is really needed, or whether your information might be transmitted just as effectively by a personal interview or a telephone call. Keep in mind that a memo creates a permanent record that may not be called for.

Format

The basic memo format is as follows:

Letterhead

Memorandum

To: _____

From: _____

Date: _____

Subject: _____

Body

_____

_____

_____

_____

_____

_____

_____

                                    Initials or signature

Style

Memos can be either formal or informal, depending on their intended use. But a single set of guidelines applies to all cases.

HEADINGS

It is customary and courteous to include the title of the person to whom a memo is addressed as well as your own title or rank. This rule applies regardless of whether the person you're addressing is of higher or lower rank than yourself.

> To: Staff Sgt. G. DiFlorio, C Division
> From: Cst. H. Sheckley, 0372, C Division

or

> To: Traffic Branch, C Division
> From: Staff Sgt. G. DiFlorio, C Division

Note that there is no salutation ("Dear Staff Sgt. DiFlorio").

SUBJECT LINE

The subject line does not have to be a complete sentence. You'll see in the discussion of formats later in this chapter that the subject line for the direct order memo refers specifically to your topic, but the subject line for the indirect order memo is more general in nature. For instance, in the case of a direct order memo that concerns the time and place of a staff Christmas party, your subject line might be as follows:

Subject: C Division Christmas party

In the case of an indirect order memo requesting payroll deductions for a charitable cause, your subject line might be as follows:

Subject: United Way campaign

CLOSING

Initial or sign your memo after you proofread it, for the following reasons:

- It personalizes the memo and indicates to the reader that you care about the topic.

- It signifies to the reader that you are responsible for its contents and for any errors it may contain.

- It verifies to the reader that the memo was sent with your authorization.

Note that there is no complimentary closing ("Yours truly," "Sincerely,") in a memo.

CONTENT

You should limit your memo to one topic. If you have two topics to discuss, send two memos. The memo should be accurate, complete, and free of confusing or irrelevant detail.

TONE

Be polite, courteous, and businesslike, even if the memo is an informal one.

CORRECTNESS

Proofread your memo for spelling and grammar mistakes.

THE "YOU" APPROACH

In your memo, point out the advantages for the reader(s) in doing what is requested, or make it clear why the information in the memo is important to those being addressed. These practices are also useful in writing letters, as Appendix B will discuss.

Writing Strategies

Depending on its purpose, a memo will take one of two forms: direct order or indirect order.

DIRECT ORDER

The direct order memo (see Figure A.1) is a short, three-section memo that conveys good news or a neutral message to a group, and usually requests information. You expect a positive, or at least a neutral, response to your message. The format for this type of memo is as follows:

1. *Section 1*: State the news, the reason for the request, or the information you are conveying.

2. *Section 2*: Explain the reasons for your position in section 1, in list form if possible.

3. *Section 3*: Write a goodwill closing paragraph, providing any details necessary, requesting additional information, or requesting action.

FIGURE A.1 DIRECT ORDER MEMO

MITCHELL'S BAY POLICE SERVICE

Memorandum

To: Officers of C Division

From: Staff Sgt. G. DiFlorio, C Division

Date: 18 November 2010

Subject: Holiday schedule 2010

The holiday schedule for 2010 is being prepared. All officers are requested to submit their holiday requests by 1 December 2010.

Submitting your requests on time
1. increases the chances we will be able to provide you with the days off you requested
2. allows us to inform you promptly should we not be able to provide you with any of the days off you requested.

Send your requests to DiFlorio@copmail.ca. Your cooperation is greatly appreciated.

—*GD*

INDIRECT ORDER

The indirect order memo (see Figure A.2) is a longer, four-section memo that is primarily used to convey unwelcome news that will likely be met with resistance or negativity. It is also appropriate in cases where you expect a lack of interest in your message. This type of memo takes the "bad news" approach.

Unlike the direct order memo, the indirect order memo states the point of the memo in the third section. Also, the subject line is of a more general nature, since a more specific indicator of the memo's contents might cause readers to discard it unread. The format for this type of memo is as follows:

1. *Section 1*: Write a "goodwill" opening, which may introduce the general subject of your memo, but doesn't yet specify a request, refusal, or complaint.

2. *Section 2*: Give detailed reasons for the message to follow, but don't yet convey it. You may imply it.

3. *Section 3*: State your request, refusal, or complaint, showing (if possible) how your message is for the benefit of the reader.

4. *Section 4*: Write a goodwill closing, where you offer alternatives to what you have suggested, or politely request that some action be taken.

Consider the following features of the indirect order memo shown in Figure A.2:

1. There is no mention made of payroll deductions or contributions in the subject line. There is merely a general reference to the Canadian Cancer Society.

2. The first section of the memo talks about the good works of the Society and, by reminding readers that the Society relies on voluntary contributions, hints that a request is coming.

3. The second section gives detailed reasons for the request that follows in section 3. It discusses the fact that contributions from the Police Service have fallen off (possibly a bit of guilt is being applied here), reviews the Service's history of generosity, and indicates that it's time to be generous again.

4. The third section contains the request. The emphasis here is on the following facts:

    a. the amount requested is small,

    b. management will handle all the administrative work,

    c. the police service will match contributions, and

    d. the contributions are tax-deductible.

FIGURE A.2   INDIRECT ORDER MEMO

MITCHELL'S BAY POLICE SERVICE
Memorandum

To: Officers of C Division

From: Staff Sgt. G. DiFlorio, C Division

Date: 18 November 2010

1 Subject: Canadian Cancer Society

2 As you know, the Canadian Cancer Society has made a significant contribution toward lowering the rate of cancer deaths in Canada over the past number of years. Possibly you know someone who has been helped by the Society. You also likely know, then, that private contributions are the Society's main source of revenue.

3 Employees of the Mitchell's Bay Police Service have contributed a great deal of money in the past to the Canadian Cancer Society, entirely through volunteer donations. However, over the past five years, contributions have dropped from an average of over $20 per person to just over $10. The Mitchell's Bay Police Service would like to make a more significant contribution to the Society's very important work.

4 In order to increase C Division's commitment to the Society, the chief has arranged to deduct a small weekly contribution from your paycheques to the Canadian Cancer Society. This would result in a contribution of $30 per person over the course of the year. We urge you to sign the payroll forms authorizing this deduction. The Mitchell's Bay Police Service will match all employee contributions to the Society. Your contribution is tax-deductible.

5 **Please fill out the appropriate forms by February 15. These forms will be included in your next paycheques. The contributions that you make will have a significant impact on the fight against cancer in Canada.** —GD

5. The fourth section contains a final goodwill gesture and makes the following points:

   a. the deadline is far enough away that employees will have time to give the matter some thought;

   b. forms will be provided, making it easy for employees to respond; and

   c. the significance of the contribution is appreciated.

Staff Sergeant DiFlorio could have included other things in this memo in order to persuade employees to contribute to the Canadian Cancer Society, such as the fact that the Society may offer a free "quit smoking" campaign. He might have used a specific case study to show how the Society has helped a particular individual. He might even have devised a contest whereby all those who contribute are eligible for a free trip. These would all be effective methods of overcoming resistance to the measures outlined in the memo.

Note that reports can also be written in memo or letter form.

EXERCISE 1

WRITING MEMOS

1. You are a constable with your local police service. During your time off, you volunteer as president of a club that provides recreational activities to disadvantaged children. You have decided to hold a fundraiser, and you would like your chief of police to be a guest speaker. The fundraiser will be held on February 1 next year, and numerous local athletes have already agreed to be speakers. The theme of the fundraiser is "Don't do time with crime." Write a memo to the chief, asking him or her to be a speaker. You will have to fill in some of the details, such as the location of the event, the time, and any other information that you feel might help convince the chief to participate.

2. As a first-year probationary inspector with your local customs service, you are the employee with the least seniority. Vacation schedules for next year have already been set, and you find that you're working the evening shift next New Year's Eve. However, family members from Newfoundland, including your mother, whom you haven't seen in five years, have decided to visit you for the holidays and plan to spend New Year's Eve at your home. Write a memo to your superior asking for the time off.

3. Assume that you are the personnel director of Deltex Security. Write a memo to all employees, inviting them to a retirement party in honour of Antonia Morris. Antonia has worked for the company for 23 years, initially as a security officer, now as the director of the company's mobile security units. The party will be held at the Holiday Inn on the 15th of next month. A cash bar will open at 7 p.m., followed by dinner at 7:30. Tickets cost $30 each, part of which will go toward a retirement gift for Antonia.

APPENDIX B

Letters

Introduction

We all write and receive letters, although email is making the traditional letter less common. The focus of Appendix B is not on the general letter you write to friends and acquaintances or on the more specific cover letter you may write to accompany a resumé. The purpose of Appendix B is to look at the letter as it applies to law enforcement situations.

Where the memo is written exclusively for interoffice communication, the letter is used for correspondence sent outside the organization. Like the memo, the letter requires that a few rules be followed.

Purpose

In a law enforcement environment, letters are written mainly to convey information; however, they are also written to deal with complaints and to request information. Your letters are more likely to be answered completely and promptly if you follow commonly accepted practices for letter writing and adopt the philosophy of the "Three Cs": be *clear*, *concise*, and *courteous*.

Formats

The basic business letter format is reproduced in outline form in the box below.

Letterhead

Date
_____

Receiver's name and address
_____

Salutation
_____

Body
_____

Complimentary closing
_____

There are three formats that can be developed from this outline: the modified block style, the traditional style, and the full block style. In addition, there are three different types of punctuation that can be used: modified open punctuation, closed punctuation, and open punctuation. Some of these stylistic variations are shown in Figures B.1, B.2, and B.3.

■ Style

As you are writing letters, there are a few matters of style that should be taken into consideration.

HEADINGS

Avoid abbreviations such as "St." for "Street," not only in your headings but also in other parts of your letter (with the exception of titles such as "Dr." for "doctor" in your salutation). Abbreviations indicate a certain informality on your part, or a desire to get through the letter quickly. Be sure to include your postal code in the return address (if you are not using letterhead) so that a return letter can be addressed correctly.

SALUTATION

You can use the receiver's given name or a number of courtesy titles (Ms., Miss, Mrs., and Mr.) in the salutation. Much will depend on how the person wishes to be addressed. For instance, if you receive a letter signed "Mrs. Edna Jones," send a reply to "Mrs. Edna Jones." Otherwise, "Ms." is now the standard courtesy title for women. When addressing both men and women, it may be easier to use the person's full name (e.g., "Dear Edna Jones") along with the person's business title and department, if you know it, in the inside address. Avoid "Dear Sir or Madam" or "Ladies and Gentlemen."

CLOSING

Use a neutral closing in your letter, such as "Yours truly" or "Sincerely yours," and note that the first letter on the second word is not capitalized.

CONTENT

Organize your material. If the information in your letter is accurate, complete, and free from confusing or irrelevant detail, the recipient will respond more quickly.

TONE

Adopt a courteous, businesslike tone. The overall impression created by your letter is important. A courteous tone will elicit a much quicker response than will a threatening or sarcastic tone.

READABILITY

The ease and speed with which your reader can grasp the main points and supporting details of your letter will often determine how the letter is handled. Check carefully for errors: spelling and grammar mistakes are unacceptable.

THE "YOU" APPROACH

When writing your letter, consider your reader's point of view. Don't tell the reader what he or she can do for you; tell readers what you can do for them.

FIGURE B.1 MODIFIED BLOCK STYLE WITH MODIFIED OPEN PUNCTUATION

MITCHELL'S BAY POLICE SERVICE
1237 Chieu Street
Mitchell's Bay, Ontario N0P 1V0

November 16, 2010

Dr. Geraldine Kehnon
22 Cherry Lane
Mitchell's Bay, Ontario N0P 1V0

Dear Dr. Geraldine Kehnon:

XXX XXXXXXXXXXXXXX XXXXXX XXXXXXXXXXXX XXXXXXX XXXXXX XXXXX
XXXXXXXXXXXXX.

XXX XXXXXXXXXXXXXX XXXXXX XXXXXXXXXXXX XXXXXXX XXXXXX XXXXX
XXXXXXXXXXXXX. XXX XXXXXXXXXXXXXX XXXXXX XXXXXXXXXXXX XXXXXXX XXXXXX
XXXXX XXXXXXXXXXXXX.

XXX XXXXXXXXXXXXXX XXXXXX XXXXXXXXXXXX XXXXXXX XXXXXX XXXXX
XXXXXXXXXXXXX.

XXX XXXXXXXXXXXXXX XXXXX XXXXXXXXXXXX XXXXXXX XXXXXX XXXXX
XXXXXXXXXXXXX.

Sincerely,

Cst. J. Allison
Community Relations

Note: Use punctuation between items (such as city and province) within a line and within the body of the letter. End the salutation with a colon, and end the complimentary closing with a comma. Do not indent paragraphs.

FIGURE B.2 TRADITIONAL STYLE WITH CLOSED PUNCTUATION

MITCHELL'S BAY POLICE SERVICE
1237 Chieu Street
Mitchell's Bay, Ontario N0P 1V0

November 16, 2010

Dr. Geraldine Kehnon
22 Cherry Lane
Mitchell's Bay, Ontario N0P 1V0

Dear Dr. Geraldine Kehnon,

    XXX XXXXXXXXXXXXXX XXXXX XXXXXXXXXXX XXXXXXX XXXXX XXXXX
XXXXXXXXXXXXX.

    XXX XXXXXXXXXXXXXX XXXXX XXXXXXXXXXX XXXXXXX XXXXX XXXXX
XXXXXXXXXXXXX. XXX XXXXXXXXXXXXXX XXXXX XXXXXXXXXXX XXXXXXX XXXXXX
XXXXX XXXXXXXXXXXXX.

    XXX XXXXXXXXXXXXXX XXXXX XXXXXXXXXXX XXXXXXX XXXXX XXXXX
XXXXXXXXXXXXX.

    XXX XXXXXXXXXXXXXX XXXXX XXXXXXXXXXX XXXXXXX XXXXX XXXXX
XXXXXXXXXXXXX.

Sincerely,

Cst. J. Allison
Community Relations

Note: Use punctuation between items within a line (the date, for example) and within the body of the letter. End the salutation and the complimentary closing with a comma, and indent paragraphs.

FIGURE B.3   FULL BLOCK STYLE WITH OPEN PUNCTUATION

MITCHELL'S BAY POLICE SERVICE
1237 Chieu Street
Mitchell's Bay, Ontario N0P 1V0

16 November 2010

Dr. Geraldine Kehnon
22 Cherry Lane
Mitchell's Bay, Ontario N0P 1V0

Dear Dr. Geraldine Kehnon

XXX XXXXXXXXXXXXX XXXXX XXXXXXXXXXX XXXXXX XXXXX XXXXX
XXXXXXXXXXXX.

XXX XXXXXXXXXXXXX XXXXX XXXXXXXXXXX XXXXXX XXXXX XXXXX
XXXXXXXXXXXX. XXX XXXXXXXXXXXXX XXXXX XXXXXXXXXXX XXXXXXX XXXXXX
XXXXX XXXXXXXXXXXX.

XXX XXXXXXXXXXXXX XXXXX XXXXXXXXXXX XXXXXXX XXXXXX XXXXX
XXXXXXXXXXXX.

XXX XXXXXXXXXXXXX XXXXX XXXXXXXXXXX XXXXXXX XXXXXX XXXXX
XXXXXXXXXXXX.

Sincerely

Cst. J. Allison
Community Relations

Note: No punctuation is used with the date, receiver, salutation, and complimentary closing. Use punctuation within the text and at the ends of sentences. Do not indent paragraphs.

Letter-Writing Strategies

As with memos, you should use the indirect order format for bad news and the direct order format for good or neutral news. A brief overview of these formats is set out below. For a complete explanation of the direct and indirect order writing strategies, refer to Appendix A.

1. Direct order

   a. *Section 1*: State the reason for your communication.

   b. *Section 2*: Provide details.

   c. *Section 3*: Write a goodwill closing.

2. Indirect order

   a. *Section 1*: Write a "goodwill" opening.

   b. *Section 2*: Provide a detailed discussion of your reasons for writing.

   c. *Section 3*: State your request, refusal, or complaint.

   d. *Section 4*: Write a goodwill closing.

Note that the sections may consist of more than one paragraph.

Examples of the direct and indirect order letter are set out in Figures B.4 and B.5 respectively.

EXERCISE 1

WRITING LETTERS

1. You are applying for a job. Write a letter to your local police service, the Canada Border Services Agency, Corrections Canada, or a local private security firm to request application information. Obtain addresses from the Internet.

2. Write a letter to your local police service requesting permission for you and your class to view the service's facilities. Be sure to give the reason for your request, the number of people involved, the name of your instructor, and suggested dates for the visit.

3. Write a letter to your local police service complaining about cars speeding in front of your house and asking that a radar trap be placed there.

4. You have applied for a position both with the Canada Border Services Agency and with Corrections Canada, and you have been accepted by both agencies. Write an indirect order letter to one of the agencies, stating that you have decided not to accept its offer of employment. Write a direct order letter to the other agency that is offering you employment, accepting the offer.

FIGURE B.4 DIRECT ORDER LETTER

MITCHELL'S BAY POLICE SERVICE
1237 Chieu Street
Mitchell's Bay, Ontario N0P 1V0

16 November 2010

Mori and Associates
Barristers and Solicitors
886 Lorente Avenue
Hamilton, Ontario L7P 3R5

Dear Harold Mori:

Re: Your file # 33465

I am responding to your request for information, our file 02-011.

Thank you for your payment of our fee for this information, which was received today. Your receipt and the records you requested are enclosed.

If you have any questions, please contact this office at 905-566-2652.

Sincerely,

PC D. Wedmark
Freedom of Information Branch

FIGURE B.5   INDIRECT ORDER LETTER

MITCHELL'S BAY POLICE SERVICE
1237 Chieu Street
Mitchell's Bay, Ontario   N0P 1V0

16 November 2010

Mori and Associates
Barristers and Solicitors
886 Lorente Avenue
Hamilton, Ontario   L7P 3R5

Dear Harold Mori:

Re: Your file # 33465

Thank you for your request for information regarding our file 02-011.

The *Freedom of Information Act* allows law enforcement agencies to release certain information to the public that will not materially harm the person or organization named in the information. Law enforcement agencies are unable to release information that will affect the prosecution of an ongoing criminal investigation, specifically if the person making the request has no direct link with either the Crown or the defence in a criminal matter, or is not a lawyer representing either the Crown or the accused.

Since your client cannot show a relationship to the matter under consideration, I must deny your request for information.

I am returning your payment for this service. Please contact me at 905-566-2652 if I can provide you with additional information.

Sincerely,

PC D. Wedmark
Freedom of Information Branch

APPENDIX C

Emails

Introduction

Today, memos and letters are often sent electronically as email. For this reason, it's important to understand that professional email differs from personal email in some important ways. When we write to family and friends, we focus on quick responses, writing and organizing our messages casually. We anticipate quick responses from them, and we count on their making correct assumptions since they know us well. At work, however, our relationships are professional, not personal. We can't assume that readers will make correct assumptions. Therefore, we must take care to write and organize our electronic messages as carefully as we would other professional documents. Furthermore, we must understand the purpose of email in a law enforcement context.

Purpose

In law enforcement, email may be used either to send memos, for interoffice communication, or to send letters, for correspondence outside the organization. The same principles discussed in Appendix A: Memos and Appendix B: Letters apply. However, there are some additional points to consider when using email. Because electronic documents are always recoverable, email provides a permanent record of statements, reports, and agreements. This fact means that email is often used to ensure accountability—it's easy to check the history and details of email exchanges. Furthermore, email is discoverable in the case of a lawsuit. Your messages may be entered into court as evidence.

For these reasons, avoid the temptation to "dash off" a quick memo you may later regret. Remember, once you send your message, you can't retrieve it. One advantage of email systems is that they generally contain a "Drafts" folder for incomplete messages. Use it to your advantage. Save email messages in the "Drafts" folder for a "second look"; this way, you can consider your message and minimize unexpected consequences.

Format

The basic email memo format is reproduced below.

Send	Save as Draft	Add Attachments	Delete
To:			
Cc:			
Bcc:			
Subject:			
Attachments:			

Salutation

Body

Closing

Style

There are some important style points to consider when sending email correspondence.

HEADINGS

To:

This section contains the receiver's email address.

Cc:

"Cc" stands for "Carbon copy." This section contains the email addresses of secondary recipients—others you wish to copy on the message. These addresses are visible to everyone receiving the message.

Bcc:

"Bcc" stands for "Blind carbon copy." This section contains the email addresses of other recipients whose email addresses are invisible to everyone receiving the message. Generally, this function is used for batch messages and offers privacy protection.

Subject:

The subject line indicates the contents of the message. The same guidelines for subject lines discussed in Appendix A apply to emails.

Attachments:

This section displays any files attached to the message. Attach a letter to the message for formal messages, and use the body of the email simply to request that the reader open the attachment. Review Appendix B: Letters for details.

SALUTATION

Since the "To:" and "From:" fields of an email can't contain title and rank, include this information at the beginning of your message. This approach is especially important when writing to superiors. For example, you can begin your message with "Staff Sgt. Smith," and continue with your message.

BODY

Write using complete sentences and organized paragraphs. Choose the direct order approach for routine or good news messages, and the indirect order approach for bad news or persuasive messages. (Review Appendixes A and B for details.)

CLOSING

End your email message by typing your title, name, and division or branch at the bottom of the message. Most email software packages offer a simple way to create an electronic signature that automatically inserts this material into your message.

Replying

A WORD OF WARNING

When replying to an email message, be careful that you choose the correct button: using "Reply All" will send your message to all the addresses inserted into the original email—including addresses in the "Cc:" and "Bcc:" sections. Use "Reply" if you want to send your response only to the address in the "To:" section of the original message. It is common for people to mistake these two functions, and often leads to unintended consequences. Unless you want everyone to read your reply, be careful to check the address sections of your message.

As with email memos, carefully consider the implications before hitting the "Send" button. It's particularly easy to "fire off" a quick response you may later regret, especially when you have received a hostile message or unwelcome news.

CONTEXT AND CLARITY

To avoid confusion when replying to a message, quote the original document to provide context. For example, rather than simply typing

Yes

in response to a question, include the original message or line to which you are responding, and respond using a complete sentence so that your meaning is clear:

Did you find someone to help you with the report, or would you like to meet to discuss the specifics?

Yes, I met Officer Davies and completed the report. I don't think a meeting is necessary. I'll put the report on your desk tomorrow.

Formatting and Attaching Documents

Because people use a variety of software platforms to receive electronic messages, it is best to keep formatting simple. Format your message so that the person with the simplest setup will have no problems understanding your message.

The same idea applies to attachments. Make sure the receiver can open your attachment. Use well-accepted formats and avoid sending attachments saved in cutting-edge versions of programs unless you know in advance that the receiver can read the document.

Spell Checks

Most email systems include a spell-checking program. The review function is useful for pointing out potential errors. The review feature allows you to choose from suggestions for each potential correction. However, avoid automatic correction because this process often makes mistakes. Computers can't grasp the context of law enforcement, and must be trained to recognize specialized language such as acronyms. If you use the spell-check feature, always read over your work yourself to catch errors that the program itself may have created.

References

Adamson, R. (2006, January 1). Is Canadian justice system too soft on violent crime? Pro. *Sunday Star* [Toronto], p. A16.

American Psychological Association. (2009). *Publication manual of the American Psychological Association* (6th ed.). Washington: Author.

Beazley, D. (2000, September 14). Lawyers wary of proposal: Suggestion cops be allowed to break laws met with reservations. *The Edmonton Sun*. Retrieved from http://www.mail-archive.com/ctrl@listserv.aol.com/msg50684.html.

Canada. Statistics Canada. (2010). *Education indicators in Canada: An international perspective*. Retrieved from http://www.statcan.gc.ca/daily-quotidien/090908/dq090908b-eng.htm.

Canadian Policy Research Networks. (2009). *Diversity*. Retrieved from http://www.cprn.org/theme.cfm?theme=58&l=en.

Community Dispute Resolution Services of Hamilton. (n.d.). Mediation information. *Cultural sensitivity and its significance to communication*, p. 5 [Brochure]. Hamilton, ON: Author.

Gendreau, P., Coggin, C., & Cullen, F. (1999). *The effects of prison sentences on recidivism*. Ottawa: Solicitor General Canada.

Gibaldi, J. (2009). *MLA handbook for writers of research papers* (7th ed.). New York: MLA.

Gillespie, K. (2003, October 19). Police fume at security firms. *Sunday Star* [Toronto], p. A1.

How to prevent counterfeit money from falling between the cracks. (2004, July 29). *The Hamilton Spectator*, p. A6.

Ingerman, E. (2001). *On the subject of security incompetence*. Retrieved from http://www.securityprofessionalssite.com/securityarticles/security_articles_list.html.

Jones, R.C. (2001). Strategies for reading comprehension: Summarizing. *ReadingQuest.org*. Retrieved from http://www.readingquest.org/strat/summarize.html.

Lester, J.D. (1976). *Writing research papers: A complete guide* (2nd ed.). Glenview, IL: Scott, Foresman.

Lipschutz, G., Roberts, J., Scarry, J., & Scarry, S. (2004). *The Canadian writer's workplace* (5th ed.). Toronto: Thomson Nelson.

McQuaig, L. (2006, January 1). Is Canadian justice system too soft on violent crime? Con. *Sunday Star* [Toronto], p. A16.

Mohawk College. (n.d.). Written communication test: Practice test. Hamilton, ON.

Northey, M. (1998). *Impact: A guide to business communication* (4th ed.). Scarborough, ON: Prentice Hall, p. 220.

Purdue Online Writing Lab. (2010). *Paraphrase: Write it in your own words.* Retrieved from http://owl.english.purdue.edu/owl/resource/619/01/.

Purdue Online Writing Lab. (2010). *Quoting, paraphrasing, and summarizing.* Retrieved from http://owl.english.purdue.edu/owl/resource/563/1/.

Sheppard, R. (2001, April). Growing old inside. *Maclean's, 114*(15), 30.

Shusta, R.M., Levine, D.L., Wong, H.Z., & Harris, P.R. (2005). *Multicultural law enforcement: Strategies for peacekeeping in a diverse society.* Upper Saddle River, NJ: Pearson.

Wall, L. (2003). *Documenting research sources using MLA style; Documenting research sources using APA style* [Pamphlet]. Hamilton, ON: Mohawk College.

Index

#

10-codes, 194

A

accused statement, 212
antonyms, 44
APA reference style, 136–139
apostrophes
    contractions, and, 86
    possessives, and, 84–86

B

barriers to communication
    general, 2
    listening, 23
bias, 104–106
body language, 19
body orientation, 157
brainstorming, 119

C

capital letters, 90
clause
    defined, 72
    dependent clause, 74
    independent clause, 74
closed questions, 17
colons, 88
comma splice, 76
commas, 83–84
communication
    barriers to, 2, 23
    grammar, 61–93
    listening, 11–32
    multicultural society, and, 2–5
    people with disabilities, and, 5
    process of, 1

speaking, 145–173
spelling, 33–60
summary and paraphrase, 95–107
theory of, 1
writing, 111–139
communication process, 1
contractions, 86
correlatives, 82
court testimony, 163
Crown brief, 224–225

D

dangling modifiers, 77, 78
dependent clause, 74
diagrams, 183–186
direct speech, 98

E

emails, 273–276
essay writing
    audience, 112–113
    brainstorming, 119, 120
    checklist, 140–141
    comparison/contrast essay, 127
    descriptive essay, 118, 126
    expository essay, 118, 127
    narrative essay, 118, 126
    organization, 121–123, 125
    outline, 119, 129
    persuasive essay, 118, 127
    purpose, 111–112
    structure, 113
        body, 124
        conclusion, 128–130
        introduction, 123–124
        transitions, 125–126
        writing strategies, 126–128

essay writing (cont.)
    thesis statement, 120–121
    types of, 118
    use of, 117–119
exclamation points, 87
eye contact, 156

F

facial expression, 156
facts in issue, 202–203

G

gerund, 66
gestures, 157
grammar
    capital letters, 90
    importance of, 61
    punctuation
        apostrophes, 84–87
        colons, 88
        commas, 83–84
        exclamation points, 87
        periods, 87
        question marks, 87
        quotation marks, 88
        semicolons, 88
    sentences
        correlatives, 82
        modifiers, 77–78
        parallel structure, 81–82
        pronoun references, 78–81
        run-on sentences, 75–77
        sentence fragments, 72–75
        subject of, 66–67
        subject–verb agreement, 70–72
        verb of, 68–70
    voice, 90

H

homographs, 40
homonyms, 40

I

impromptu speaking, 159
incident report, 203, 205–208
independent clause, 74
indirect speech, 98
infinitive, 69
irregular verb, 68

L

letter writing, 265–272
linking verb, 68
listening
    additional principles, 22
    barriers to, 23
    memory, and, 23–24
    nine rules, 14–22
    profile, 12–14
loudness, 157

M

memo book
    10-codes, 194
    checklist, 192–193
    guidelines for entries, 187–190
    note taking
        diagrams, 183–186
        guidelines, 187
        irrelevant material, 181
        listening, and, 21–22
        strategies for, 182
        use of notes in court, 182–183
memorandum writing, 233–239
memos
    general purpose, 257
    necessity for, 258
    specific purpose, 257
    style, 258–259
    writing strategies, 260
misplaced modifiers, 77
MLA reference style, 131–135
modifiers
    dangling, 77, 78
    misplaced, 77
motor vehicle accident statement, 212
multicultural society, 2–5

N

nervousness, 154
non-verbal communication
    spatial elements, 158
    visual elements, 156–157
    vocal elements, 157–158
note taking
    diagrams, 183–186
    guidelines, 187
    listening, and, 21–22
    strategies for, 182
    use of notes in court, 182–183

O

objective pronouns, 80
open questions, 17
oral presentations
    answering questions, 153–154
    mechanics, 152–153
    narrowing the topic, 147
    nervousness, 154
    organization, 152
    preparation, 150–151
    purpose, 146
    research, 148–149
    topic selection, 146–147
    visual aids, 155
outline, 119

P

paragraphs, 114–117
parallel structure, 81–82
paraphrase
    bias, and, 104–106
    methods, 101–103
    use of, 101
periods, 87
possessive pronouns, 80
possessives, 84–86
posture, 157
pronoun
    indefinite pronoun, 71
    references, 76–81
    relative pronoun, 71

pronoun references, 76–81
punctuation
    apostrophes, 84–87
    colons, 88
    commas, 83–84
    exclamation points, 87
    periods, 87
    question marks, 87
    quotation marks, 88
    semicolons, 88

Q

question marks, 87
questioning
    broadening questions, 18
    clarifying questions, 18
    closed-ended questions, 17, 179
    open-ended questions, 17
    techniques, 178–180
quotation marks, 88

R

reflective listening, 17
regular verb, 68
report writing
    chronological reporting, 199
    common errors, 203
    composition, 200
    Crown briefs, and, 224–225
    facts in issue, 202–203
    memo book, transfers from, 204
    organization, 198–201
    outline, 199
    parts of, 196–197, 201
    rules, 197–198
research paper
    citing sources
        APA, 136–139
        MLA, 131–135
    finding facts, 130
    note taking, 130–131
run-on sentences, 75–76

S

selective listening, 16
semicolons, 88
sentence fragments
    clauses, and, 72–75
    defined, 72
sentences
    correlatives, 82
    modifiers, 77–78
    parallel structure, 81–82
    pronoun references, 78–81
    run-on sentences, 75–77
    sentence fragments, 72–75
    subject of, 66–67
    subject–verb agreement, 70–72
    topic sentences, 114–117
    verb of, 68–70
speaking
    application, speaking techniques, 163–164
    impromptu speaking, 159
    non-verbal communication, and
        spatial elements, 158
        visual elements, 156–157
        vocal elements, 157
    one-on-one communication
        conferencing with peers, 162
        difficult people, dealing with, 160–162
    oral presentations
        answering questions, 153–154
        mechanics, 152–153
        narrowing the topic, 147
        nervousness, 154
        organization, 152
        preparation, 150–151
        purpose, 146
        research, 148–149
        topic selection, 146–147
        visual aids, 155
spelling
    antonyms, 44
    frequently misspelled words, 37–38
    frequently misused words, 44–48
    homographs, 44
    homonyms, 44, 49
    importance of, 33–34
    plurals, 41–44
    rules, 40–41
    steps to improve, 34
    synonyms, 44
    troublesome words, 35, 36, 44
statement forms, 211–219
subject
    agreement with verb, 70–72
    complete subject, 67
    simple subject, 66
subjective pronouns, 80
summary
    direct to indirect speech, 98
    rules, 96–97
    samples, 98–101
    use of, 96
    word counts, 98
supplementary report, 204–205, 208–211
synonyms, 44

T

tense, 68
thesis statement, 120–121
tone of voice, 19–20
topic sentences, 114–117

V

verb
    agreement with subject, 70–72
    infinitive, 69
    irregular verb, 68
    linking verb, 68
    regular verb, 68
    tense of, 68
verbal noun, 66
visual aids, 155
voice, 90

W

witness statement, 211–212
word counts, 98

Acknowledgments

The following individuals and publishers have been generous in giving their permission to reproduce works in this text. If we have inadvertently overlooked any acknowledgment, we offer our sincere apologies and undertake to rectify the omission in any future editions.

Rondi Adamson   Adamson, R. (2006, January 1). Is Canadian justice system too soft on violent crime? Pro. *Toronto Star*, p. A16. Reprinted by permission of Rondi Adamson.

The Hamilton Spectator   How to prevent counterfeit money from falling between the cracks. (2004, July 29). *The Hamilton Spectator*, p. A6. Reprinted by permission of The Hamilton Spectator.

Linda McQuaig   McQuaig, L. (2006, January 1). Is Canadian justice system too soft on violent crime? Con. *Toronto Star*, p. A16. Reprinted by permission of Linda McQuaig, author and journalist.

Jo-Anne Procter, Associate Dean, Brantford Campus, Mohawk College   Material in Chapter 9 that was originally generated for Mohawk College.

Thomson Nelson   Lipshutz, G., Roberts, J., Scarry, J., & Scarry, S. (2004). *The Canadian writer's workplace* (5th ed.) (pp. 158, 176). Toronto: Thomson Nelson. From ROBERTS/LIPSCHUTZ/SCARRY ET AL. *Canadian Writer's Workplace 5/E.* © 2004 Nelson Education Ltd. Reproduced by permission. www.cengage.com/permissions.

Torstar Syndication Services   Gillespie, K. (2003, October 19). Police fume at security firms. *Toronto Star*, p. A1. Reprinted with permission—Torstar Syndication Services. From an article originally appearing in the *Toronto Star*, October, 1993.